CAN COURTS BE BULWARKS OF DEMOCRACY?

Liberal concepts of democracy envision courts as key institutions for the promotion and protection of democratic regimes. Yet social science scholarship suggests that courts are fundamentally constrained in ways that undermine their ability to do so. Recognizing these constraints, this book argues that courts can influence regime instability by affecting inter-elite conflict. They do so in three ways: by helping leaders credibly reveal their rationales for policy choices that may appear to violate legal rules; by encouraging leaders to less frequently make decisions that raise concerns about rule violations; and by encouraging the opposition to accept potential rule violations. Courts promote the prudent use of power in each of these approaches. This book evaluates the implications of this argument using a century of global data tracking judicial politics and democratic survival.

Jeffrey K. Staton is Professor of Political Science and Senior Associate Dean of Laney Graduate School, Emory University. He is the author of *Judicial Power and Strategic Communication in Mexico* (Cambridge University Press, 2010). His research has been supported by the National Science Foundation.

Christopher Reenock is Associate Professor of Political Science at Florida State University. He is the coauthor of *Democratic Policymaking* (Cambridge University Press, 2017). His work has been supported by the National Science Foundation, and he has been the recipient of the Herbert Kaufman Award and the Beryl Radin Award.

Jordan Holsinger received his Ph.D. in Political Science from Florida State University. His research focuses on the role of NGOs as promoters of civil society in authoritarian regimes. His research agenda also includes projects on the role of NGOs in authoritarian contexts and the politics of repression.

COMPARATIVE CONSTITUTIONAL LAW AND POLICY

Comparative constitutional law is an intellectually vibrant field that encompasses an increasingly broad array of approaches and methodologies. This series collects analytically innovative and empirically grounded work from scholars of comparative constitutionalism across academic disciplines. Books in the series include theoretically informed studies of single constitutional jurisdictions, comparative studies of constitutional law and institutions, and edited collections of original essays that respond to challenging theoretical and empirical questions in the field.

Books in the Series

The Fall of the Arab Spring: Democracy's Challenges and Efforts to Reconstitute the Middle East
Tofigh Maboudi

Filtering Populist Claims to Fight Populism: The Italian Case in a Comparative Perspective
Giuseppe Martinico

Constitutionalism in Context
David S. Law

The New Fourth Branch: Institutions for Protecting Constitutional Democracy
Mark Tushnet

The Veil of Participation: Citizens and Political Parties in Constitution-Making Processes
Alexander Hudson

Towering Judges: A Comparative Study of Constitutional Judges
Edited by Rehan Abeyratne and Iddo Porat

The Constitution of Arbitration
Victor Ferreres Comella

Redrafting Constitutions in Democratic Orders: Theoretical and Comparative Perspectives
Edited by Gabriel L. Negretto

From Parchment to Practice: Implementing New Constitutions
Edited by Tom Ginsburg and Aziz Z. Huq

The Failure of Popular Constitution Making in Turkey: Regressing Towards Constitutional Autocracy
Edited by Felix Petersen and Zeynep Yanaşmayan

A Qualified Hope: The Indian Supreme Court and Progressive Social Change
Edited by Gerald N. Rosenberg, Sudhir Krishnaswamy, and Shishir Bail

Reconstructing Rights: Courts, Parties, and Equality Rights in India, South Africa, and the United States
Stephan Stohler

Constitutions in Times of Financial Crisis
Edited by Tom Ginsburg, Mark D. Rosen, and Georg Vanberg

Hybrid Constitutionalism: The Politics of Constitutional Review in the Chinese Special Administrative Regions
Eric C. Ip

Constitution-Making and Transnational Legal Order
Edited by Tom Ginsburg, Terence C. Halliday, and Gregory Shaffer

The Invisible Constitution in Comparative Perspective
Edited by Rosalind Dixon and Adrienne Stone

The Politico-Legal Dynamics of Judicial Review: A Comparative Analysis
Theunis Roux

Constitutional Courts in Asia: A Comparative Perspective
Edited by Albert H. Y. Chen and Andrew Harding

Judicial Review in Norway: A Bicentennial Debate
Anine Kierulf

Constituent Assemblies
Edited by Jon Elster, Roberto Gargarella, Vatsal Naresh, and Bjorn Erik Rasch

The DNA of Constitutional Justice in Latin America: Politics, Governance, and Judicial Design
Daniel M. Brinks and Abby Blass

The Adventures of the Constituent Power: Beyond Revolutions?
Andrew Arato

Canada in the World: Comparative Perspectives on the Canadian Constitution
Edited by Richard Albert and David R. Cameron

Constitutions, Religion and Politics in Asia: Indonesia, Malaysia and Sri Lanka
Dian A. H. Shah

Courts and Democracies in Asia
Po Jen Yap

Proportionality: New Frontiers, New Challenges
Edited by Vicki C. Jackson and Mark Tushnet

Constituents before Assembly: Participation, Deliberation, and Representation in the Crafting of New Constitutions
Todd A. Eisenstadt, A. Carl LeVan, and Tofigh Maboudi

Assessing Constitutional Performance
Edited by Tom Ginsburg and Aziz Huq

Buddhism, Politics and the Limits of Law: The Pyrrhic Constitutionalism of Sri Lanka
Benjamin Schonthal

Engaging with Social Rights: Procedure, Participation and Democracy in South Africa's Second Wave
Brian Ray

Constitutional Courts As Mediators: Armed Conflict, Civil-Military Relations, and the Rule of Law in Latin America
Julio Ríos-Figueroa

Perils of Judicial Self-Government in Transitional Societies
David Kosař

Making We the People: Democratic Constitutional Founding in Postwar Japan and South Korea
Chaihark Hahm and Sung Ho Kim

Radical Deprivation on Trial: The Impact of Judicial Activism on Socioeconomic Rights in the Global South
César Rodríguez-Garavito and Diana Rodríguez-Franco

Unstable Constitutionalism: Law and Politics in South Asia
Edited by Mark Tushnet and Madhav Khosla

Magna Carta and Its Modern Legacy
Edited by Robert Hazell and James Melton

Constitutions and Religious Freedom
Frank B. Cross

International Courts and the Performance of International Agreements: A General Theory with Evidence from the European Union
Clifford J. Carrubba and Matthew J. Gabel

Reputation and Judicial Tactics: A Theory of National and International Courts
Shai Dothan

Social Difference and Constitutionalism in Pan-Asia
Edited by Susan H. Williams

Constitutionalism in Asia in the Early Twenty-First Century
Edited by Albert H. Y. Chen

Constitutions in Authoritarian Regimes
Edited by Tom Ginsburg and Alberto Simpser

Presidential Legislation in India: The Law and Practice of Ordinances
Shubhankar Dam

Social and Political Foundations of Constitutions
Edited by Denis J. Galligan and Mila Versteeg

Consequential Courts: Judicial Roles in Global Perspective
Edited by Diana Kapiszewski, Gordon Silverstein, and Robert A. Kagan

Comparative Constitutional Design
Edited by Tom Ginsburg

Can Courts Be Bulwarks of Democracy?

JUDGES AND THE POLITICS OF PRUDENCE

JEFFREY K. STATON
Emory University

CHRISTOPHER REENOCK
Florida State University

JORDAN HOLSINGER
Florida State University

CAMBRIDGE
UNIVERSITY PRESS

CAMBRIDGE
UNIVERSITY PRESS

University Printing House, Cambridge CB2 8BS, United Kingdom

One Liberty Plaza, 20th Floor, New York, NY 10006, USA

477 Williamstown Road, Port Melbourne, VIC 3207, Australia

314–321, 3rd Floor, Plot 3, Splendor Forum, Jasola District Centre, New Delhi – 110025, India

103 Penang Road, #05–06/07, Visioncrest Commercial, Singapore 238467

Cambridge University Press is part of the University of Cambridge.

It furthers the University's mission by disseminating knowledge in the pursuit of education, learning, and research at the highest international levels of excellence.

www.cambridge.org
Information on this title: www.cambridge.org/9781316516737
DOI: 10.1017/9781009030939

First published 2022

A catalogue record for this publication is available from the British Library.

Library of Congress Cataloging-in-Publication Data
NAMES: Staton, Jeffrey K., author. | Reenock, Christopher, author. | Holsinger, Jordan, 1991– author.
TITLE: Can courts be bulwarks of democracy? : judges and the politics of prudence / Jeffrey K. Staton, Emory University, Atlanta; Christopher Reenock, Florida State University; Jordan Holsinger, Florida State University.
DESCRIPTION: [New York] : Cambridge University Press, 2022. | Series: Comparative constitutional law and policy | Includes bibliographical references and index.
IDENTIFIERS: LCCN 2021035307 (print) | LCCN 2021035308 (ebook) | ISBN 9781316516737 (hardback) | ISBN 9781009015264 (paperback) | ISBN 9781009030939 (ebook)
SUBJECTS: LCSH: Political questions and judicial power. | Political questions and judicial power–United States.
CLASSIFICATION: LCC K3367 .S73 2022 (print) | LCC K3367 (ebook) | DDC 347/.012–dc23
LC record available at https://lccn.loc.gov/2021035307
LC ebook record available at https://lccn.loc.gov/2021035308

ISBN 978-1-316-51673-7 Hardback

Contents

Acknowledgments *page* ix

1 **Introduction** 1
- 1.1 Defenders of Democracy 3
- 1.2 Defensive Failures 6
- 1.3 Argument Summary 10
  - 1.3.1 Methodological Approach 12
- 1.4 Plan of the Book 13

2 **Democratic Regimes and Their Survival** 15
- 2.1 What Is Democracy? 15
  - 2.1.1 Democracy as Political Compromise 19
  - 2.1.2 What Does It Mean to Defend Democracy? 20
- 2.2 The Fundamental Problem of Democratic Governance 20
- 2.3 How Can Courts Influence the Fundamental Problem? 22
  - 2.3.1 Judges as Trustees 23
  - 2.3.2 Judges as Mediators 23
  - 2.3.3 Courts as Settings for Information Transmission 24
  - 2.3.4 Information and Judicial Review 25
- 2.4 The Argument 26
- 2.5 The Path Forward 29

3 **Political Competition and Judicial Independence** 31
- 3.1 Measuring De Facto Judicial Independence 32
- 3.2 Measuring De Jure Judicial Independence 35
- 3.3 Courts as Political Insurance: A Process 39
  - 3.3.1 Competition, Judicial Independence, and Regime Transitions 39
  - 3.3.2 An Exogenous Intervention: The Fall of the Wall and Judicial Independence 41
  - 3.3.3 Instrumentation 48
- 3.4 Conclusion 53

3.A Complete Tables for Instrumented Analysis 55
4 Judicial Effects on Democratic Regime Stability 60
4.1 An Informational Model of Regime Breakdown 62
4.1.1 Baseline Model 62
4.1.2 Judicial Review Model 68
4.1.3 A Model with a Stronger Version of Autonomy 76
4.2 Discussion 76
4.2.1 Policy Failure and Opportunism Trade-Offs 77
4.2.2 When Can Courts Help the Parties Reveal Information? 77
4.2.3 Can Courts Influence Regime Conflict If They Do Not Influence Information? 79
4.A Proofs 81
5 Imprudent Politics 84
5.1 Extraordinary Actions of Leaders 88
5.1.1 Electoral Reform 88
5.1.2 Investigating Former Leaders 89
5.1.3 States of Emergency 91
5.2 Extraordinary Reactions: Coups 98
5.3 The Survival of Democracy 102
5.3.1 An Alternative Interpretation of Judicial Attacks 105
5.4 Conclusion 106
5.A Tables 109
5.B Sensitivity to Measurement Error 118
6 Will Courts Be Bulwarks of Democracy in the United States? 120
6.1 The Case for US Courts as Bulwarks 124
6.2 Caveats 128
6.2.1 Judicial Appointments 129
6.2.2 Attacks on the US Judiciary 130
6.2.3 The Supreme Court as a Republican Agent 135
6.3 Where the American Judiciary Stands and What This Means 137
7 Conclusion 140
7.1 How Courts May Defend Democracy 140
7.2 Courts as Defenders of Democracy: Important Implications 142
7.2.1 Courts Cannot Police Nonexistent Bargains 142
7.2.2 Courts Cannot Police Bargains That Have Already Broken Down 143
7.2.3 Noncompliance, Courts, and Democracy? 144
7.3 Open Questions 144
Bibliography 146
Index 154

Acknowledgments

Over the years, many colleagues have offered both insights and unbridled criticisms of our early thoughts and drafts, and we thank them here. Despite our best efforts to recall everyone who has offered assistance along the way, we apologize to anyone who has been inadvertently overlooked. The origins of this book lie in unstructured conversations held over countless lunches and coffees at Florida State University. We thank Sona Golder, Matt Golder, Mark Souva, Amanda Driscoll, Jens Grosser, and Robert J. Carroll. We also wish to thank our colleagues at Emory University for their encouragement and support. We thank Clifford Carrubba, Tom Clark, Jennifer Gandhi, Adam Glynn, Greg Martin, Richard Doner, Miguel Rueda, and Nancy Arrington.

We have presented elements of our book at conferences, workshops, and departmental colloquia over the years and we would like to thank our audience members for their feedback and patience with us. We are particularly grateful for suggestions from Julio Ríos Figueroa, Gretchen Helmke, Monika Nalepa, Georg Vanberg, Emilia Powell, Daniel Brinks, Emily Hafner-Burton, Kim Lane Scheppele, Milan Svolik, Abel Iscribà Folch, Brad Epperly, John Katellec, Mariana Llanos, Steven Levitsky, M. Victoria Murillo, Charles Cameron, Barry Weingast, Anna Harvey, Gustavo Torrens, Anthony DeMattee, Lee Alston, Emily Hencken Ritter, Courtenay Conrad, Nathan Monroe, Thomas Hansford, and Jessica Tournstine.

We thank Stefan Voigt and Christian Bjørnskov for their willingness to share data with us so that we could replicate their work and build on it. We thank Donna Bahry for sharing a draft of her paper on criminal investigations.

We are deeply indebted to the Varieties of Democracy team for core intellectual and organization support, so necessary to the development of our project. We thank Staffan Lindberg, Michael Coppedge, John Gerring, Jan Teorell, Josefine Pernes, Natalia Stepanova, Kelly McMan, David Altman, Carl Henrik Knutsen, Daniel Pemstein, Allen Hicken, Steve Fish, Michael Bernhard, Patrik Lindenfors,

Brigitte Zimmerman, Svend-Erik Skaaning, Rachel Sigman, Kyle Marquardt, Anna Lührmann, Megan Reif, Richard Morgan, Fernando Bizzarro, and Lisa Gastaldi.

We would also like to thank Anisha Koilpillai and Giulia Venturini for their capable research assistance.

As always, despite all of this generous assistance, any errors, sins of commission or omission are our responsibility.

We wish to thank our families for giving us the time and space to pursue new ideas and for demanding that we bring our study to a conclusion. We are especially grateful for toboggans, real and imagined..

1

Introduction

If, then, the courts of justice are to be considered as the bulwarks of a limited Constitution against legislative encroachments, this consideration will afford a strong argument for the permanent tenure of judicial offices, since nothing will contribute so much as this to that independent spirit in the judges which must be essential to the faithful performance of so arduous a duty.

Alexander Hamilton, Federalist 78

The election of Donald J. Trump to the presidency of the United States disrupted the otherwise abstract and politically disconnected world of American political science. Scholars once content to publish in journals hidden behind paywalls began writing opinion pieces in print media sources and granting interviews with broadcasters, radio stations, and podcasts, all questioning whether American democracy was indeed in danger. With the assistance of a young journalist core committed to evidence-based reporting, scholars mobilized to bring decades of research on the nature of authoritarianism to the public discourse.[1] As the field promoted past research, it also created new measurement strategies designed to characterize changes in important elements of democratic life, engaging the whole discipline in the process of data production.[2]

In a global context in which right-wing populist leaders are stressing democratic projects in a diverse set of states including Hungary, Poland, France, Italy, Austria, the Philippines, and Brazil, scholars have questioned the durability of the American system. In a *New York Times* opinion piece in December of 2016, Steven Levitsky and Daniel Ziblatt put the matter bluntly, writing

> Is our democracy in danger? With the possible exception of the Civil War, American democracy has never collapsed; indeed, no democracy as rich or as established as America's ever has. Yet past stability is no guarantee of democracy's future

1 See, for example, the reporting in Amanda Taub's "The Rise of American Authoritarianism," www.vox.com/2016/3/1/11127424/trump-authoritarianism

2 See, for example, the work of John Carey, Gretchen Helmke, Brendan Nyhan, and Susan Stokes developing Bright Line Watch, http://brightlinewatch.org/about-us-new/

> survival. We have spent two decades studying the emergence and breakdown of democracy in Europe and Latin America. Our research points to several warning signs.[3]

Noting that many Americans place their faith in the US system of checks and balances, Levitsky and Ziblatt remind us that the ultimate success of formal checks on the politically powerful depends on a variety of informal norms, including the notion of a legitimate opposition, partisan and presidential restraint. To this list, we should add respect for general rule of law values, including a deep societal commitment to an independent judiciary as the arbiter of fundamental constitutional norms.

Just eight days after President Trump's inauguration, the American system of checks and balances was tested. On January 27, 2017, with little input from the Departments of State, Homeland Security or Defense, President Trump issued Executive Order 13769, which immediately prohibited entry into the United States for nationals from Iran, Iraq, Libya, Somalia, Sudan, Syria, and Yemen.[4] The order also suspended the US Refugee Admissions Program (USRAP) for a period of 120 days, widening the policy's impact beyond the seven named states. As a consequence of requiring the immediate implementation of the order hundreds of individuals were detained at the nation's airports, some of whom enjoyed permanent US residency status.

Almost immediately, dozens of legal challenges to the executive order were launched. Many of the initial challenges took the form of habeas corpus petitions seeking the release of individuals who were detained at the nation's airports.[5] The State of Washington filed for declaratory and injunctive relief in order to protect its "residents, employers and educational institutions," which it argued would be powerfully harmed by the executive order. On January 28, Judge Ann Donnelly of the US District Court for the Eastern District of New York issued an emergency stay of removal, which arguably halted the continued enforcement of Trump's order; and on February 3, US District Court Judge for the Western District of Washington James L. Robart issued a temporary restraining order on a nationwide basis enjoining the most important sections of Executive Order 13769. This decision was affirmed by a three-judge panel of the Ninth Circuit Court of Appeals on February 9. Reflecting on Judge Donnelly's emergency stay, American Civil Liberties Union (ACLU) Executive Director Anthony Romero exclaimed,

3 www.nytimes.com/2016/12/16/opinion/sunday/is-donald-trump-a-threat-to-democracy.html?_r=0

4 Executive Order: Protecting the Nation from Foreign Terrorist Entry into the United States, January 27, 2017.

5 For example, *Aziz* v. *Trump* No. 1:17-cv-00116 (E.D.Va. 2017) involved two Yemini brothers, Tareq Aqel Mohammed Aziz and Ammar Aqel Mohammed Aziz, who were detained by US Customs and Border Protection at Washington-Dulles Airport pursuant to the executive order despite having been previously granted lawful permanent resident status by the State Department. Similarly, *Darweesh* v. *Trump* involved two Iraqi men who were detained at John F. Kennedy International Airport despite having valid US visas.

"What we've shown today is that the courts can work. They're a bulwark in our democracy."[6]

Weeks after the Ninth Circuit's decision, the Trump administration issued a second executive order in March and a proclamation in late September 2017, which modified the original order, changing the states subject to the ban and adding a variety of exemptions resulting in a more limited travel ban. Revisions to the first executive order ultimately produced more than fifty separate litigations carried out across most of the country's legal system. In June 2018, a divided Supreme Court upheld the proclamation, finding among other things that there was a facially valid rationale for the administration's restrictions.[7]

Ultimately, the Trump administration succeeded in some aspects of its original plan. Travelers from a number of majority Muslim countries have been effectively banned from entry. The court declined to find an unconstitutional religious rationale for the restrictions. Instead the court found a facially neutral explanation based in the president's authority to protect national interests through immigration policy. Yet the policy that survived judicial scrutiny was considerably changed from the original. Lawful permanent residents and individuals who will be granted asylum are exempted, among many other cases.

Our book considers Anthony Romero's claim that the courts of the United States are a bulwark of democracy. Under what conditions, if any, can courts be defenders of democratic regimes? If they can, how do they do it?

1.1 DEFENDERS OF DEMOCRACY

The notion that judges should act as defenders of democratic systems, their values, and their processes is a common and well-developed position. Writing in the *Harvard Law Review*, former Israeli Supreme Court President Aharon Barak clarifies the breadth of Anthony Romero's proposition, placing it in historical context. He writes:

> The [role] of the judge in a democracy is to protect the constitution and democracy itself. Legal systems with formal constitutions impose this task on judges, but judges also play this role in legal systems with no formal constitution. Israeli judges have regarded it as their role to protect Israeli democracy since the founding of the state, even before the adoption of a formal constitution. In England, notwithstanding the absence of a written constitution, judges have protected democratic ideals for many years. Indeed, if we wish to preserve democracy, we cannot take its existence for granted. We must fight for it. This is certainly the case for new democracies, but it is also true of the old and well. Anything can happen. If democracy was perverted and destroyed in the Germany of Kant, Beethoven, and Goethe, it can

6 www.latimes.com/nation/la-na-aclu-profile-20170131-story.html

7 *Trump* v. *Hawaii*, 585 US (2018).

> happen anywhere . . . I do not know whether the supreme court judges in Germany could have prevented Hitler from coming to power in the 1930s. But I do know that a lesson of the Holocaust and of the Second World War is the need to enact democratic constitutions and ensure that they are put into effect by supreme court judges whose main task is to protect democracy. (Barak, 2002)

Judge Barak's position reflects a consensus that developed in the twentieth century among the global legal community, which mobilized around the goal of promoting democratization and human rights. A highly professional and independent judiciary came to be understood as one of the central pillars of rule of law advocacy efforts aimed at supporting new democracies and encouraging reform in authoritarian contexts. The clear recognition of an obvious theoretical tension between majoritarian values and legal limits on authority notwithstanding (e.g. Friedman, 2002), judges exercising various forms of constitutional review came to be viewed as key defenders of democratic norms. In the introduction to its 2002 report on the promotion of judicial independence and impartiality, the US Agency for International Development writes

> Judicial independence is important for precisely the reasons that the judiciary itself is important . . . In democratic, market-based societies, independent and impartial judiciaries contribute to the equitable and stable balance of power within the government. They protect individual rights and preserve the security of person and property. They resolve commercial disputes in a predictable and transparent fashion that encourages fair competition and economic growth. They are key to countering public and private corruption, reducing political manipulation, and increasing public confidence in the integrity of government. (Miklaucic, 2002)

In times when core democratic norms appear to be threatened, when historical understandings of the limits of state power are suddenly called into question, there is an undeniable optimism in these perspectives. Norms of legislative and executive constraint may be violated, perhaps discarded entirely, yet as long as the courts of law are open for business and judges are willing to constrain the state, democracies may backslide but they are unlikely to collapse. It is a comforting story.

The story is comforting not only because of its clear normative appeal but also because of well-known examples in which courts have either claimed or been explicitly delegated a role for protecting democratic norms. In its 1951 Southwest States Case (1 VBerfGE 14), the German Federal Constitutional Court was asked to invalidate two federal statutes designed to reorganize three Laender created during the period of allied occupation, Baden-Württemberg, Baden, and Württemberg-Hohenzollern, into the single Land Baden-Württemberg. The first statute extended the lives of the Laender parliaments until the reorganization could be completed, thus suspending upcoming elections. The second statute laid out the procedures for the reorganization. In its opinion, the court wrote

> An individual constitutional provision cannot be considered as an isolated clause and interpreted alone. A constitution has an inner unity, and the meaning of any one part is linked to that of the other provisions. Taken as a unit, a constitution reflects certain overarching principles and fundamental decisions to which individual provisions are subordinate ... Thus this Court agrees with the statement of the Bavarian Constitutional Court, "That a constitutional provision itself may be null and void, is not conceptually impossible just because it is part of the constitution. There are constituent principles that are so fundamental and such an extent an expression of a law that precedes even the constitution that they also bind the frame of the constitution, and other constitutional provisions that do not rank so high may be null and void because they contravene these principles." (As quoted in Jackson and Tushnet, 2006, p. 588)

Against the backdrop of the principle that the Basic Law ought to be thought of as a logical whole, the nature of which is itself limited by certain higher principles of law, the court continued, writing

> The Basic Law has decided in favor of a democracy as the basis for the governmental system ... As prescribed by the Basic Law, democracy requires not only that parliament control the Government, but also that the right to vote of eligible voters is not removed or impaired by unconstitutional means ... It is true that the democratic principle does not imply that the life of a Landtag must not exceed four years or that it cannot be extended for important reasons. But this principle does require that the term of a Landtag, whose length was set by the people in accepting their constitution, can only be extended through procedures prescribed in that constitution, i.e., only with the consent of the people. (As quoted in Jackson and Tushnet, 2006, p. 588)

By extending the Laender parliaments' life without consent of the voters in the affected areas, the federation had violated the right to vote. Beyond invalidating federal statues in order to preserve fundamental democratic liberties, the court endorsed a powerful principle restricting amendments to the Basic Law that might contravene fundamental norms of a democratic society. Conceived of in this way, constitutional review serves as a backstop against any legislative effort that might undermine basic democratic principles.

An extraordinary variant of this power was conferred upon the South African Constitutional Court during its transition to democracy. A key element of the compromise that allowed for the relatively peaceful transition to democracy involved an agreement at the Multiparty Negotiating Process to 34 Constitutional Principles which would guide the drafting of South Africa's new constitution. The constitutional court was explicitly delegated the power to certify that the constitution conformed to the thirty-four principles (see Constitutional Court of South Africa Case 23/96).

By the end of the twentieth century, providing a form of constitutional review had become a common piece of transitioning states' institutional architecture. Notably, democratic reforms across post-communist Europe were accompanied by forms of constitutional control relying on powerful constitutional courts whose initial appointments were drawn from pools of highly qualified and well-regarded jurists (see the excellent discussion in Schwartz, 2000). Despite clear variation in the level of activism, courts across the region were credited with decisions helping transition from an authoritarian past to a democratic form of government. Indeed, the Constitutional Court of Hungary played such an important role in the provision of social and economic rights during the 1990s that Kim Scheppele called it "arguably more democratic than the Parliament even though the judges are not directly elected" (Scheppele, 2005).

So too in Latin America have courts been a part of the story through which democratic norms come to be fully adopted. The Constitutional Court of Colombia is recognized internationally for giving meaning and force to core commitments of the 1991 Constitution, requiring the state to provide the social and economic rights which the highest law demands (e.g. Cepeda-Espinosa, 2004; Uprimny, 2003). The constitutional court is also credited for developing a flexible jurisprudence on the limits of military jurisdiction, which has allowed for the successful negotiation of civil–military relations during a prolongated period of violent conflict (Ríos-Figueroa, 2016). Similarly the Constitutional Chamber of the Costa Rican Supreme Court is credited with massively expanding access to justice over social and economic rights claims, especially in the context of health (Wilson and Rodríguez Cordero, 2006). And following a notorious delay, in the late 1990s, the judiciary of Chile eventually began to investigate credible claims of gross human rights abuses under the Pinochet regime, a critical source of accountability in the aftermath of the democratic transition (e.g. Huneeus, 2010; Sikkink, 2011).

Across many years and multiple political contexts, courts have been empowered to speak to the nature of a state's democratic practices. They have developed jurisprudence identifying the limits of state authority under democratic constitutions, and they have provided access to citizens seeking redress for violations of core democratic principles. In all of these ways, judges look to be defenders of democracy.

1.2 DEFENSIVE FAILURES

Just as there are powerful stories of judges coming to the defense of democratic states, it is clear that courts, even courts that are formally independent and unconnected politically from sitting governments, are far from successful sources of democratic restraint in all cases. Created by the communist regime in 1982, the Polish Constitutional Tribunal (CT) emerged through the democratic transition as an important source of constitutional control. Beginning in the middle of the 2000s, the CT would become a locus of conflict in the political competition between the Christian democratic Civic Platform (PO) and the conservative, national Law and

Justice Party (PiS). The battle would come to a dramatic head in the weeks following the October 2015 parliamentary election.

Following eight years as the dominant coalition partner in Poland's government, public opinion polling in the summer of 2015 strongly suggested that PO was likely to lose a considerable number of seats in the October parliamentary elections. In June, the PO government enacted a new statute on the CT, which permitted it to replace five judges, all of whom had terms that were set to expire after the pending election. Two terms would expire after the seating of the new parliament. Under the prior institutional framework, the new government would have been empowered to appoint these judges.

The five additional PO appointments meant that it had appointed fourteen out of fifteen CT judges; however, Andrzej Duda, the president of Poland, refused to administer the oath of office for the five new appointees. After taking office following an election that gave it a majority of seats in the Sejm, the PiS amended the PO's constitutional court act, annulling the appointment of the five PO judges. The amendment created five new positions, limited the term of office for the president of the tribunal, ended the tenure of the sitting president and vice president, and stipulated that a judge's term begins only after the administration of the oath of office before the president of Poland. On December 2, the PiS-controlled Sejm appointed five new judges in direct defiance of a CT order demanding the Sejm abstain from doing so until the constitutionality of the amendment could be reviewed. President Duda administered the oath of office to the new PiS judges.

On December 3, a five-judge panel of the CT found that the three PO-appointed judges who replaced judges whose terms were expiring prior to the new parliamentary session were validly appointed. On December 9, the CT found multiple aspects of the PiS amendments to the Constitutional Tribunal Act to be unconstitutional, including the termination of the president and the vice president's terms. The government rejected the decision, refusing to publish it in the state's Journal of Laws.

By the end of January 2016 the government had passed a budget bill cutting the CT's yearly budget by roughly 10 percent. Ignoring concerns expressed by the European Commission that it was undermining judicial independence and democracy, the PiS continued its efforts to reform the judiciary well into 2018, amending rules for appointing and removing judges across the system and at all levels (Venice Commission, n.d.).

The Polish experience is far from unique. Courts seeking to constrain leaders are often the target of institutional attacks. Judges are removed from their posts. Key institutions of judicial powers are reformed or eliminated altogether. Appointment rules are changed so as to concentrate staffing authority in a single power center (Helmke, 2010; Pérez-Liñán and Castagnola, 2009). Some of the attacks are so serious that they effectively eliminate the courts as a source of constraint. Indeed, in 2007, Bolivia's Constitutional Tribunal was rendered inquorate as a consequence of

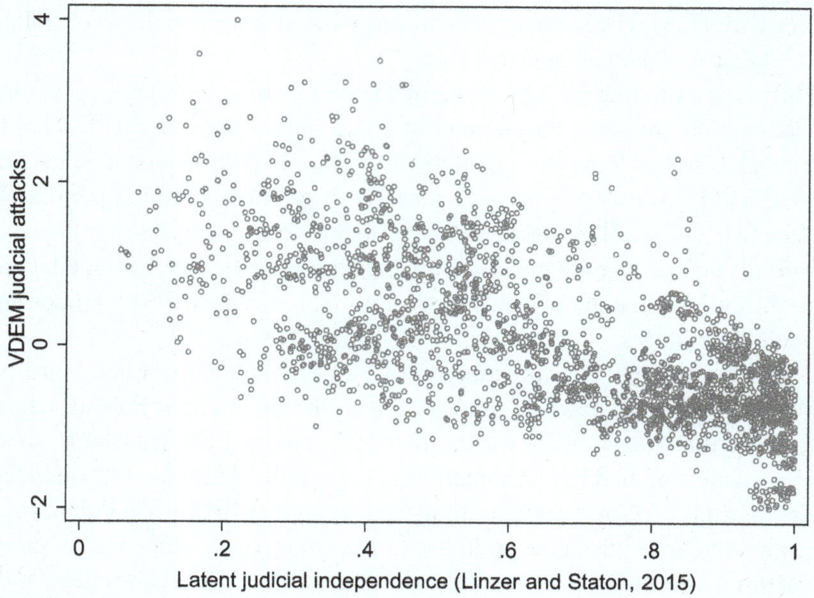

FIGURE 1.1 Attacks on the judiciary and de facto judicial independence

politically motivated impeachments and resignations in the context of major conflict between the judiciary and President Evo Morales (Castagnola and Pérez-Liñán, 2011).

Figure 1.1 reveals a key empirical pattern. It shows a plot of an index of attacks on judicial institutions on a measure of de facto judicial independence (Coppedge et al., 2018; Linzer and Staton, 2015). The points in the figure show the combination of judicial attacks and judicial independence for all states of the world in 2015. As the figure displays, judiciaries are less likely to be the target of government attacks as independence increases; however, the integrity of courts is called into question and judges are purged for political reasons even on courts that enjoy a relatively high level of independence.

The Polish case also reminds us that judicial orders are broadly understood to not be self-enforcing, a challenge that is particularly pressing when the target of an order is the state itself (Becker and Feeley, 1973; Birkby, 1966). Critically, although there are many examples of noncompliance in settings characterized by low levels of the rule of law (Ginsburg and Moustafa, 2008), courts are not always obeyed in states characterized by high levels of the rule of law (Carrubba, Gabel, and Hankla, 2008; Chilton and Versteeg, 2018; Vanberg, 2005). The Constitutional Bench of Costa Rica's Supreme Court confronts a variety of compliance challenges in its amparo jurisdiction (Staton, Gauri, and Cullell, 2015). The Netanyahu government's pattern of evading high court and administrative court decisions across a very wide set of issue areas is particularly notorious (Association for Civil Rights in

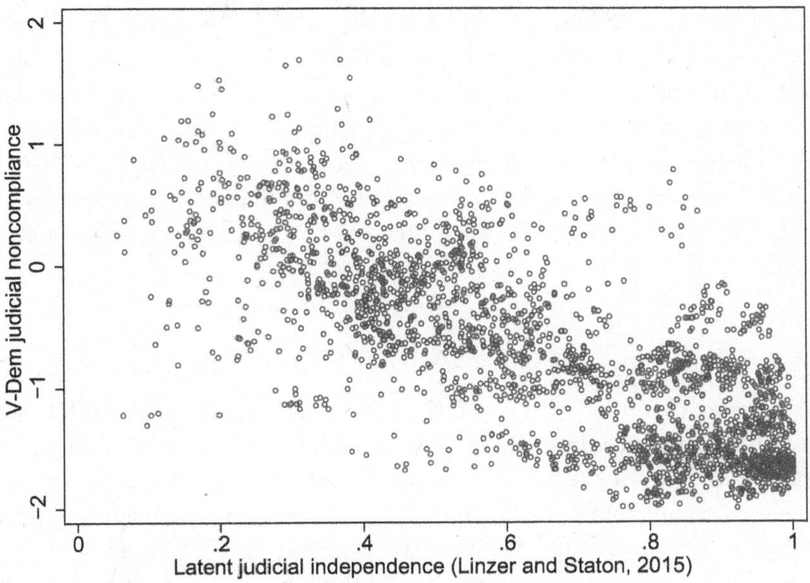

FIGURE 1.2 *Noncompliance and de facto judicial independence*

Israel, 2010). Figure 1.2, which plots the Varieties of Democracy (V-Dem) measure of high court noncompliance on judicial independence underscores the point. There is a negative association between noncompliance and judicial independence, but independent courts are not always obeyed.

Perhaps of greatest concern, scholars have suggested that in order to avoid conflict and noncompliance, judges often engage in politically deferential patterns of decision-making, at least in particularly salient cases, which render the constraints they might place on governments practically nonbinding (e.g. Bill Chávez, Ferejohn, and Weingast, 2011; Carrubba, Gabel, and Hankla, 2008; Rodríguez-Raga, 2011). Summarizing these challenges, the United States Agency for International Development's (USAID) Office of Democracy and Governance writes:

> [I]n several countries, governments have refused to comply with decisions of the constitutional court (e.g. Slovakia and Belarus) and substantially reduced the court's power (e.g. Kazakhstan and Russia). This illustrates the dilemma constitutional courts often face: Should they make the legally correct decision and face the prospect of non-compliance and attacks on their own powers, or should they make a decision that avoids controversy, protects them, and possibly enables them to have an impact in subsequent cases? Bold moves by constitutional courts can be instrumental in building democracy and respect for the courts themselves. However, the local political environment will determine the ability of the courts to exercise independent authority in these high stakes situations. (Office of Democracy and Governance, 2002)

These facts raise serious questions about the capacity of courts to serve as defenders of democracy. If judges attempting to hold leaders accountable are often the target of institutional attacks; if courts are constructed to represent the political interests of appointers; if jurisdiction can be tailored to reduce constraints of courts on political power; if court orders can be ignored even in states with seemingly significant commitments to the rule of law; and if politically savvy judges avoid conflict precisely when they are needed, how is it that courts can serve as bulwarks of democracy?

1.3 ARGUMENT SUMMARY

Our argument knits together and elaborates upon ideas from related but separate research traditions. Understanding whether, and if so under what conditions, courts might be bulwarks of democracy requires a model of what democracy is, what challenges groups confront when they organize themselves democratically, and an account of how courts influence these challenges, if they do so at all.

Drawing on a robust literature on political regimes, we conceive of democracy as a kind of social equilibrium in which groups exchange risky and violent lotteries over complete control of the state for peaceful lotteries over the transfer of power via elections (Acemoglu and Robinson, 2006; Boix, 2003; Boix, Miller, and Rosato, 2012; Przeworski, 2005). Favorable outcomes of conflict are more profitable and potentially more enduring than the favorable outcomes of elections; however, the unfavorable outcomes of conflict can be worse than electoral losses. At its core, democracy requires compromise across a community's salient political cleavage(s). Supposing that compromises necessary to sustain democracy are possible, a fundamental challenge of sustaining these compromises will involve policing limits on the authority of the state. Democracies commonly institutionalize compromises over the allocation of resources and values via a series of limits on the powers of governing parties. These limits, which we refer to as "regime rules," are typically entrenched in constitutions. If it were possible to classify every action of the state with respect to the regime's rules – that is, if it were clear when a policy has exceeded a limit on the authority of the state – groups out of power could police regime rules alone (e.g. Przeworski, 2005). Yet, because there is uncertainty about what governments do, why they do it, and in many cases what regime rules genuinely imply, policing the rules that structure democratic compromises involves resolving a critical informational problem over whether leaders are in fact remaining faithful to regime rules (Carrubba and Gabel, 2014; Reenock, Staton, and Radean, 2013).

We argue that courts can influence regime instability by affecting the informational problem inherent in policing regime rules. They do so in three ways: (1) by providing a mechanism through which private information about the rationale for policy choices that arguably violate a regime rule can be clearly communicated between leaders and the opposition, (2) by encouraging leaders to less frequently make decisions that raise concerns about rule violations, and (3) by encouraging the opposition to more often accept potential rule violations. The central implication of this argument is that courts influence democratic regime survival primarily by encouraging prudence on the part of leaders and the opposition. Although we can identify instances in which courts make decisions stopping arguably undemocratic actions, it is the second face of judicial power that is ultimately essential to the ability of a judicial system to make democratic regimes stable.

In making this argument, we draw on three literatures in judicial politics. The first claims that independent courts are products of democratic political competition (Epperly, 2019; Ginsburg, 2003; Hanssen, 2004; Stephenson, 2003). Independent courts emerge and are sustained when competing groups expect turnover in power via free and fair elections. From this perspective, independent courts offer a kind of "insurance policy" against electoral losses. We will argue that when the underlying social, economic, and cultural conditions for broad democratic compromises in the sense of Przeworski are met, then elites will have incentives to build and sustain independent judicial bodies.

A second literature in judicial politics suggests a way in which courts provide the kind of insurance envisioned by the first literature on which we draw. They do so by influencing the ability of parties to police the boundaries of fundamental regime rules. Scholars argue that judicial processes can help resolve uncertainty for parties in conflict in a variety of ways (e.g. Carrubba and Gabel, 2014). On Julio Ríos-Figueroa's account, constitutional courts can act as a kind of mediator by creating jurisprudence that avoids creating clear winners and losers, instead inviting parties to experiment with possible solutions. This experimentation helps parties credibly reveal to each other what types of legal interpretations will be politically feasible. Clifford Carrubba and Matthew Gabel also suggest that judicial processes give competing parties a centralized means of transferring information to each other about the kinds of compromises regarding the meaning of regime rules that are politically feasible. We draw on these ideas, arguing that courts offer insurance by helping political groups more peacefully police the boundaries of their fundamental democratic compromises. They do so by influencing the information problem essential to managing regime instability.

We also draw on a third literature that considers how political pressures influence judicial decision-making (e.g. Epstein and Knight, 1998; Helmke, 2005; Martin, 2006; Rodríguez-Raga, 2011; Vanberg, 2005). Courts can be rendered dependent on governments through the appointment of political allies; however, courts need not be packed in order to function like extensions of the government. If judges care about their posts, their jurisdiction, and potentially compliance with their decisions, this literature tells us that judicial decision-making will be tied to the interests of officials with control over these matters. In order to influence regime outcomes, courts must overcome these routine political pressures.[8]

An immediate implication of our argument is that while courts *can be* bulwarks, it certainly does not follow that they *will be* bulwarks in all cases. Courts can also be important sources of social control and repression. They can be used to neutralize opposition leaders and to render the powerful immune from prosecution. Judicial systems can be penetrated and judges can be co-opted. When commitments to democratic compromises waiver, courts are natural targets. In such environments, when key groups of political actors no longer find it useful to sustain commitments to the peaceful transfer of power, we ought not to expect judges to be useful defenders of democracy. They may, in fact, be used to undermine the regime.

Elites might also wish to continue transferring power via elections while rejecting limits on their powers while they govern. In such cases, courts may be called upon to check government policy decisions. Lacking independent sources of violent or financial power, the ability of courts to influence political conflicts will always be subject to particular conditions (Epstein and Knight, 1998; Rodríguez-Raga, 2011; Staton and Moore, 2011). If judges are unwilling to be effective checks or if their decisions can be ignored by governments without consequence, courts will not meaningfully influence either policy-making, or more importantly, the interactions between governments and the opposition that risk democratic regime collapse.

We develop this argument further in Chapters 2 and 4, focusing on the conditions necessary to support this system and the variety of ways in which it can break down. For the mechanism we envision to work, like Ríos-Figueroa, we will argue that judges must have preferences that are sufficiently distinct from at least the sitting government. We also share with Ríos-Figueroa a belief that noncompliance must be consequential for state leaders. But we will stress that judges must also be willing to risk noncompliance. The risk of noncompliance, as well as noncompliance itself, is a critical part of the mechanism by which judges help stabilize regimes. Indeed, the simple threat of noncompliance (1) creates incentives for more prudent elite behavior, and (2) can create the possibility for elites to credibly communicate about their intentions.

1.3.1 *Methodological Approach*

We confront two core empirical challenges in evaluating our argument's implications. A natural challenge is whether we will be able to identify exogenous variation in some of our core concepts, such that we can estimate causal effects. Second, as

[8] Ginsburg and Huq (2018) recognize this limitation on judicial authority in practice, and for that reason, they are justifiably skeptical about the ability of courts to serve as saviors of democracy (see discussion in Ginsburg and Huq, 2018, pp. 141–148).

will become clear later, if we are correct about the role that courts play in reinforcing democratic compromises, direct evidence for the mechanism will be hard to come by. The reason for this is that the primary effect of independent courts is to incentivize political prudence on the part of state and opposition leaders. Finding evidence of roads considered but not taken or even roads that were simply never considered at all is a fundamental empirical challenge. In many cases the best evidence we could marshal will not make it into the historical record.

The empirical strategies that we employ address both of these challenges. We pursue two primary strategies. First, whenever possible we adopt credible observational designs for causal identification. Specifically we rely on matching, instrumental variables and difference-in-difference techniques when we can. When this is not possible, we are careful with the interpretation of our findings. In some cases, we are confident that we have identified causal evidence, and when we are not we attempt to provide interpretation in light of our theoretical argument while identifying potential alternative explanations. Our second approach is to look for behaviors and events that indirectly reveal the mechanisms that we propose. In these cases, our goal is not necessarily causal inference but rather description that is consistent with our theoretical account.

1.4 PLAN OF THE BOOK

Chapter 2 begins by defining terms. What do we mean by democracy? What does it mean to defend democracy? What is an independent court? We then present our argument in general terms. When groups in society wish to compete for power peacefully via free and fair elections, they will have strong incentives to construct and support independent judicial bodies. Independent courts, in turn, can cause leaders to pursue policy initiatives more prudently and cause the opposition to police democratic compromises less aggressively. This reinforces commitments to democracy. To have these effects, courts must be staffed by judges who are sufficiently independent of (at least) sitting governments. Judges must also be willing to risk noncompliance with their orders. If judges are not incentivized to independently evaluate the cases before them, regimes will be less stable. Similarly and more transparently, if the background conditions necessary for democratic compromises are not met, elites will no longer have incentives to support independent courts. Just as walls can be constructed, they can be torn down.

In Chapter 3, we investigate the first key element of our argument: the well-known claim that increases in political competition cause judicial independence. This is the primary subject of Brad Epperly's (2019) recent work. In some cases, we draw on research designs that Epperly employs, fit to a larger sample of states. In other cases, we present new designs. We present evidence of a causal relationship between political competition de facto judicial independence. We argue that this relationship is best interpreted as coming from the transition from autocracy to democracy. Basically, judicial independence is a feature of democracy. Interestingly, we do not find a causal relationship between the formal rules that are supposed to incentivize independent judicial behavior and independent behavior itself.

In Chapter 4, we present a theoretical model that is designed to shed light on whether, and if so how, courts might protect democratic regimes from collapse. The model identifies conditions under which courts can influence the exchange of information between leaders and the opposition. It also identifies the conditions under which courts can help stabilize democratic regimes even when they cannot influence information exchange.

In Chapter 5, we present evidence bearing on key empirical predictions implied by the model developed in Chapter 4. We both summarize existing scholarship and offer new evidence on the relationship between judicial independence and a variety of policy choices that can be destabilizing: electoral system reform, the investigation of political rivals, and declarations of states of emergency. We also investigate relationships between judicial independence, coups, and democratic breakdown. We show that judicial independence is associated with lower probabilities of governments declaring emergencies when there is a greater likelihood for disagreement over the need for extraordinary responses but not when this likelihood is lower. We show that judicial independence is associated with lower probabilities of coups and democratic breakdowns. We also show that attacks on courts increase the likelihood of coups and breakdowns. Critically, we show that noncompliance is not positively associated with coups or breakdowns. Indeed, we observe a small negative association. These findings suggest that while attacking courts in democracy can be profoundly destabilizing, some degree of noncompliance with judicial orders can be a part of a healthy democratic system.

Chapter 6 considers the recent pattern of attacks on courts around the world in light of the argument we make in the book. We describe where courts are being attacked. We return to the case of the United States and speculate on the ability of the US federal judiciary to serve as a bulwark of US democracy. Finally, Chapter 7 offers three general lessons that our study suggests for research on political regimes and judicial politics.

2

Democratic Regimes and Their Survival

In framing a government which is to be administered by men over men, the great difficulty lies in this: you must first enable the government to control the governed; and in the next place oblige it to control itself.

James Madison, Federalist 51

This chapter answers four questions: What do we mean by democracy? What does it mean to say that a court has defended democracy? What is the threat democracies confront that courts might defend against? How might courts address this threat? With answers to these questions, we then present our conceptual framework in broad prospective. The first part of our argument connects political incentives to opt for democratic political competition with incentives to create and support independent judicial bodies. It also explains how independent courts influence an important informational challenge that is critical to the survival of democratic regimes.

The second part of our argument raises theoretical questions that require more space than we can devote in this chapter. Therefore we return to it in Chapter 4, where we present a formal model that accounts for how different degrees of judicial independence affect the ability of courts to promote democratic peace through information transmission. Our model also identifies the conditions under which courts influence democratic peace even when they cannot influence information.

2.1 WHAT IS DEMOCRACY?

Recognizing that democracy's meaning is essentially contested (Gallie, 1956), our conceptual goal is limited. We will adopt a concept that both clarifies a fundamental problem for democratic regime survival and makes the measurement of key ideas tractable.

Definitions of democracy are conceived of as either minimalist-procedural or maximalist-substantive. The minimalist definition, best associated with Schumpeter (1942), conceives of democracy as nothing more than a political system in which elites compete for mass support via free and fair elections. Although the meaning of democracy is vigorously contested by political theorists, scholars agree that free and fair elections are essential components of any concept. Disagreements emerge over whether to include in the definition substantive values that democracies might advance, and if so, which values. Democracy in the maximalist or substantive sense is Schumpeterian political systems that also, for example, protect private property, promote economic equality, and require clear and vigorous public debate, among many other features. In light of the large number of combinations of potential substantive criteria, it is possible to conceive of a very large number of maximalist varieties of democracy (Coppedge et al., 2011).

The Minimalist Concept of Democracy

We adopt the minimalist definition for several reasons. First and foremost, the definition focuses our attention on a critical normative outcome. A social commitment to transferring power via elections means that groups shun violence as a means of seeking state power. We take it as obvious that avoiding violence is a normatively appropriate goal (Przeworski, 2003).

Second, the minimalist concept allows us to consider connections between the independence of the judiciary and democracy. Ginsburg and Huq (2018) study the survival of liberal constitutional democracies. A liberal constitutional democracy on this account is a political regime in which there are free and fair elections, robust associational rights (speech, association, and assembly), as well as a bureaucracy governed by the rule of law (pp. 9–15). Our thinking on the connection between courts and democracy has been influenced considerably by Ginsburg and Huq's analysis. They offer an account of democratic erosion, which complements Levitsky and Ziblatt's (2018) focus on democratic norms by connecting it to scholarship on constitutional jurisprudence and empirical studies of constitutional courts around the world. That said, we will separate the concept of democracy from the concept of judicial independence, which is, after all, a common component of the rule of law concepts on which Ginsburg and Huq draw (e.g. Raz, 1997). We do so in order to consider how, if at all, undermining rule of law institutions influences political commitments to elections.

Third, the minimalist concept links nicely to research on judicial independence as political insurance, which forms the first link in our argument. Under conditions of democratic competition via elections, elites turn to courts as insurance against the loss of political power. We develop an account of how courts help reinforce commitments to democracy, and in that way provide a mechanism through which insurance is provided.

Fourth, the minimalist concept simplifies a series of important measurement challenges. On a minimalist account, courts defend democracy in so far as they reinforce social commitments to the peaceful transfer of power via elections. How they might do this will require some explication, and drawing inferences connecting courts to regime survival will require a mix of strong theory and credible research design. Yet measuring the collapse of a democratic regime under a minimalist concept, though not without difficulty, is a common and largely solved problem in comparative politics (Boix, Miller, and Rosato, 2012; Przeworski et al., 2000).

The measurement challenges implied by arguments envisioning courts as protectors of substantive concepts of democracy are significantly more complicated. Arguments about courts as protectors of substantive concepts of democracy focus on the ways particular decisions are in line with substantive democratic values. Consider Kim Scheppele's discussion of the Hungarian Constitutional Court's democratic role in the 1990s. She writes, "the new post-Soviet citizens would not believe that a democracy was real until the *substance* of the previous policies had changed. The new constitutions not only guaranteed this, but also gave these institutions more radically democratic *content* through the 'thickness' of the post-Soviet constitutions" (p. 38). The Hungarian court's primary function was to invalidate both old and new laws that were inconsistent with the substantive goals of the founding document. The court required the privatization of nationalized property, constrained the Parliament's investigations of former communist leaders in order to protect a principle against retroactive justice, and undermined state control of the media (p. 41). In each of these ways, the court protected, in fact it enhanced, a Hungarian view of democracy. As Scheppele understands it, this democracy is much more than a commitment to free and fair elections.

Scheppele's account of the Hungarian Constitutional Court suggests that courts defend democracy by vetoing policies that violate core substantive provisions of a democratic system or by requiring that governments adopt policies that bring the state in line with its commitments to particular values. This is a highly reasonable perspective. No doubt, it captures what many people believe courts are doing when they claim that they are defending a democratic system. We are drawn to this language in cases where courts are called upon to review arguably unconstitutional state behavior on matters that are highly salient. And yet consider what it would mean for a general account of courts as defenders of democracy. In order to conceptualize the extent to which a court, or perhaps the judiciary as a whole, has defended democracy in a maximalist sense will require precise interpretations of the many substantive features of a political system that a court might be called upon to protect.

Suppose that we adopt a liberal conception of democracy. Here democracy is understood to involve both the competition for power via free and fair elections as well as a commitment to limited government that respects a series of individual rights and freedoms. Suppose further that we imagine that liberal democracy also requires a commitment to free market exchange. The constitutions of many countries guarantee some elements of market freedom. The tenth amendment to the US Constitution prohibits laws "impairing the obligation of contracts." Article 314 of the Bolivian Constitution prohibits monopoly. Article 45 of the Constitution of Ireland prohibits "the concentration of the ownership or control of essential commodities in a few individuals to the common detriment." Article 333 of the Constitution of Colombia and Article 27 of the Egyptian Constitution ensure that all individuals have the right to free economic competition (Elkins et al., 2014). Article 42 of the Constitution of Argentina provides specifically that state authorities must provide for the "defense of competition against any type of market distortion, for the control of natural and legal monopolies." Article 42 also provides consumers the right to "adequate and truthful information" in their relationships with the providers of goods and services.

With our liberal concept in hand, one might naturally look to cases in which, say, the Supreme Court of Argentina is called upon to review the regulation of public utilities with respect to Article 42. In August of 2016, the Supreme Court of Argentina invalidated energy price increases on residential users, finding that government had failed to hold "obligatory" public hearings prior to the price hike, in violation of Article 42's public information provision.[1] Did this decision protect Argentina's liberal democracy? One's interpretation of the meaning of Article 42 in light of the facts of the case, and here we mean a researcher's interpretation, will critically affect how one views a decision permitting or striking down the regulation. The researcher's interpretation is not merely an important consideration; it is essential to the entire enterprise. Absent a clear understanding of how particular substantive values constitute democracy in a regime, it will be impossible to know whether a court has defended the regime or not.

Deepening the challenge, we must recognize that legal scholars, lawyers, and judges commonly disagree over the precise meaning of constitutional terms. For this reason, it is not immediately obvious how a researcher will choose the correct interpretation of a rule governing a substantive value for a court to defend, much less a group of scholars working in a research program.[2] Yet this kind of term-by-term constitutional analysis would have to be carried out for many judicial decisions across multiple policy areas in order to say anything meaningful about the ability of the judiciary to protect the substantive aspects of democracy via its decisions.

Making matters worse is the issue of aggregation. Suppose for the sake of argument that there is consensus over the meaning of every substantive term of every state's constitution (written or unwritten) in every year. States will violate some

1 Fallo 339:1077, "Centro de Estudios para la Promoción de la Igualdad y la Solidaridad y otros c/Ministerio de Energía y Minería s/ amparo colectivo."

2 Law and Versteeg (2013) offer one potential solution. In a study of state commitments to constitutional promises, the authors characterize state constitutions as "shams" by identifying mismatches between a state's constitutional promise (e.g. right to vote) and its observed behavior (limitations on voting rights) as judged by experts such as Cingranelli and Richards (2008). Here Cingranelli and Richards, with help from the US Department of State and Amnesty International, give us an evaluation of the state's behavior. But the kind of arguments that are made about courts as protectors of the substantive aspects of democracy would need to be far more careful. We would require an account of whether placing an election on a Tuesday or whether districts that are drawn with political considerations in mind violate a constitutional right to participate. These are questions that reasonable people can disagree about.

of these terms in some years, perhaps in all years (Law and Versteeg, 2013). Yet they likely will not violate all of them. How should we aggregate across the different dimensions of a maximalist view of democracy? Do some elements, e.g. voting rights, speech rights, access to justice, quality health care, or housing, count more than other elements? If so, how much more? On the other hand, if all substantive elements are considered equal, what proportion of them must be respected in a particular state and year in order for democracy to "survive"? We view the Varieties of Democracy Project measures of liberal, egalitarian, participatory, and deliberative variations on democracy as plausible measures of substantive concepts; however, they are very clearly aggregations of a tremendous amount of information. We can envision a study attempting to connect courts to these substantive measures, but for the reasons we have summarized, we strongly prefer to focus on courts as protectors of the Schumpeterian core.

2.1.1 *Democracy as Political Compromise*

Our minimalist definition focuses on democratic procedures; however, it is important to stress that the substantive concerns on which Scheppele focuses play a role in our account. We define democracy as a political regime in which groups, typically parties, compete for power by winning votes. This definition eases the challenge of measuring regime types and their failure, but it does not have much to say about why groups commit to the peaceful transfer of power via elections. By taking a position on this issue, we clarify the link between the substantive values that democratic regimes might respect even if we only consider democracy itself to involve a commitment to selecting leaders via elections. We also illuminate the core problem of democratic governance.

Following Przeworski (2005), we envision democracy as a broad compromise between groups over the control of the authoritative allocation of values and resources. It is an equilibrium in which competing groups opt for peace and the corresponding lotteries over election outcomes instead of pursuing control over the state via violence. Whereas the outcome, i.e. free and fair electoral competition, is procedural, democracy conceived of in this way is influenced by many substantive concerns.

Substantive considerations influence the choice to continue contesting power via elections, precisely because what holding power means is control over substantive outcomes, e.g. the language in which our children are taught, our religious freedoms, our ability to speak and publish freely, our rights when we are accused, the tax burdens we confront. The democratic compromise we envision is predicated on choices to limit the state's power. All but five countries in the modern world have codified constitutions, which identify rights, grant powers, and limit state authority (Miaschi, 2017). We will refer to these limits on state authority as "fundamental regime rules." Violations of these rules, many of which are substantive in nature, can call into question a leader's commitment to elections.

To summarize, we adopt a Schumpeterian, minimalist concept of democracy. Although democracy for us only requires free and fair competition for state power, we view democracy as involving compromises over the uses of state authority, which have implications for substantive outcomes that people value. Competing groups in society strike an agreement, which involves trading a violent struggle for unconstrained governance for a peaceful struggle for constrained governance. This trade depends critically on believing that the parties that enjoy power will be constrained during their period in office. Uncertainty about whether this is true in practice can be significantly destabilizing.

2.1.2 *What Does It Mean to Defend Democracy?*

When we say that a judiciary has defended a democratic regime, we will mean that courts have positively influenced the survival of the regime as conceived of under a minimalist or maximalist concept. Otherwise put, we mean to say that the regime would have been less stable in the absence of courts. The counterfactual is important here. To defend a democracy does not imply that the regime would have *failed* in the absence of courts. Democratic regimes might survive for many years in the absence of a well-functioning judicial system, and democratic regimes may collapse even if courts are working well. Well-functioning judicial systems are neither necessary nor sufficient for regime survival. To defend democracy simply implies that courts have made the system more robust, more stable than they would have been without courts.

2.2 THE FUNDAMENTAL PROBLEM OF DEMOCRATIC GOVERNANCE

Democracies are threatened by failures to resolve a fundamental governance problem. The problem, stated succinctly by Publius in *Federalist* 51, involves seeking a balance between two seemingly irreconcilable goals. We want a government powerful enough to ensure social peace, defend the territory from outside aggressors, produce public goods, and generally meet the social challenges that communities confront, without being so powerful that it cannot be controlled. We want a powerful but constrained state.

To clarify for leaders the extent of their powers and to help opposition groups police potential violations of regime rules, written constitutions specify the nature and limits of state authority; however, no constitution can completely and precisely characterize all limits on state actions. Some limits and powers will be implied. Naturally, there will be disagreements over claims about implied powers. Similarly there will be uncertainty and corresponding disagreements about the meaning of the fundamental regime rules that political communities actually do write down. In so far as some leaders do not act in good faith, opposition groups must police the limits on state power. And yet since there will be uncertainty about these limits, it is possible for a democratic compromise to break down as a consequence of mutual misunderstandings about whether leaders are acting within the constraints of fundamental regime rules. The key point is that managing the right balance between constrained and powerful states will necessarily involve solving an *informational problem* over whether leaders are committed to regime rules.

Complicating the informational challenge, many regime rules are context dependent. Public health or economic crisis, natural disasters, domestic disturbances, and war all typically require a leader to pursue extraordinary actions, which might not be ordinarily tolerated.[3] Informational asymmetries between governors and the governed make this problem particularly vexing. Leaders often have more precise information about the possibility for implementing policy initiatives. This advantage makes it possible for leaders to be less than truthful about the true reasons behind a change in policy, and for that reason skepticism is a sensible reaction to government actions that plausibly violate regime standards. The Israeli Interior Ministry's rationale for failing to comply with high court decisions on a variety of policies dealing with the separation barrier, treatment of migrant workers, and educational equality between the Arab and Jewish populations highlighted practical difficulties and relied on appeals about impracticalities. Specifically, the ministry claimed that delays in changing their policies were due to the

> [E]xtreme complexity of these cases, some of which entail significant budget expense, some of which have implications for third parties, some of which require the establishment of new procedures and various complex administrative actions. Because of their complexity, these court rulings require an extended period during which they can be implemented. (Association for Civil Rights in Israel, 2010)

Was this true? Were the conditions such that these policies could not be amended or was the Interior Ministry simply refusing to do what it surely could have? In the absence of the Interior Ministry's information, opposition groups would have had to draw an inference about whether compliance would have been too complicated or expensive.

Also, consider the Peruvian constitutional crisis of the early 1990s. After nearly a decade of attempting to bring to heel elements of the Shining Path and the Tupac Amarú Revolutionary Movement (MRTA), newly elected Peruvian president Alberto Fujimori sought to enhance his powers via emergency power legislation. By the president's account, "his emergency measures were needed both to battle

[3] Of course, some constitutional arrangements typically anticipate this problem, calibrating the state powers so as to properly meet economic crises, natural disasters, or security threats (Gross, 2011); however, even when present, these "states of exception" are themselves open to interpretation.

terrorism and to restructure the state and economy. He required an iron hand to reform the judiciary and break the gridlock created by the opposition in Congress" (Cameron, 1998, p. 127). Suspicious that President Fujimori's plea for greater authority to fight domestic terrorism was in actuality a raw power grab, Congress resisted. It altered the legislation to "subordinate the executive to the rule of law, assert congressional supremacy over law-making, and require the executive to justify its use of emergency powers" (p. 127). Soon after, Fujimori, in conjunction with the intelligence community and the military, initiated his *autogulpe*.

2.3 HOW CAN COURTS INFLUENCE THE FUNDAMENTAL PROBLEM?

Efforts to strike a balance between powerful and constrained states have looked to legal solutions to police the boundaries of fundamental regime rules. The twentieth century witnessed the development of a variety of constitutional review mechanisms in nearly all states. Indeed, Ginsburg and Versteeg (2013) report that by the second decade of the twenty-first century 83 percent of the world's constitutions contained some form of constitutional review, permitting courts to set aside statutes, regulations, decrees, and international treaties for their violation of constitutional rules.

Although this monitoring function is most associated with constitutional review powers, administrative law and judicial review in the sense of that practiced historically in the United Kingdom serves a similar purpose (Vanhala, 2012). As Peter Cane (2004, p. 16) writes, judicial review can be defined as "scrutiny by the judicial branch of government of decisions and actions of the executive branch to police compliance with rules and principles of 'public law' (including, but not limited to, 'higher law')." This kind of authority can also be used to police what we are calling fundamental regime rules. Importantly, it will be more limited than that exercised under jurisdiction that, say, permits a court to strike down an act of Parliament as begin inconsistent with a state's constitution. However, since democracies are commonly threatened by uncertainty whether executive actions are lawful, judicial review in the sense that Cane means it, can be an extremely powerful tool.

The basic institutional logic is straightforward. The problem to be solved is one of policing the boundaries of regime rules. Judicial processes provide a centralized and public venue for raising claims that rules have been violated. Thus, a judicial solution to the problem involves creating a kind of fire alarm monitoring system for democratic compromises. Judges are asked to police the boundaries of regime rules. We are led to ask how the process of reviewing state actions might change beliefs about whether a potential violation of regime rules ought to be tolerated or challenged outside the context of normal democratic rules for leadership selection.

2.3.1 *Judges as Trustees*

One simple possibility is that once the power to review acts of the state has been delegated to courts (or a particular court) designed to be independent, the informational challenge is solved. Actors in the system simply rely on the judgment of courts. This argument follows from scholarship that conceptualizes judges as trustees of the constitutional system rather than as agents of their appointers (e.g. Stone Sweet, 2000; Stone Sweet and Brunell, 2013). Karen Alter (2008) writes,

> Trustees are actors created through a revocable delegation act where the Trustee is: (1) selected because of their personal and/or professional reputations; (2) given authority to make meaningful decisions according to the Trustee's best judgment or the Trustee's professional criteria; and (3) is making these decisions on behalf of a beneficiary.

Judges appointed because of their expertise, who are given authority to exercise judicial review powers and who do so with the interests of the public generally in mind, might simply be granted the authority to resolve uncertainty about the meaning of regime rules and the conditions that might give rise to particular kinds of powers of leadership. As long as judges are not perceived to be doing the work of leaders or the opposition, i.e. they are assumed to be independent, we resolve the informational problem by simply deciding not to worry about it.

People will certainly hold different views about the finer points of regime rules in light of new circumstances. Some facts of the world are simply impossible to convey with perfect credibility to another person. What it means to use an independent judiciary to police the boundaries of regime rules is to recognize that the informational challenge to be overcome is simply unresolvable. In so far as that is true, we agree to let judges solve these difficult problems for us so that we can go on living in peace. This is the essential logic of triadic dispute resolution (Shapiro, 1981).

The argument may well be part of the overall story of how courts help democracies survive. Yet, it is helpful to see that this account is hard to square with some key facts presented in Chapter 1. If independent courts are trustees, why are independent courts attacked? Why is the integrity of respected jurists called into question? Why would respected judges face noncompliance with their decisions? And why would we observe patterns of decisions that raise questions about whether judges are strategically avoiding conflict on occasion? These facts suggest that the authority of judges is not a settled matter at the point of delegation or appointment. It should be thought of as an ongoing concern.

2.3.2 *Judges as Mediators*

Ríos-Figueroa (2016) offers a compelling alternative. Drawing on international relations scholarship on the role of mediation in the resolution of interstate conflicts,

Ríos-Figueroa claims that constitutional courts can help resolve seemingly intractable domestic political conflicts by offering creative jurisprudential frameworks, which create incentives for competitors to explore potential resolutions through experimentation and dialogue. In developing this argument, Ríos-Figueroa draws a distinction between courts as "arbitrators" and courts as "mediators." He writes, "A court behaving as an arbitrator simply determines the outcome of a case based on the record adjudicating responsibility between disputing parties." In contrast, when courts behave as mediators their decisions are "not case circumscribed, ... creative, forward looking, nonshaming, and transparent in [their] argumentation that should be robustly grounded on constitutional principles and norms" (p. 34).

Courts acting in this way do not create clear winners and losers. They look for compromises and establish incentives to continue a dialogue moving forward. For courts to act as mediators, Ríos-Figueroa emphasizes that they must be independent, accessible, and ultimately powerful. Indeed, he refers to courts as a particular species of mediator: they are mediators with power. Accessibility allows courts to learn about how law works on the ground across a very wide variety of situations (Clark and Staton, 2015; Rogers, 2001; Whittington, 2009). Independence in turn gives courts credibility in their evaluation of constitutional conflicts. And finally, courts that enjoy significant control over their docket possess the discretion they require to pick the kinds of cases that best allow them to engage in the flexible kind of jurisprudence associated with mediation. Courts that satisfy these conditions can reduce uncertainty about "the legal consequences of certain actions," "the bounds of the exceptions and the weight of extraordinary circumstances," and "how to balance clashing constitutional principles or rules in particular cases."

2.3.3 *Courts as Settings for Information Transmission*

Another possibility is that the judicial review process reveals special information to judges about the true nature of the political conflict they resolve. Judges might then consider revealing what they learn to uncertain parties. Carrubba's (2005) model of judicial review assumes such a role for a court. As long as judges are reasonably certain that governments will comply with their decisions, they will be willing to reveal the information that they learn via the litigation process. It is no doubt common to assume that litigation, generally speaking, reveals information about the case facts and parties' motivations (Bull and Watson, 2004; Clark and Kastellec, 2013). So, perhaps all that is necessary is to assume that some information will be revealed about a leader's motives during the course of a case. The difficulty with this assumption is that regime misunderstandings follow from beliefs that some kinds of leaders have incentives to dissemble. And if that is true, it is unclear why a litigation process that involves a party believed to be less than truthful would necessarily convince another party that what has been presented or said or recorded is in fact true. This lack of trust is exactly what causes the problem of managing regime understandings.

It is the problem we are trying to solve. Assuming that courts simply provide this information does not answer why and how they might do it.

Carrubba and Gabel (2014) provide a mechanism by which information could be revealed in the process of litigation. They develop a model in which regime rules are managed via litigation before a court. The particular setting that they have in mind is the Court of Justice of the European Union. The problem on which they focus is that in some years some member states of the European Union will confront local challenges that make it inefficient to comply with long-run commitments to European regulations. Other governments in the system might agree with this state's interest in violating the treaty under these facts, at least in the short-run; however, there is an informational asymmetry. Only the noncompliant state truly knows whether the local challenge it confronts is sufficient to render its long-run commitments inefficient. Carrubba and Gabel suggest that the litigation process provides states with an opportunity to send costly signals about their private information.

2.3.4 *Information and Judicial Review*

In Chapter 4, we offer a formal analysis of the ways in which judicial review can influence the fundamental problem of democratic governance. It draws on ideas developed by Ríos-Figueroa (2016) and Carrubba and Gabel (2014). Here we highlight what our account shares with their accounts. We also highlight ways in which we depart from their work. We conclude by specifying four conditions that are necessary for courts to influence democratic regime survival.

We agree with Ríos-Figueroa that courts lacking independence, at least from sitting governments, are unlikely to influence conflicts between leaders of the state, the political opposition, or other interests in society. We agree with both Ríos-Figueroa and Carrubba and Gabel that influencing the ability of parties to deal with their uncertainty about the underlying nature of a political conflict can be an important element of the way in which courts stabilize democratic regimes. And with Carrubba and Gabel, we share the view that judicial processes can influence the credibility of communication even if courts do not behave as mediators in the sense of Ríos-Figueroa.

Our account also differs from their work, but in complementary ways. As we show in Chapter 4, judicial review can help reduce political conflict even if courts act in ways that would be classified as "arbitrators" on Ríos-Figueroa's account. The model of judicial review we develop is sparse. Judicial decisions act as a kind of veto only. There is no dialogue. Indeed, there is no jurisprudence at all. This does not imply that mediator-like courts are no better than the type of court we imagine. They may very well be. Nevertheless, we believe it is useful to identify the conditions under which an arbitrator style court can work to promote peace as well.

Our model identifies conditions under which courts are able to incentivize the revelation of private information. This, as it turns out, has a lot to do with how we conceive of judicial preferences, and ultimately judicial independence. As we show, for courts to influence the informational problem directly by helping the parties to the conflict communicate credibly, they must be not only independent of the sitting government but independent of all parties. Whether it is politically feasible to imagine a court that is somehow independent of all political cleavages in society is not completely clear; however, if courts do operate largely independently of all interests, then there are conditions under which they can incentivize leaders to fully reveal their private information in ways that the opposition will find credible.

We will also depart slightly from Ríos-Figueroa on the issue of judicial power and compliance with court orders. He writes, "In this framework compliance goes hand in hand with the transmission of information ... Transmitting information effectively does not assume compliance, but arguably simply issuing creative and forward-looking jurisprudence would incentivize the actors in the conflict to apply the solution suggested by the mediator" (p. 40). We do not disagree with this logic, but in our model it is the threat of noncompliance and the costs that leaders can sometimes bear for defying court orders that creates the costs necessary to send credible signals about their reasons for acting in extraordinary ways. Indeed, this argument provides a simple rationale for understanding where the costs associated with the signals in Carrubba and Gabel's account come from. In our argument, courts are defied and yet defiance can be part of a mechanism through which democracy is stabilized.

Finally and critically, the model we develop in Chapter 4 shows how judicial review can promote democratic peace even when courts do not in fact influence the information that leaders transmit to the opposition. As long as noncompliance is sufficiently costly, judicial review will incentivize leaders to less frequently engage in extraordinary policy-making, thus making the scenarios that can result in conflict less likely to observe. This effect in turn will make opposition leaders less likely to aggressively police potential violations of regime rules when they observe them. In short, judicial review lowers the temperature of political conflicts even when courts cannot influence information transmission.

2.4 THE ARGUMENT

We are now in a position to recombine the preceding ideas in support of courts as bulwarks of democracy. Figure 2.1 summarizes our argument. The first link in our account recognizes that democratic governance can be usefully conceived of as a social equilibrium, where competing groups forego violence in exchange for some degree of limited state power (Przeworski, 2005). If nothing else, democracy requires a commitment to the peaceful transfer of power. Underlying this equilibrium are fundamental compromises or understandings made between groups on the nature of power in a democratic state. Modern democratic governance is indeed limited

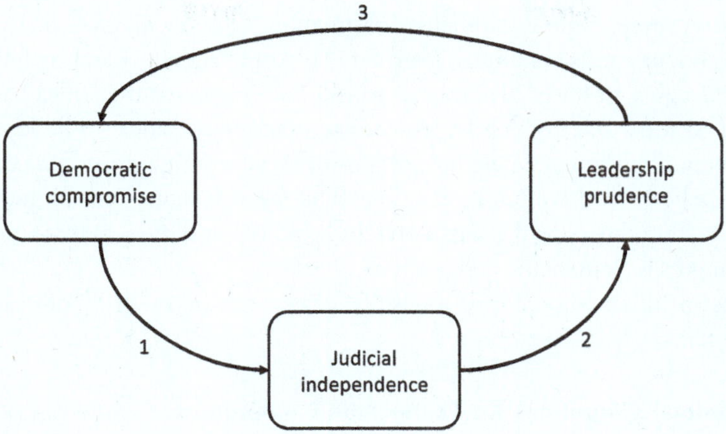

FIGURE 2.1 Courts and democracy

in a variety of ways, with limits often expressed formally in written constitutions but sometimes only understood implicitly by members of society (Weingast, 1997). Judicial systems are constructed to solve a monitoring problem inherent in this arrangement. Groups out of power will find it useful to have some mechanism for revealing violations of regime commitments (Reenock, Staton, and Radean, 2013). Critically, as monitoring solutions, courts will be useful only in so far as competing groups wish to sustain democratic cooperation.

The incentives to construct effective monitoring systems are heightened when competition in a democracy is strong. Where elites might find themselves in control of the state one year and yet out of power the next, monitoring systems are in great demand. A generation of scholarship on the determinants of judicial independence suggests that courts operated by independent judges are particularly useful in this role (Epperly, 2013, 2019; Finkel, 2008; Ginsburg, 2003; Hanssen, 2004; Stephenson, 2003). Thus, communities that compete in competitive electoral environments have strong incentives to build independent judiciaries. This relationship constitutes the first link in Figure 2.1.

The second and third links in the argument address how independent courts influence a critical information challenge that must be addressed to render democratic regimes stable. One opposition party leader's claim that a president has fundamentally violated the constitution may be the president's necessary use of power under exigent circumstances. Failing to communicate clearly and credibly about the reasons for arguably unconstitutional behavior can be fundamentally destabilizing for a regime. By offering a centralized and visible venue for raising claims that officials have violated limits on their authority, courts present a potentially useful means of coordinating beliefs about whether limits on authority have been violated. In Chapter 4, we develop a model that identifies how courts can help parties reveal regime stabilizing information. Our key claim is that in doing so independent courts encourage leaders to be more prudent, adopting fewer policies or engaging in fewer actions that would raise concerns that rules have been violated. At the same time courts encourage opposition leaders to be less aggressive in their efforts to police regime compromises, accepting more often potentially extreme policies in the interests of peace. The result is that courts promote more prudent politics, lowering the stakes of holding power; and this prudence reinforces commitments to democratic competition.

To sustain this reinforcing relationship, several conditions of a political system are essential.

1. **Minimal Conditions for Democratic Compromise:** Courts can only help reinforce democratic arrangements if competing parties are in principle committed to peaceful, democratic competition. A monitoring system is not useful is if there is no agreement to monitor. We will discuss and provide evidence for the claim that minimal conditions of economic development, necessary to sustain broad redistributional compromises between economic groups, remain essential for democratic stability. In states where the economic conditions for democratic compromise are met, we will suggest that independent courts can be particularly useful mechanisms for monitoring state power. To be fair, independent courts may help promote economic development in underdeveloped states, but it is less clear that courts will be effective monitors of the state. In such contexts, courts may be more effective tools of social control than monitors of state behavior.
2. **Minimal Judicial Independence:** Our argument highlights the need for a monitoring system that can solve informational problems that complicate democratic compromises (Carrubba and Gabel, 2014; Ríos-Figueroa, 2016). A judicial system whose judges can be separated politically from both current governments as well as opposition parties can powerfully influence the ability of competing parties to communicate credibly about the true rationales behind potentially destabilizing policy choices. Of course, this claim immediately raises a question about the conditions under which judges can truly be separated from major competing interests in a political system. Although the appointment mechanisms for judges vary considerably (Brinks and Blass, 2018), no system completely purges politics from the process, and it is not clear how it could be done. So, we might be skeptical about the ability of courts to fully resolve a regime's informational challenges. Critically, we will show that merely disconnecting judges from sitting governments can nevertheless incentivize political prudence and by so doing promote peace and regime stability. The absence of independence, whether because judges share the preferences of sitting governments or because judges behave as if they

do in order to protect their posts, will not necessarily result in the demise of a democratic regime. It will mean that democratic regimes will only be as robust as the parties' noninstitutionally assisted efforts to sustain democratic compromises.

3. **Costly Noncompliance:** The model we develop envisions courts as offering leaders a visible way of credibly signaling a sincere rationale for engaging in behavior that might be interpreted as violations of fundamental limits on authority. Leaders can do this by defying court orders. For this mechanism to work there must be consequences to noncompliance. We argue that a robust civil society that mobilizes public support for judicial authority commonly serves this purpose.
4. **Judges Who Tolerate Noncompliance:** To sustain the mechanism we develop, judges must be willing to accept defiance of their orders. In this way we will depart from existing literature in which the democracy-promoting revelation of information follows from judges being politically prudent (e.g. Carrubba and Gabel, 2014). On our account, judges impact democratic compromises through sincerely resolving their cases, by inviting some degree of interbranch conflict. Our argument shares the perspective of Ríos-Figueroa (2016) where the ability of a court to successfully mediate depends on its independence. We will show that in order to defend democracy, judges simply must accept some degree of noncompliance with their orders. Indeed, on this account some level of noncompliance with judicial decisions can be a healthy part of a functional system of judicial review. By accepting a degree of noncompliance in exchange for issuing decisions that invite leaders to violate orders, judges permit the translation of violent interparty conflict into more peaceful interinstitutional conflict.

2.5 THE PATH FORWARD

This chapter has provided a conceptual framework for our account. We adopt a minimalist concept of democracy and state the fundamental problem of democratic governance. In doing so we also describe how the substantive values that make up maximalist concepts of democracy are precisely what creates the fundamental problem. With the problem stated, we propose that judicial review, broadly defined, might be a part of the solution.

In the subsequent chapter, we consider the first link in our argument. We consider evidence associated with the claim that elites have incentives to build and sustain independent courts when they opt to compete for power via elections. In Chapter 4, we develop a formal model of the ways in which judicial review can influence conflict in democracy. We show how different degrees of judicial independence affect the ability of courts to promote democratic peace through information transmission, and we identify the conditions under which courts influence democratic peace even when they cannot influence information. We evaluate key empirical implications of that model in Chapter 5. Chapter 6 considers the implications of our argument for the survival of democracy in the United States. Chapter 7 concludes.

3

Political Competition and Judicial Independence

Again, there is no liberty, if the power of judging be not separated from the legislative and executive powers. Were it joined with the legislative, the life and liberty of the subject would be exposed to arbitrary control, for the judge would then be the legislator. Were it joined to the executive power, the judge might behave with all the violence of an oppressor.

The Spirit of the Laws, Baron de Montesquieu 1748

This chapter addresses the first link in our argument. Are independent courts a direct product of the incentives that democracy provides? Or, are they simply epiphenomenal, occurring in conjunction with, but not generated by, competitive political arrangements? The most widely accepted explanation of judicial independence suggests that democratic competition causes judicial independence. Under conditions of increasing democratic competition for political office, elites face strong incentives to construct, fund, support, and sometimes simply tolerate independent judicial bodies. On this account, courts are understood as a kind of political "insurance" against losses of political power (Epperly, 2013, 2019; Finkel, 2008; Ginsburg, 2003; Hanssen, 2004; Stephenson, 2003). Although independent courts might frustrate leaders while they hold office, they are important sources of protection for the opposition.

A few empirical predictions follow from this argument. First, we ought to observe associations between politically competitive environments and the formal rules that are thought to enhance judicial independence. These de jure judicial institutions ought to appear when politically competitive regimes emerge and deepen as competition grows. Second, we ought to observe associations between politically competitive environments and the de facto judicial independence with which courts operate. We expect these associations both to surface and to develop as products of competition.

We begin this chapter with a discussion of our measurement approach for judicial independence. We then take up the predictions we have just identified. Our primary goal is to evaluate the empirical validity of these claims with creative research designs that enable us to draw causal inferences when possible. Our secondary goal is to explore associations between the key variables operating within the "courts as insurance" literature, making use of newly available data from the Varieties of Democracy (V-Dem) project. At the broadest scope, V-Dem data is available for all countries for over 110 years, offering the widest data coverage ever put to these questions. Accordingly, throughout the chapter, we introduce visualizations that draw on these new data to explore the foundational claims of the insurance model. We offer three separate causally oriented empirical analyses to triangulate on whether and to what degree political competition encourages judicial independence.

3.1 MEASURING DE FACTO JUDICIAL INDEPENDENCE

Judicial autonomy is the ability of a judge to render a decision that reflects their sincere preferences (Ríos-Figueroa and Staton, 2014, p. 107) We require a measure of judicial independence that reflects autonomy or whether a judge resists undue pressures to resolve cases with a particular interest in mind. Scholars have produced a large number of de facto judicial independence measures, but each confronted notable limitations as a consequence of related patterns of measurement error and data missingness.[1]

Prior research teams assessed de facto judicial independence with different conceptual definitions. As a result, variations in how the operational concepts are measured are common. Moreover, different teams often possessed varying levels of expertise both across cases and across time. Most critically, despite the potential for measurement error to propagate through a research team's work, no estimate of the uncertainty around the final measures are provided. Last, prior measures also offered spatially or temporally incomplete data coverage. Critically, this missingness was often correlated with measurement error and other features of a country (e.g. economic development).

Linzer and Staton (2011) offer a measurement model of de facto judicial independence (LJI, latent judicial independence) that builds upon the insights and data of prior work but improves upon the limitations discussed in the previous section. This approach offers wider spatial and temporal coverage, providing measures of judicial independence for 200 countries between 1948 and 2012. Their original measurement model did face, however, a rather unfortunate limitation. Due to temporal restrictions on data availability prior to 1948, any attempt to estimate their measurement model prior to that year would need to rely on only a single indicator spanning this earlier period – Polity's measure of executive constraints. We remedy this limitation by updating the Linzer and Staton (2011) judicial independence scores, taking advantage of newly available data from the V-Dem project.

V-Dem measures offer a temporal domain from 1900 to 2015 and provide several additional variables to incorporate into the Linzer and Staton (2011) model, prior to 1948. To update their scores, we began by identifying any datasets, used

[1] For a complete review of available measures of de facto independence see Linzer and Staton (2011).

in the original model, that offer more recent versions of their data. Accordingly we included newer versions of Cingranelli–Richards (CIRI) judicial independence variable (Cingranelli and Richards, 2008), Polity's executive constraints variable (Marshall et al., 2002), the "law and order" variable from the PRS Group (Political Risk Group, 2004), Feld–Voigt (Feld and Voigt, 2003), and Global Competitiveness Report (GCR) are included.

We also include two new variables from the V-Dem project: an indicator of high court independence (V-Dem variable *v2juhcind*) and an indicator of high court compliance (V-Dem variable *v2juhccomp*). The high court independence item asks expert coders to answer the following question, "When the high court in the judicial system is ruling in cases that are salient to the government, how often would you say that it makes decisions that merely reflect government wishes regardless of its sincere view of the legal record?" (Coppedge and Ziblatt, 2018, p. 153). The compliance questions asks, "How often would you say the government complies with important decisions of the high court with which it disagrees?" (p. 154).[2] By updating LJI with the most current indicators, including Polity before 1948, and adding two V-Dem indicators, we nearly double the country-year coverage of de facto judicial independence.

A potential concern of estimating a new latent variable model is whether or not the updated version corresponds to the original estimates. In the aggregate, these two models are quite consistent. The original and the update both have means of .45. Likewise, the average posterior standard deviation changes from .05 to .04, suggesting equal or even greater certainty across estimates. Moreover, at the country level, the updated measures are quite consistent with the originals.

Consider the original and updated LJI data for Spain displayed in Figure 3.1. The first obvious benefit of the updated data is the longer time frame. With the newly available V-Dem data, we were able to backdate the LJI data to 1900, providing additional insights into how judicial independence developed in the earlier half of the twentieth century. Where the series overlap, we have a very tight correspondence between the two, save the 1950s through 1970s, during the Franco years. The original data registers slightly lower LJI scores during this period compared to our updated version. In the newly extended period however, the LJI data pick up the dynamics of the last remnants of the constitutional monarchy under the reign of Alfonso XIII and the eventual coup and dictatorship of Primo de Rivera between 1923 and 1930. The series grows in accordance with

2 Unless otherwise stated, all coding conventions from the original estimation were used. In the case of GCR, a new interval measure was used containing seven categories instead of the ten that were used in the original dataset. In all estimations in our update, the new GCR measure is treated as an additional indicator to the original eight. For Feld–Voigt, if a value in the update differed from the original dataset, the more current value was used for the entirety of the 1980–2015 time period. Unless otherwise stated, all coding conventions from the original estimation were used.

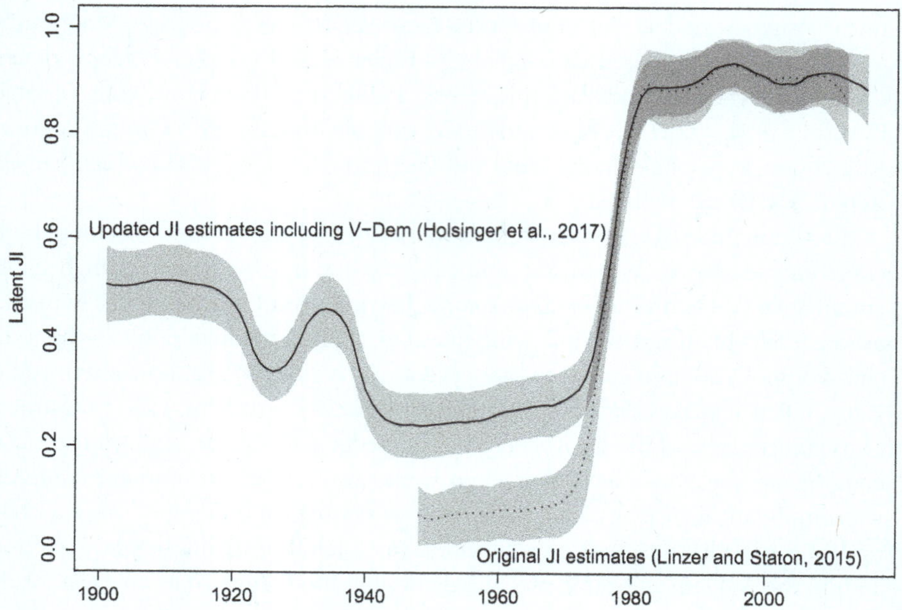

FIGURE 3.1 Original and V-Dem-updated LJI estimates for Spain: 1900–2015

the Second Spanish Republic and the commitment to constitutional principles between 1931 and 1939 and then descends again as Franco's dictatorship takes hold after 1939.

Consider as well the original and updated LJI data for the United States displayed in Figure 3.2. With the updated LJI data, we gain a different perspective on the US courts, providing additional insights into how the they grappled with challenges to their authority in the middle of the twentieth century. The original LJI data portrays US de facto judicial independence as highly independent and essentially static from 1948 to 2015.

The inclusion of the new V-Dem indicators, however, reveals a slightly different story. While the series suggests that the US courts were highly independent throughout the century, they did weather a challenge beginning in the 1950s. These data are likely picking up the challenges that the US courts, particularly the Warren Court, faced to their authority over cases dealing with racial segregation in education, voting, and housing. It is important to note, of course, that the range on the y-axis for the US plot in Figure 3.2 is restricted compared to the Spain plot in Figure 3.1. This is because despite the challenges that the US courts may have faced during this time, they never registered an LJI score in the entire series lower than .79 in 1961. This suggests that, despite the challenges the US system faced, if we were to adopt a dichotomous threshold approach to coding judicial independence, it is likely that any research team would have still coded the US system as "independent."

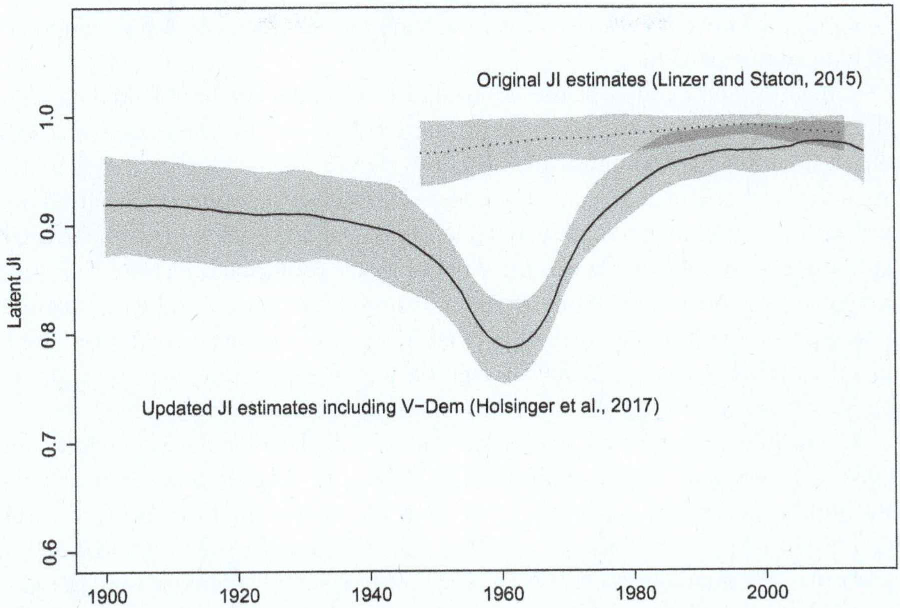

FIGURE 3.2 Original and V-Dem-updated LJI estimates for the United States: 1900–2015

Our updated and expanded LJI data offer superior spatial and temporal coverage over the original Linzer and Staton (2011) data. Accordingly, for the remainder of this book, we make use of our updated version of LJI to measure de facto judicial independence in all contexts.

3.2 MEASURING DE JURE JUDICIAL INDEPENDENCE

De jure conceptualizations of judicial independence focus on the formal rules or institutions that have direct consequences for judicial insulation from undue interference by actors external to the court. By this conceptualization, a more independent judiciary is one in which any number of formal rules incentivize nonjudicial actors to respect the court's autonomy. These rules are thought to accomplish this goal by raising the costs that nonjudicial actors bear in attempting to violate the constitutional boundaries vis-á-vis the court (Hayo and Voigt, 2007).

De jure conceptualizations of judicial independence immediately confront two challenges when migrating to the empirical world. The first challenge is, among the many rules regarding judicial operation that might contribute to a court's independence, e.g. lifetime tenure and nonpolitical appointment, which precise formal rules are likely to raise the costs of court interference? The second challenge is whether any one rule is sufficient alone to ensure judicial independence or whether a given rule complements or compounds the contribution of another to the development of judicial independence.

Scholarship on de jure measures of judicial independence has focused on identifying features of the political system that are believed to limit external actors' ability to influence members of the court. These features are reflected in the legal foundations of the court as expressed in either statutory or constitutional provisions. Imagining judicial independence as a latent variable that is not observable directly, scholars have identified a variety of institutional features that were designed to promote judicial independence from other actors. And while the precise inputs to de jure measures of judicial independence have varied, over nearly two decades of research, a relatively high degree of consensus exists across various applications.

The early 2000s witnessed an uptick in the empirical explorations of de jure judicial independence. An early application by Linda Camp Keith (2002) examined the relationship between judicial independence and human rights by focusing on seven constitutional provisions across all states from 1976 to 1996. She found that one in particular, the guarantee of tenure in office, was related to enhanced human rights protection.[3] In addition, she also noted a synergy between four inputs in particular. When adopted jointly, guaranteed terms, separation of powers, a ban on military courts, and fiscal autonomy had particularly strong associations with human rights protections. Apodaca (2004) applied these data as well but with an additive scale across Keith's seven items.

Feld and Voigt (2003) provide another empirical innovation of de jure judicial independence. Using a questionnaire administered to country experts, they assessed a variety of features of the court's power as found in legal documents in the aggregate over the period 1960–2002.[4] They used twelve inputs as represented in legal documents and constitutional provisions to yield an index of de jure independence that was eventually summed across all available inputs and normalized by the total inputs available, resulting in a scale that ranged from 0 to 1.[5]

La Porta et al. (2004) provided a measure of de jure judicial independence and constitutional review gathered over seventy-one states for the year 2003. Their judicial independence measure consists of three inputs: supreme court judicial tenure, administrative court judicial tenure, and whether case law serves as precedent; and

3 Keith's seven inputs were terms of office, finality of decisions, exclusive authority, ban against military of exceptional courts, fiscal autonomy, separation of powers, and enumerated qualifications

4 These indicators were not gathered annually but rather are aggregate estimates of a country's de jure judicial independence over the entire time period.

5 The twelve inputs included in their index were: whether the high courts is "anchored" in the constitution and the ease with which it could be amended, appointment procedures, lifetime appointment, removal only through legal process, renewable terms, salary independence, competitive salary, court accessibility, rules on case allocation, constitutional review, and whether the court publishes its decisions.

their constitutional review measure consists of two: the difficulty to amend the constitution, and judicial review of government action.

Across each of these empirical treatments of de jure judicial independence the correspondence between inputs is quite high. Indices often include items related to the relative ease with which judicial institutions can be amended, judicial appointment and tenure, the political insulation of judicial salaries, the process of allocating cases, the existence of constitutional review, and the extent to which the court publishes its decisions, including minority decisions.

In addition to their inputs, each measure possesses another, familiar, similarity: nonrandom missingness in their data. The temporal and spatial scope over which various inputs for each judicial independence measure are available is nonrandom. Some measures offer more complete spatial coverage including a great number of countries around the world but select nonrandomly on time. Others offer detailed legal documentation of various institutions over longer periods of time but select nonrandomly on cases. The challenge for users looking to apply any of these de jure measures is that often this nonrandom missingness is correlated with features of the political system under study (e.g. data is unavailable for developing states or states for which legal documentation was not readily available). As a result the analyst must theorize carefully about the impact of the nonrandom patterns in the data on the question at hand.

The Comparative Constitutions Project (CCP) described in Elkins, Ginsburg, and Melton (2009) provides a solution to several of these challenges. Founded in 2005, the CCP has spent the last decade collecting and analyzing constitutional texts for all independent states since 1789. The CCP uses the information contained in constitutional texts in conjunction with a survey instrument and a coding team to generate a comprehensive dataset of government institutions.[6] These publicly available data, first released in 2010, allow scholars to extract any combination of constitutional institutions believed to be linked to judicial independence.

Figure 3.3 displays the relative advantages in geographic coverage across these datasets. Panel A displays the countries that are covered by the suite of variables included in the CCP. Compared to prior datasets, the CCP offers more complete geographic coverage without the standard trade-offs of either a limited time period or number of institutions covered. In fact, the temporal coverage, relative to prior data is equally impressive.

We use the CCP to generate a measure of de jure judicial independence that Elkins, Ginsburg, and Melton (2014) used. This measure utilizes six aspects of constitutions believed to contribute to judicial autonomy. These include constitutional statements on judicial independence, judicial tenure, selection procedures,

6 See http://comparativeconstitutionsproject.org/

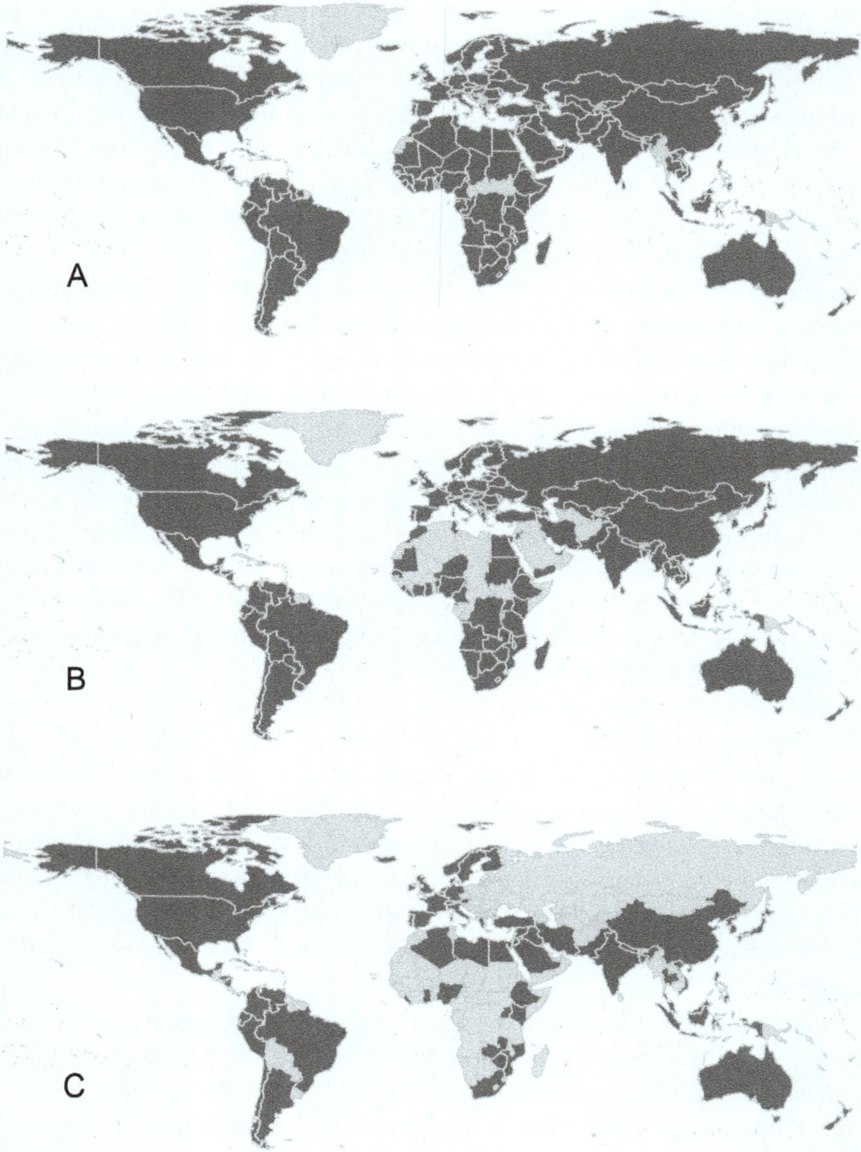

FIGURE 3.3 Data availability across de jure judicial independence datasets. Panel A represents Elkins, Ginsburg, and Melton (2014); Panel B represents Feld and Voigt (2003), and Panel C represents La Porta et al. (2004).

removal procedures, limited removal conditions, and salary insulation. These data offer superior spatial and temporal coverage. Accordingly, for the remainder of this book, we make use of the CCP data and these six inputs to construct our measure de jure judicial independence in all contexts.

3.3 COURTS AS POLITICAL INSURANCE: A PROCESS

We begin by considering whether prima facie evidence supports the expectation that policymakers construct independent courts under competitive political environments. If policymakers construct courts as devices of political insurance, then we ought to observe more formal de jure institutions associated with independent courts under democracy compared to autocracy as well as more de facto independent courts.

In this section, we consider three empirical exercises focused on how shifts in competition lead to changes in judicial independence. First, we consider the dynamic responses of de jure and de facto judicial institutions in the lead-up to and the aftermath of democratic transitions and breakdowns. While we acknowledge that democratic transitions and breakdowns are not exogenous to judicial independence, we do believe there is value in assessing whether these judicial institutions vary in the immediate aftermath of a regime transition. Second, we consider how judicial institutions changed in Eastern Bloc countries in the wake of the collapse of the Berlin Wall compared to matched autocratic regimes that did not experience such political shocks. Last, we utilize an instrumentation strategy to identify the relationship between shifts in political competition and judicial independence. We instrument political competition with per capita production of petroleum, coal, natural gas, and metals, and we examine its effect on de jure and de facto judicial independence. We proceed with each of these strategies in turn.

3.3.1 *Competition, Judicial Independence, and Regime Transitions*

How might large-scale shifts in political competition be associated with the formal institutions believed to help construct independent courts? To consider this question we examined the relationship between de jure judicial independence using the Elkins, Ginsburg, and Melton (2014) data and regime dynamics. Figure 3.4 displays a count of the number of de jure judicial independence indicators as noted by Elkins, Ginsburg, and Melton (2014) in the lead-up to and aftermath of a transition to democracy (top panel) and a breakdown from democracy (bottom panel).

The shaded area in Figure 3.4 represents one standard deviation around the series mean for a given year, and the figure is centered around the point of transition. The data suggest that formal institutions designed to enhance judicial independence are not particularly likely to be strengthened after a transition to democracy nor eradicated after a breakdown. In the top panel, we see that after a transition to democracy there is indeed a rise in the formal institutions associated with an independent court. But there is a good deal of variance among newly inaugurated regimes within the first twenty-five years on this measure, and this institutional advantage appears to weaken with regime age. Older democratic regimes appear to possess fewer of these indicators compared to their younger compatriots. In the bottom panel, we

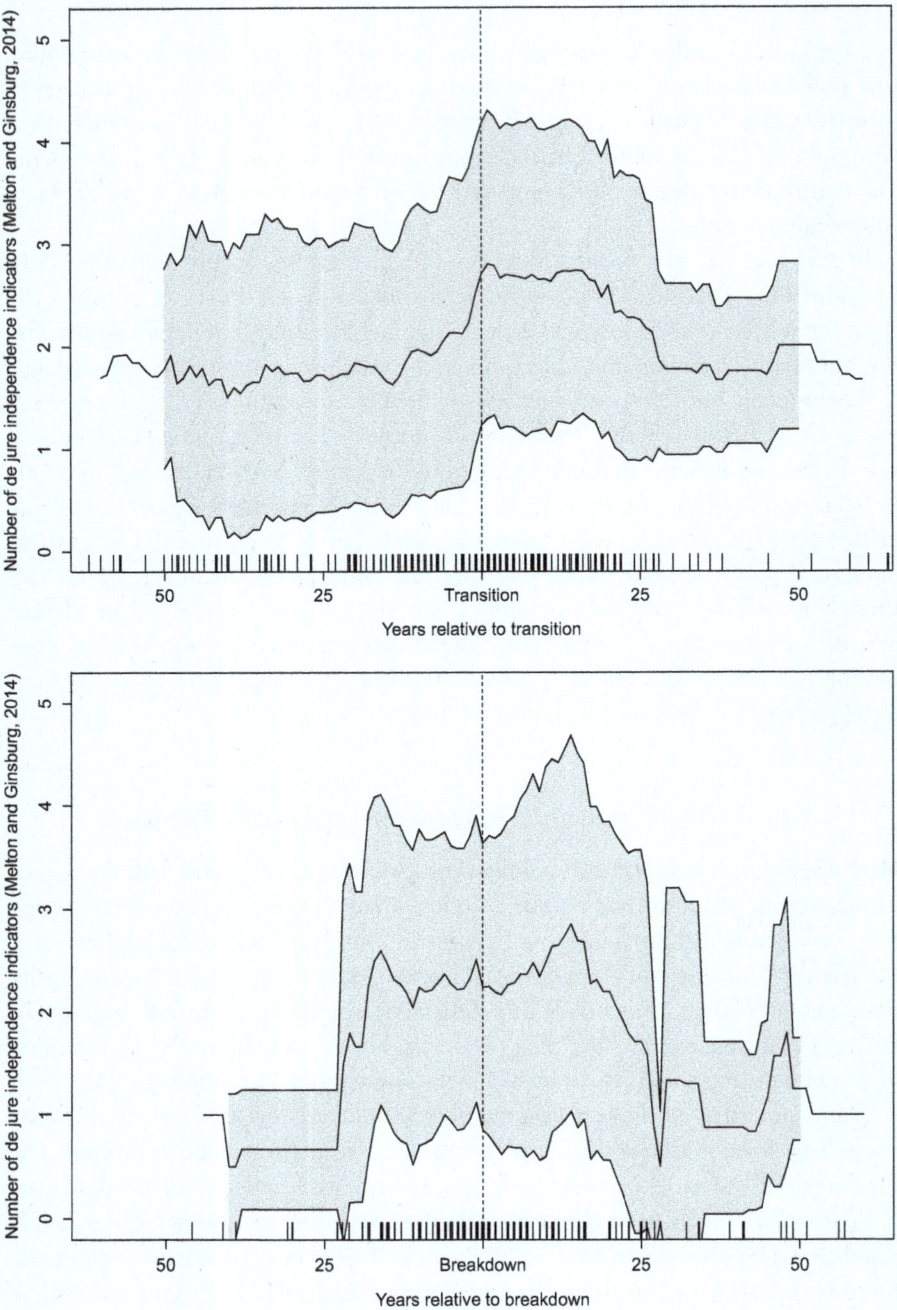

FIGURE 3.4 De jure judicial independence pre- and post-democratic transitions (top panel) and breakdowns (bottom panel). Shaded area represents one standard deviation around series mean.

see hardly any effect of democratic regimes that break down into authoritarianism on the number of indicators associated with de jure judicial independence.

Now we turn to Figure 3.5, which summarizes the changes in de facto judicial independence following transitions to democracy, and we see a striking difference from Figure 3.4. Figure 3.5 displays the mean levels of de facto judicial independence using the Linzer and Staton (2015) measure in the lead-up to and aftermath of a transition to democracy (top panel) and a breakdown from democracy (bottom panel). The shaded area in Figure 3.5 represents one standard deviation around the series mean for a given year. The plot provides simple but striking support for the notion that de facto judicial independence responds to large scale shifts in democratic competition reflected in the transition between democratic and autocratic regimes. We see in the top panel that after transitioning to democracy, de facto judicial independence experiences rather rapid growth in the first twenty years, continuing to climb until roughly fifty to sixty years under democracy where it plateaus at or near its measurable limit. Enhanced political competition appears to be associated with increased de facto judicial independence.

The plot showing change in judicial independence around the aftermath of a democratic collapse also shows a decline. Yet it is important to stress that the average LJI score for states that would experience a breakdown dropped prior to the fall of democracy. While the top panel suggests that increases in judicial independence lags transitions to democracy, the bottom panel suggests that decreases in independence may lead to breakdown.

We can examine more carefully the relationship between competition and judicial independence by considering an empirical model that not only accounts for their causal relationship but also recognizes the potential for endogeneity between political competition and judicial independence. After all, while the insurance model suggests that political competition ought to breed more independent courts, it may also be the case that less independent courts, as mere extensions of the executive branch, are less likely to protect opposition parties from government harassment. Therefore any association between political competition and judicial independence presents a challenge to identify the causal direction between the two. We pursue two strategies to assess this possibility in the next two sections. First, we consider the response of judicial independence to the fall of the Berlin Wall and the transition of the Eastern Bloc countries. Next, we consider an instrumentation strategy that uses petroleum endowments to identify the relationship between autocratic transitions to democracy.

3.3.2 *An Exogenous Intervention: The Fall of the Wall and Judicial Independence*

To evaluate the relationship between political competition and judicial independence, we require an exogenous shock of competitive elections being introduced

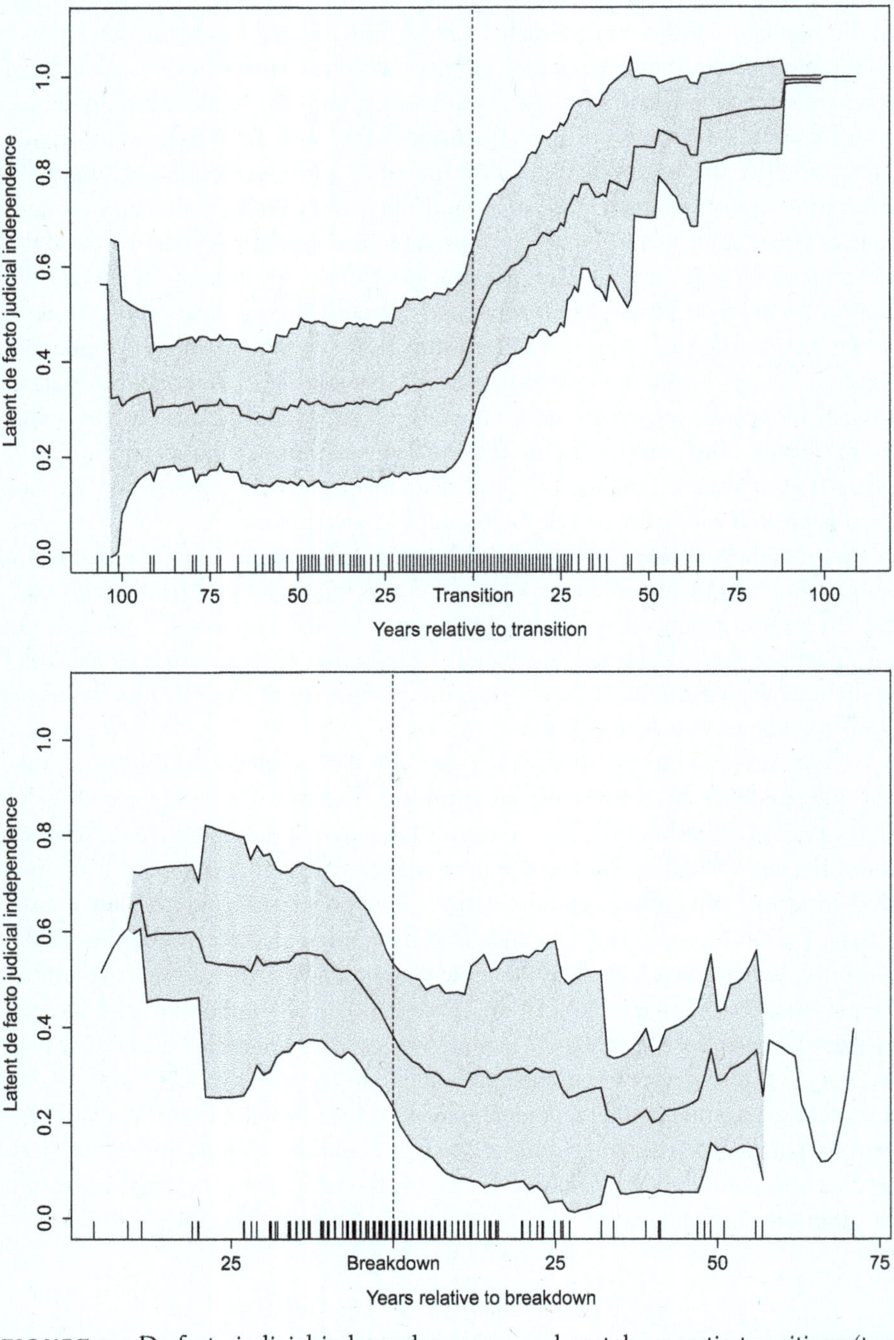

FIGURE 3.5 De facto judicial independence pre- and post-democratic transitions (top panel) and breakdowns (bottom panel). Shaded area represents one standard deviation around series mean.

in an otherwise closed political system. Identifying the introduction of competitive elections is relatively straightforward; being convinced that such introductions are exogenous is another matter entirely. One instance that we believe approximates the rapid onset of an exogenous shock to a set of states was the fall of the Berlin Wall and the transition of Eastern Bloc countries toward democracy after 1989.

As the decade of the 1980s drew to a close, most regimes in the Eastern Bloc, while economically anemic, were nevertheless believed to be relatively secure from imminent regime change. A best case might be made that Poland was an outlier. By 1988, Poland had already experienced years of economic stagnation accompanied with political protests, strikes, and resistance. The regime's response over the decade was characterized by fits and starts of repression and liberalization. In a short window the regime that featured political openings for workers to organize and strike, as with Solidarity, also featured crackdowns in the form of martial law and political murders. Attempts to stabilize the regime bore little fruit. Increased resistance in the form of national strikes, the failure of a nationwide referendum in the fall of 1987, and interventions by the Catholic church all laid the groundwork for the regime to request additional negotiations with Solidarity (Linz and Stepan, 1996). Eventually the Round Table negotiations led to the first free election in the summer of 1989. This election would set the tone for the events that reshaped Eastern Europe in November of that same year.

Still, only now, from our vantage point with perfect hindsight, did Poland appear to have been steadily marching toward an inevitable democratic transition. For the other Eastern Bloc regimes, the vision of an imminent democratic transition was blurrier. In Albania, Bulgaria, Hungary, and Romania, the lead-ups to their democratic transitions were briefer and less strewn with signs of the potential political shock that was to hit in the fall of 1989. Kuran (1991) famously diagnosed the failure of intelligence agencies, professional political scientists and journalists alike to foresee the events of 1989 as a case of "imperfect observability" due to preference falsification among the citizens. In short, predicting the timing of such revolutions was and continues to be difficult when citizens have incentive to falsify their support for the regime and dissemble their thresholds for taking to the streets. Given the wide failure to predict these regime transitions in 1989, we are reasonably confident to treat the onset of political competition within them as exogenous.

To understand how political competition informed the development of judicial independence in the wake of the events of 1989, we consider how de jure and de facto independence changed relative to other autocratic states that experienced no such shock. To match states that did not experience a transition against the Eastern Bloc states, we identified authoritarian counterparts in the pre-intervention period (i.e. 1987) using a Coarsened Exact Matching algorithm (Iacus et al., 2009). For each Eastern Bloc country we matched on GDP per capita, GDP growth, and ethnic fractionalization, using a coarsened binning procedure in which we segmented each variable into three bins. We also utilized binary indicators for regime type

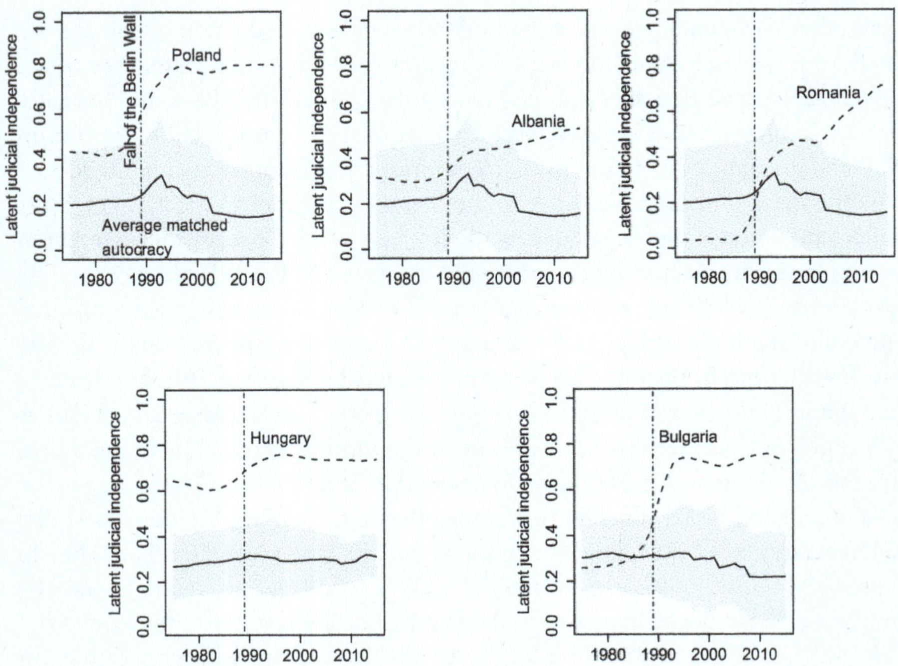

FIGURE 3.6 Eastern Bloc states' de facto judicial independence compared to pre-1989 intervention coarsened exact matched autocracies

(authoritarian/democratic) and whether or not the state was experiencing a civil war. Three of the five states, Poland, Albania, and Romania, each matched to the same group; as a result we have three distinct comparison strata.[7]

Figure 3.6 displays separate plots for each of these states and their matched cohorts. Our measure of de facto judicial independence is plotted on the y-axis, with time plotted on the x-axis. A dashed vertical line marks the 1989 collapse of the Berlin Wall. Each Eastern Bloc country series is displayed with a dashed line, while the mean for their autocratic-matched cohort is displayed with a solid line, bordered with gray shaded confidence bands plotted around the mean.

Visually, the results are compelling. With varying degrees of intensity, the Eastern Bloc states responded to the rapid onset of political competition after 1988 with increases in judicial independence. Albania and Hungary registered fairly muted increases, while Poland, Bulgaria, and Romania experienced pronounced shifts

7 Strata 1: Paraguay, Poland, Albania, Romania, Republic of the Congo, South Africa, Egypt, North Korea, and Indonesia. Strata 2: Hungary, Serbia, Mali, Burkina Faso, Togo, Nigeria, Gabon, Central African Republic, Democratic Republic of Congo, Kenya, Tanzania, Rwanda, Zambia, Malawi, Swaziland, Madagascar, Comoros, Libya, Qatar, United Arab Emirates, China, Mongolia, Taiwan, South Korea, and Bangladesh. Strata 3: Bulgaria, Guinea-Bissau, Equatorial Guinea, Senegal, Liberia, Sierra Leone, Ghana, Lesotho, Yemen, Kuwait, and Nepal.

TABLE 3.1 *Change in Eastern Bloc states' de facto judicial independence compared to pre-1989 intervention coarsened exact matched autocracies*

			Δ JI		
	1 yr	2 yr	3 yr	4 yr	5 yr
(Intercept)	0.03**	0.05***	0.06***	0.07***	0.08***
	(0.01)	(0.01)	(0.01)	(0.02)	(0.02)
Treatment	0.07**	0.09*	0.11*	0.12*	0.13*
	(0.02)	(0.03)	(0.05)	(0.06)	(0.06)
			Δ JI		
	6 yr	7 yr	8 yr	9 yr	10 yr
(Intercept)	0.09***	0.09***	0.07***	0.07***	0.07***
	(0.02)	(0.02)	(0.02)	(0.02)	(0.02)
Treatment	0.13*	0.14*	0.15*	0.16**	0.15*
	(0.06)	(0.06)	(0.06)	(0.06)	(0.06)

***$p < .001$, **$p < .01$, *$p < .05$

in de facto judicial independence. These descriptive data are consistent with the claim that competitive environments provide incentives for leaders to support an independent judiciary.

To consider the effect of this shift in competition more precisely we calculated the average treatment effect among the treated with a pooled sample across all five Eastern Bloc states. Ten models were fit on ten windows of change in de facto judicial independence, starting with the difference between 1988 and 1990 and ending with 1988 and 1999. Table 3.1 displays the estimates of the average treatment effects among the treated as a difference of means test comparing the judicial independence of Eastern Bloc states experiencing exogenous shocks of political competition (treated) to that of matched authoritarian states (control) across ten increasingly large windows of time. The only complication is that the resulting estimates are weighted according to the relative sizes of the three strata. These ten time frames characterize the increasing cumulative effect of more years with political competition. The estimated shifts in de facto judicial independence displayed in Table 3.1 offer additional support to evidence displayed in Figure 3.6. The opening of political competition after just one year (1988–1990) results in a .07 increase in a state's latent judicial independence. After ten years post-treatment (1988–1999), the effect increases to .15 or 7.5 percent of the entire range of LJI.

Do we observe similar changes in the formal institutions believed to protect judicial independence? To consider this possibility, we conducted an identical analysis on the observed changes in the number of de jure institutions in response to the fall of the Berlin Wall. Figure 3.7 displays separate plots for each of the Eastern Bloc states and their matched cohorts. However, we now

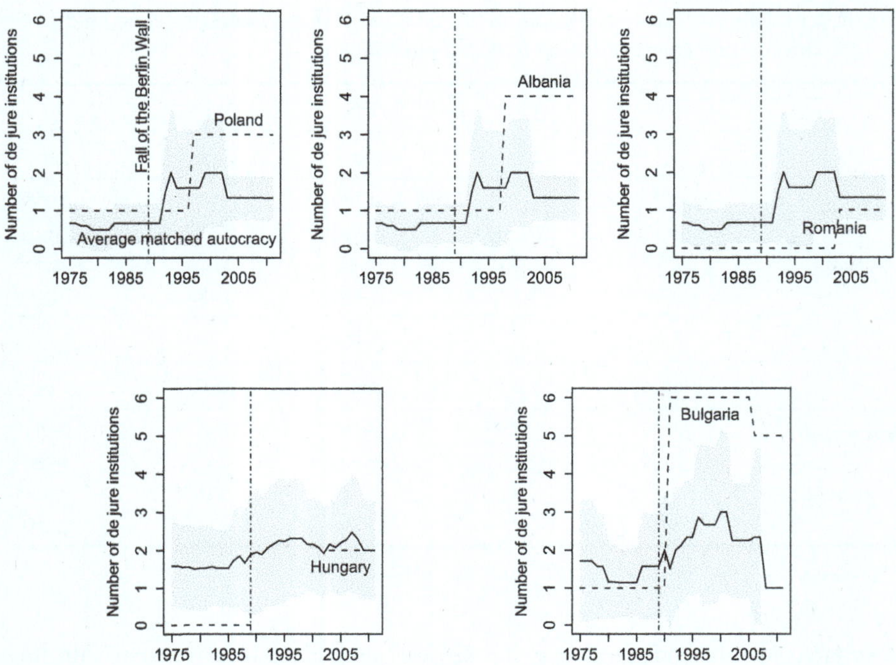

FIGURE 3.7 Eastern Bloc states' de jure judicial independence compared to pre-1989 intervention coarsened exact matched autocracies

plot our measure of de jure judicial independence on the y-axis, with time plotted on the x-axis. As before, a dashed vertical line marks the 1989 collapse of the wall.

Similar to the de facto results, the panels suggest that, in the wake of the 1989 shock, newly inaugurated regimes that amended or completely rewrote their constitutions included new rules designed to enhance de jure judicial independence. Prior to the adoption of a new constitution, each of these regimes either included no formal rules regarding judicial independence or included only one – a statement that the courts are to be independent. However, after adopting new or significantly amended constitutions, these inaugural democratic regimes included several additional provisions. The most frequent new appearance, observed in Poland, Hungary, Bulgaria, and Albania, was the inclusion of a statement on the independent procedures for nominating judges. Three additional rules were adopted by two states each. These rules included statements regarding independence of tenure (i.e. Poland and Bulgaria), removal conditions (i.e. Albania and Bulgaria), and independence of judicial salaries (i.e. Albania and Bulgaria).

One notable difference between the de facto panels and the de jure rules is the lag between the shock of the wall falling and the adoption of these new formal rules. Most new constitutions were not formally adopted until several years after the shock.

TABLE 3.2 *Change in Eastern Bloc states' de jure judicial independence compared to pre-1989 intervention coarsened exact matched autocracies*

	Δ De jure institutions				
	1 yr	2 yr	3 yr	4 yr	5 yr
(Intercept)	0.05	0.06	0.78**	1.12***	1.18***
	(0.05)	(0.14)	(0.26)	(0.28)	(0.00)
Treatment	−0.05	1.6**	0.47	0.13	0.07
	(0.19)	(0.51)	(0.80)	(0.86)	(0.88)
	Δ De jure institutions				
	6 yr	7 yr	8 yr	9 yr	10 yr
(Intercept)	1.18***	1.35***	1.35***	1.34***	1.34***
	(0.28)	(0.31)	(0.30)	(0.30)	(0.30)
Treatment	0.07	−0.10	0.40	1.16	1.16
	(0.88)	(0.96)	(0.95)	(0.93)	(0.93)

***$p < .001$, **$p < .01$, *$p < .05$

In the interim, states operated under constitutional rules that were holdovers from the Communist regimes, from which they just emerged, or under provisional rules.

To consider the effects of the 1989 shock on the development of de jure judicial independence we again conducted an analysis that estimated the average treatment effect among the treated with a pooled sample across all five Eastern Bloc states. Table 3.2 reports the results of this analysis.

Our analysis suggests that the patterns displayed in Figure 3.7 are merely suggestive as only one specification suggests that de jure institutions increased with an opening of competition in the Eastern Bloc states. We cannot confidently reject that possibility that all of the other changes in de jure judicial independence are any different from changes occurring within the matched control group.

In sum, our investigation using the fall of the Berlin Wall as an exogenous shock supports the claim that political competition provides leaders with incentives to enhance judicial independence. Similar to our analysis in the previous section, however, we find that competition has uneven effects across our indicators of judicial independence. While competition uniformly enhances de facto judicial independence, it appears to provide less consistent incentives for de jure rule adoptions.

Given the restricted domain of our sample, we are, of course, cautious about overgeneralizing from this analysis. To consider a broader domain of cases, both spatially and temporally, however, will require a different tactic to address endogeneity concerns. In the next section, we consider the link between political competition and judicial independence of all states from 1900 to 2015, using an instrument for political competition.

3.3.3 Instrumentation

In this section we adopt the approach suggested by Epperly (2019). Specifically, we appeal to an instrumental variable for political competition – the per capita production of petroleum, coal, natural gas, and metals. Under what conditions would per capita production of these fixed assets offer a valid instrument for political competition? First, the instrument would need to be relevant to the endogenous regressor, political competition. This is a reasonable expectation given the dynamics between regimes and natural resources assets, and as we demonstrate in Tables 3.3 and 3.4 this is borne out empirically. Second, the instrument must itself be exogenous. On this point, it would again appear reasonable for us to assume that the natural deposits of these resources are "randomly assigned" by nature and therefore are as-if random and predetermined with respect to any regime's judicial independence. Last, our instrument must meet the exclusion restriction. We must be able to rule out any direct effect of the instrument, natural resources, on our outcome variable, judicial independence, other than through the path of political competition. On theoretical grounds we believe this to be a reasonable assumption.

In the analyses that follow, we present our instrumentation analysis for the effect of political competition on both de facto and de jure judicial independence. For each analysis, we first consider the relationship between competition and judicial independence across all regimes, and then we consider the nature of this relationship within democracies and autocracies, in turn. We consider four measures of political competition. First, we include an index created from Polity's PARREG and PARCOMP variables, which combines information about a system's regulation government restrictions on political competition. Second, we include a competition based on Vanhanen and extracted from Coppedge et al. (2017). This variable is generated by "subtracting from 100 the percentage of votes won by the largest party (the party which wins most votes) in parliamentary elections or by the party of the successful candidate in presidential elections." Last, we include two variables from the V-Dem Project (Coppedge et al., 2017). We include Suffrage, or the approximate percentage of enfranchised adults older than the minimal voting age, as well as a variable, Competition, that is a dichotomous variable reflecting whether elections are characterized by uncertainty.

Prior to presenting the identification analysis, we first consider a plot of the lagged changes in political competition along with the contemporary changes in de facto judicial independence.[8] Figure 3.8 displays the plot of changes in de facto judicial independence on the y-axis with lagged changes in political competition plotted on the x-axis. Autocratic regimes are displayed on the left panel, and democratic

8 We conduct this analysis for the Polity political competition index; however, the data patterns are similar across all of our competition indicators.

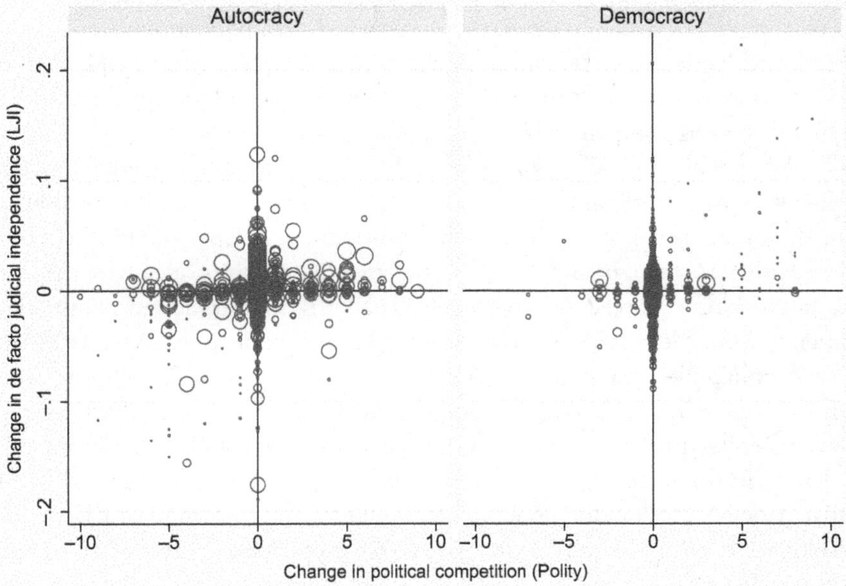

FIGURE 3.8 Changes in de facto judicial independence (LJI) plotted against changes in political competition (Polity) by regime for all states 1900–2015. Note: Circle diameter represents regime age in years.

displays are displayed on the right panel. We also scaled the diameter of the markers to reflect regime age; smaller markers denote newer regimes.

Before we turn to Figure 3.8, we should note that change in political competition is a relatively rare event within both autocratic and democratic regimes. Among democracies, 96.72 percent of our country-years experience no change in political competition, compared to 93.84 percent among autocracies. When democracies do experience a change in competition, 74 percent of the time it is an increase in competition rather than a decrease, while autocracies are more balanced, experiencing increases in competition 48 percent of the time. Among democracies, 45 percent of all increases in competition occur within the first year of the regime and 84 percent occur within the first twenty years of the regime. Reductions in competition, albeit rare, are evenly spaced throughout the lifetime of democracies. Among autocracies, competition increases evenly throughout their lifetime, whereas 35.4 percent of reductions occur in the first year and 59 percent of competition reductions occur in the first twenty years of the regime.

Turning to Figure 3.8 the right panel displays the relationship between changes in political competition and changes in de facto judicial independence. The competition–judicial independence thesis predicts data to be dominant in the upper-right quadrant of the plot. Indeed, the plot suggests prima facie evidence that changes in political competition are associated with positive shifts in de facto judicial independence, particularly among new democracies – the smaller diameter markers. Moreover, the data are less dominant in the lower-right quadrant, ruling out that increasing competition decreases judicial independence.

The left panel displays an opposite pattern. The lower-left quadrant is data dominant – particularly among new autocracies, suggesting that contractions in competition are associated with restrictions of judicial independence when autocratic regimes are inaugurated. The lack of competition is associated with newborn autocrats seeking to bring courts to heel. This pattern also underscores an important distinction from the pattern observed among democratic regimes. Any association between competition and judicial independence among autocratic regimes is more likely to be driven by reductions in competition and contractions in independence (in the lower-left quadrant) than by increases in competition and deepening of independence (in the upper-right quadrant). This interpretation is highlighted by the relative paucity of data in the upper-right quadrant of the autocratic panel.

We now turn to our identification analysis. We estimated each model with a fixed effect two-step efficient generalized method of moments (GMM) estimator that is robust to heteroskedasticity and autocorrelated disturbances. We include three time-varying covariates to further identify the relationship: GDP per capita, GDP growth, and a counter for years spent under the current regime. Our fourth competition variable, Competition (V-Dem), is a dichotomous endogenous variable. Accordingly, à la Wooldridge (2002), to avoid the so-called forbidden regression, we first estimate a probit on our endogenous first stage variable X_1 including instruments: X_2 X_3 Z_1, predict $\hat{X}_1$, and then estimate a two-stage instrumental regression with Y X_2 X_3 $(X_1 = \hat{X}_1)$.

Table 3.3 displays the results for the instrumented analysis of competition on de facto judicial independence across all regime types. The full models are reported in this chapter's Appendix, and they reveal that the instrument performs well across all regimes, with several tests for weak instruments suggesting support for fixed assets as a reasonable instrument for political competition among all regimes. The strength of this instrument, however, varies within specific regime type. Among democracies only, our instrument performs less well. Two out of four of the tests for weak instruments suggest that fixed assets is not weak, when we use Polity's ParComp or V-Dem's Competition variable. However, tests suggests that fixed assets is not a reasonable instrument for political competition as measured by our Competition (Vanhanen) or our Suffrage (V-Dem) variables. Among autocracies, our instrument performs poorly across all measures of political competition. Fixed assets does not map well onto levels of political competition within autocratic regimes. Every model suggests that fixed assets is not a reasonable instrument for political competition.

TABLE 3.3 *Instrumented estimates for political competition's impact on de facto judicial independence over regime type*

	Effects of competition on de facto JI			
	ParComp (Polity)	Competition (Vanhanen)	Suffrage (V-Dem)	Competition (V-Dem)
Instrumented competition	0.0598***	0.0073***	0.0044***	0.4024***
(all regimes)				
Instrumented competition	(0.0054)	(0.0011)	(0.0007)	(0.0696)
(democracies)	0.0645**	0.3444	0.0049**	0.2550**
Instrumented competition	(0.0138)	(2.8083)	(0.0015)	(0.0598)
(autocracies)	−0.0008	−0.0019	0.0000	0.0582
	(0.0156)	(0.0036)	(0.0006)	(0.2243)
Years covered	1900–2015	1900–2015	1900–2015	1900–2015

Note: Standard errors are clustered on country-episodes. Two-tailed tests of statistical significance are displayed: $^{*}p < .05$, $^{**}p < .01$.

The first line of Table 3.3 shows that across all regimes, enhanced political competition (instrumented), regardless of measure, appears to enhance de facto judicial independence. An increase of one standard deviation for each of our measures of political competition results in a .22, .19, .18, and .20 increase in de facto judicial independence, respectively. These effects are substantively impressive given that the mean of our de facto judicial independence measure, LJI, is .45 with a standard deviation of .28. Consider, for example, that on the ten-point ParComp index of political competition, the average democracy is located at 8.76 (e.g. Ecuador or Liberia circa 2015), while the average autocracy is located at 3.09 (e.g. Thailand or Morocco circa 2015). The results from Table 3.3 suggest that this difference of 5.67 would translate into a gain of .34 on our LJI judicial independence scale. This would be equivalent to moving Thailand from its 2015 LJI score of .56 to a 2015 LJI score of .90 – putting it on par with Finland, Japan, and Chile. The second line reports the results of our instrumented analysis for democracies only. We again see support that enhanced political competition, within democracies, enhances de facto judicial independence. These substantive effects are on the order of those estimated across all regimes. The last line reports the results for the instrumented analysis of competition on de facto judicial independence among autocratic regimes only.

Now consider the instrumented analysis for political competition on de jure institutions. In Table 3.4, we present our instrumented analysis for the effect of political competition on de jure judicial independence. For each analysis, we first consider the relationship between competition and judicial independence

TABLE 3.4 *Instrumented estimates for political competition's impact on de jure judicial independence over regime type*

	Effects of competition on de facto JI			
	ParComp (Polity)	Competition (Vanhanen)	Suffrage (V-Dem)	Competition (V-Dem)
Instrumented competition (all regimes)	0.2491* (0.0660)	0.0267** (0.0097)	0.0240* (0.0111)	4.4838* (1.1099)
Instrumented competition (democracies)	−0.2439 (0.3362)	1.1156 (18.6096)	−0.0179 (0.0221)	−0.1263 (0.9793)
Instrumented competition (autocracies)	−2.5711 (5.9942)	0.0236 (0.0170)	0.0194 (0.0178)	3.2384** (1.0588)
Years covered	1900–2015	1900–2015	1900–2015	1900–2015

Note: Standard errors are clustered on country-episodes. Two-tailed tests of statistical significance are displayed: $^{*}p < .05$, $^{**}p < .01$.

across all regimes, and then we consider the nature of this relationship within democracies and autocracies, in turn. We utilize a measure of de jure judicial independence taken from Melton and Ginsburg (2014). We coded all new de jure institutions across five de jure indicators as interventions between 1959 and 2008. These institutions included provisions for lifetime terms, selection procedures, removal conditions, removal procedures, and salary insulation. We create an additive index of these indicators, equally weighted, as our dependent variable for our investigation of the effect of political competition on de jure judicial independence. This variable ranges from 0 to 6, with a mean of 2.01 and a standard deviation of 1.33.

Table 3.4 displays the results for the instrumented analysis of competition on de jure judicial independence across all regime types. Again, the instrument performs relatively well, with several tests for weak instruments suggesting support for fixed assets as a reasonable instrument for political competition among all regimes. The one model for which the instrument may be weak is the third model, which measures competition as suffrage. The weak identification test suggests weak instrumentation for this model.

The results in Table 3.4 suggest that for all regimes, enhanced political competition, regardless of measure, appears to enhance de jure judicial independence. A one standard deviation increase in each of our measures of political competition results in a .33, .036, .03, and 5.96 increase in de jure judicial independence, respectively. These effects are less substantively impressive compared to those reported for the de facto analysis in Table 3.3. Given that the mean of our de jure judicial independence measure has a mean of 2.01 with a standard deviation of 1.33. the relative effects are quite small with most measures of political competition barely registering movement on our de jure scale. The outlier of course is the last model with the dichotomous outcome. Regimes that are politically competitive are 4.48 units higher than noncompetitive regimes for our de jure scale. Fixed assets do not function as a strong instrument for political competition for democratic of autocratic subsets. As a result, we can conclude only that political competition has a weak positive effect on de jure judicial independence across all regimes and a null relationship within democracy or within autocracy.

3.4 CONCLUSION

Our goal in this chapter was to interrogate the first link in our argument by evaluating the central predictions of the insurance model of judicial independence: that leaders in competitive electoral environments have strong incentives to build independent judiciaries. Using new data on both de jure and de facto judicial independence as well as political competition we were able to evaluate this model including all regimes across the globe for over 110 years. We employed research designs that allowed us to draw credible inferences on whether political competition is a key causal driver of independent courts.

Our findings suggest that this causal claim is credible and substantively meaningful but with provisos. Increases in political competition are causally linked to both enhanced independent judicial behavior as well as the adoption of formal rules aimed to protect judicial independence. We observe this effect primarily between democratic regimes that operate competitively and autocratic regimes that do not. Among all regimes, we saw evidence that positive changes in political competition, reflective of whether the core conditions of the democratic compromise are met, establish incentives to generate gains for both de jure and de facto judicial independence. The effect within each regime type is considerably more murky.

Within democracies, we produced evidence that competition insulates judges. But we observe this relationship only for judicial behavior not for de jure rules, suggesting that the mechanism that links competition and de facto judicial independence is unlikely to run through the formal institutions that are believed to incentivize this behavior. Within autocracies, we were unable to generate evidence that changes in competition lead to changes in either formal rules or judicial behavior. We should raise a note of caution regarding the analyses on autocratic regimes. Our instrument performs best between democratic and autocratic regimes and weakest among autocracies. So our null findings for competition and judicial independence may suffer from endogeneity. Still, the null finding for autocratic states is not particularly surprising given that while many autocratic regimes have many of the same institutional judicial forms that democracies have adopted, autocratic leaders have many more avenues available to them to navigate around these institutional protections.

Having considered incentives for supporting independent courts, the second half of the book turns to the role that courts play in democracy. Here we are primarily interested in understanding whether, and if so how, courts might protect democratic regimes from collapse.

APPENDIX

3.A COMPLETE TABLES FOR INSTRUMENTED ANALYSIS

TABLE 3.A.1 *Instrumented estimates for political competition's impact on de facto judicial independence (all regimes)*

	Effects of competition on de facto JI			
	ParComp (Polity)	Competition (Vanhanen)	Suffrage (V-Dem)	Competition (V-Dem)
Political competition (instrumented)	0.0598*** (0.0054)	0.0073*** (0.0011)	0.0044*** (0.0007)	0.4024*** (0.0696)
Time-varying controls				
ln(GDP per capita)	0.0106** (0.0053)	0.0074 (0.0101)	−0.0246* (0.0146)	−0.0032 (0.0131)
GDP growth	−0.0732*** (0.0196)	−0.0532*** (0.0170)	−0.0645*** (0.0237)	−0.0295* (0.0157)
Years under regime	0.0003** (0.0001)	0.0005*** (0.0002)	0.0002* (0.0001)	0.0011*** (0.0003)
Stock–Yogo weak ID critical value 10%	16.38	16.38	16.38	16.38
Kleibergen–Paap weak ID F-test	30.00	31.00	40.12	40.96
Stock–Wright weak instrument LM S statistic (Chi2, df(1))	28.43(1)**	27.30(1)**	27.77(1)**	44.65(1)**
C statistic, endogeneity test (Chi2, df(1))	21.054(1)**	20.815(1)**	25.228(1)**	18.588(1)**
Fixed effects	YES	YES	YES	YES
Autocorrelation robust	YES	YES	YES	YES
Heteroskedasticity robust	YES	YES	YES	YES
Number of observations	7935	8127	8248	8188
Years covered	1900–2015	1900–2015	1900–2015	1900–2015

Note: Standard errors are clustered on country-episodes. Two-tailed tests of statistical significance are displayed: $^{*}p < .05$, $^{**}p < .01$.

TABLE 3.A.2 *Instrumented estimates for political competition's impact on de facto judicial independence (democratic regimes only)*

	Effects of competition on de facto JI			
	ParComp (Polity)	Competition (Vanhanen)	Suffrage (V-Dem)	Competition (V-Dem)
Political competition (instrumented)	0.0645** (0.0138)	0.3444 (2.8083)	0.0049** (0.0015)	0.2550** (0.0598)
Time-varying controls				
ln(GDP per capita)	−0.1375** (0.0370)	−0.4221 (3.1156)	−0.1473** (0.0484)	−0.0918** (0.0244)
GDP growth	0.0257 (0.0143)	−1.3942 (11.9862)	−0.0049 (0.0284)	0.0619** (0.0089)
Years under regime	−0.0005 (0.0003)	0.0030 (0.0314)	−0.0004 (0.0003)	−0.0004 (0.0002)
Stock–Yogo weak ID critical value 10%	16.38	16.38	16.38	16.38
Kleibergen–Paap weak ID F-test	19.79	0.01	12.76	31.26
Stock–Wright weak instrument LM S statistic	6.97(1)**	5.59(1)*	5.64(1)*	17.17(1)**
C statistic, endogeneity test (Chi2, df(1))	6.764(1)**	5.470(1)*	5.548(1)*	9.834(1)**
Fixed effects	YES	YES	YES	YES
Autocorrelation robust	YES	YES	YES	YES
Heteroskedasticity robust	YES	YES	YES	YES
Number of observations	3337	3404	3432	3400
Years covered	1900–2015	1900–2015	1900–2015	1900–2015

Note: Standard errors are clustered on country-episodes. Two-tailed tests of statistical significance are displayed: $^{*}p < .05$, $^{**}p < .01$.

TABLE 3.A.3 *Instrumented estimates for political competition's impact on de facto judicial independence (autocratic regimes only)*

	Effects of competition on de facto JI			
	ParComp (Polity)	Competition (Vanhanen)	Suffrage (V-Dem)	Competition (V-Dem)
Political competition (instrumented)	−0.0008 (0.0156)	−0.0019 (0.0036)	0.0000 (0.0006)	0.0582 (0.2243)
Time–varying controls				
ln(GDP per capita)	−0.0102 (0.0160)	0.0010 (0.0227)	−0.0082 (0.0126)	−0.0088 (0.0148)
GDP growth	−0.00041 (0.0092)	−0.00098 (0.0083)	−0.0040 (0.0086)	−0.00022 (0.0052)
Years under regime	0.0007** (0.0003)	0.0008** (0.0003)	0.0007** (0.0002)	0.0006** (0.0002)

TABLE 3.A.3 *(continued)*

	Effects of competition on de facto JI			
	ParComp (Polity)	Competition (Vanhanen)	Suffrage (V–Dem)	Competition (V–Dem)
Stock–Yogo weak ID critical value 10%	16.38	16.38	16.38	16.38
Kleibergen–Paap weak ID F-test	8.72	1.45	17.37	12.05
Stock–Wright weak instrument LM S statistic	0.00(1)	0.49(1)	0.00(1)	0.07(1)
C statistic, endogeneity test (Chi2, df(1))	1.311(1)	1.108(1)	0.024(1)	0.011(1)
Fixed effects	YES	YES	YES	YES
Autocorrelation robust	YES	YES	YES	YES
Heteroskedasticity robust	YES	YES	YES	YES
Number of observations	4,594	4,720	4,812	4,784
Years covered	1900–2015	1900–2015	1900–2015	1900–2015

Note: Standard errors are clustered on country-episodes. Two-tailed tests of statistical significance are displayed: $^{*}p < .05$, $^{**}p < .01$.

TABLE 3.A.4 *Instrumented estimates for political competition's impact on de jure judicial independence (all regimes)*

	Effects of competition on de jure JI			
	ParComp (Polity)	Competition (Vanhanen)	Suffrage (V-Dem)	Competition (V-Dem)
Political competition (instrumented)	0.2491** (0.0660)	0.0267** (0.0097)	0.0240* (0.0111)	4.4838* (1.1099)
Time-varying controls				
ln(GDP per capita)	−0.0785 (0.1483)	0.1141 (0.1324)	0.1115 (0.1812)	0.3570 (0.2038)
GDP growth	−0.0306 (0.0781)	0.0196 (0.0970)	−0.3275 (0.2653)	0.5480** (0.1904)
Years under regime	−0.0001 (0.0017)	−0.0002 (0.0019)	−0.0036** (0.0012)	0.0158** (0.0056)
Stock–Yogo weak ID critical value 10%	16.38	16.38	16.38	16.38
Kleibergen–Paap weak ID F-test	16.66	60.66	11.25	24.59
Stock–Wright weak instrument LM S statistic	8.76(1)**	10.02(1)**	8.56(1)**	45.30(1)**
C statistic, endogeneity test (Chi2, df(1))	3.076(1)	3.672(1)	6.785(1)**	32.558(1)**

TABLE 3.A.4 *(continued)*

	Effects of competition on de jure JI			
	ParComp (Polity)	Competition (Vanhanen)	Suffrage (V-Dem)	Competition (V-Dem)
Fixed effects	YES	YES	YES	YES
Autocorrelation robust	YES	YES	YES	YES
Heteroskedasticity robust	YES	YES	YES	YES
Number of observations	5,390	5,525	5,6501	5,579
Years covered	1900–2015	1900–2015	1900–2015	1900–2015

Note: Standard errors are clustered on country-episodes. Two-tailed tests of statistical significance are displayed: $^{*}p < .05$, $^{**}p < .01$.

TABLE 3.A.5 *Instrumented estimates for political competition's impact on de jure judicial independence (democratic regimes only)*

	Effects of Competition on De Jure JI			
	ParComp (Polity)	Competition (Vanhanen)	Suffrage (V-Dem)	Competition (V-Dem)
Political competition (instrumented)	−0.2439 (0.3362)	1.1156 (18.6096)	−0.0179 (0.0221)	−0.1263 (0.9793)
Time-varying controls				
ln(GDP per capita)	−0.1085 (0.3435)	0.4308 (11.2944)	−0.1786 (0.2500)	−0.1884 (0.2182)
GDP growth	0.9286* (0.4371)	−1.2758 (32.1504)	0.9974* (0.4648)	0.6571** (0.0853)
Years under regime	−0.0163** (0.0052)	−0.0999 (1.4384)	−0.0152** (0.0037)	−0.0138** (0.0020)
Stock–Yogo weak ID critical value 10%	16.38	16.38	16.38	16.38
Kleibergen–Paap weak ID F-test	1.98	0.00	6.39	7.52
Stock–Wright weak instrument LM S statistic	1.56(1)	1.57(1)	1.65(1)	0.02(1)
C statistic, endogeneity test (Chi2, df(1))	2.087(1)	1.157(1)	3.542(1)	0.355(1)
Fixed effects	YES	YES	YES	YES
Autocorrelation robust	YES	YES	YES	YES
Heteroskedasticity robust	YES	YES	YES	YES
Number of observations	2,112	2,170	2,183	2,172
Years covered	1900–2015	1900–2015	1900–2015	1900–2015

Note: Standard errors are clustered on country-episodes. Two-tailed tests of statistical significance are displayed: $^{*}p < .05$, $^{**}p < .01$.

TABLE 3.A.6 *Instrumented estimates for political competition's impact on de jure judicial independence (autocratic regimes only)*

	Effects of competition on de jure JI			
	ParComp (Polity)	Competition (Vanhanen)	Suffrage (V-Dem)	Competition (V-Dem)
Political competition (instrumented)	−2.5711 (5.9942)	0.0236 (0.0170)	0.0194 (0.0178)	3.2384** (1.0588)
Time-varying controls				
ln(GDP per capita)	2.4706 (5.3354)	0.1899 (0.1501)	0.2144 (0.1888)	0.4375** (0.1679)
GDP growth	−1.1882 (2.6471)	0.0198 (0.0567)	−0.3487 (0.3214)	−0.0172 (0.0655)
Years under regime	0.0302 (0.0694)	−0.0014 (0.0022)	−0.0047 (0.0056)	−0.0021 (0.0019)
Stock–Yogo weak ID critical value 10%	16.38	16.38	16.38	16.38
Kleibergen–Paap weak ID F-test	0.20	19.98	3.62	17.22
Stock–Wright weak instrument LM S statistic	3.15(1)	3.45(1)	2.64(1)	8.86(1)**
C statistic, endogeneity test (Chi2, df(1))	3.208(1)	0.852(1)	2.221(1)	8.442(1)**
Fixed effects	YES	YES	YES	YES
Autocorrelation robust	YES	YES	YES	YES
Heteroskedasticity robust	YES	YES	YES	YES
Number of observations	3,274	3,350	3,413	3,402
Years covered	1900–2015	1900–2015	1900–2015	1900–2015

Note: Standard errors are clustered on country-episodes. Two-tailed tests of statistical significance are displayed: $^{*}p < .05$, $^{**}p < .01$.

4

Judicial Effects on Democratic Regime Stability

The art of being sometimes audacious and sometimes very prudent is the secret of success.
Napoleon Bonaparte

Democratic compromises are easier to sustain when parties out of power believe that parties in power will govern within boundaries, often explicitly stated in constitutions but also implicitly understood as part of the underlying social understandings that make it useful for opposing groups to compete for power via elections. We have referred to these boundaries as establishing fundamental regime rules, rules that leaders are expected to follow while in office. Yet fundamental regime rules cannot cover every possible contingency. Some leaders will confront scenarios that have yet to have been contemplated, and so there will be no precedent for what constitute appropriate actions. Other rules are understood to allow for a degree of discretion on the part of leaders. For example, under exigent circumstances of various types, presidents are delegated powers that they do not enjoy during normal times.

Critically, opposing parties in a system may have very different perceptions of whether observed actions of the state violate rules. This can be because there is a disagreement over the meaning of a rule. It can also arise when there is consensus about a rule but differences of opinion over the facts under which the rule is being applied. The nature of political leadership and the corresponding powers that it confers mean that leaders will have different, commonly better, information about facts. This asymmetry can be destabilizing because it creates opportunities for some leaders to take advantage of perceptions that they are better informed, and opposition party leaders know it (Svolik, 2012). This is particularly problematic when the facts determine the scope and limits of the rule itself. Solving these problems is an important part of making democracies robust.

The claim we wish to investigate is that processes that give judges powers to evaluate the appropriateness of state actions can help manage this informational challenge. Broadly, we will argue that judicial systems do so by incentivizing prudence on behalf of leaders and the opposition, and that this prudence reinforces commitments to democratic compromises. In this chapter, we consider how this might be so. Our approach draws on ideas developed by Ríos-Figueroa (2016), and Carrubba and Gabel (2015). Since our argument is most related to Carrubba and Gabel, it is useful to review it.

Recall that Carrubba and Gabel were studying the politics of the European Union (EU). They have in mind the Court of Justice of the European Union (CJEU) and the challenges of managing conflicts over whether a member state has violated treaty provisions. The argument has three steps. First, private parties (or perhaps the European Commission) file law suits alleging that an EU regulation has been violated. Second, states decide whether to file briefs in support of or in opposition to a state's legal position in a case. Third, in light of the distribution of briefs, the defendant state can take costly efforts to convince other states that have filed in opposition to their position that noncompliance with an unfavorable CJEU decision ought not to be punished collectively by the states acting together. Only states that confront significant local challenges will be willing to take the effort necessary to convince their treaty partners of the inefficiency of complying with European regulations in the current instance. The first step in this process alerts states to potential violations of law, while the second and third steps provide a coordinated process for revealing information about collective understandings of European law.

Our approach is broadly consistent with Carrubba and Gabel's account, but we depart from their model in a number of ways, which we believe helps to shed light on important parts of the problem that they do not highlight. In the Carrubba and Gabel model, judicializing the process always results in the revelation of private information held by defendant states. This happens because some types of governments (i.e. those who are being forced to pay very high costs for compliance with European law) will always be willing to make the effort necessary to convince other states of their position. Yet we should consider the possibility that judicial processes do not result in information revelation. A core feature of the politics of managing regime rules is that it is sometimes impossible to discern a leader's type because the information they reveal is consistent with what all leaders would say.

We develop a model that identifies conditions under which courts are able to incentivize the revelation of private information. This, as it turns out, has a lot to do with how we conceive of judicial preferences, and ultimately judicial independence. Second, we ask whether judicial processes might reduce regime conflict even if they do not materially affect information transmission. We find that they do, and yet in doing so courts produce other challenges for regimes. Third, the costly signal that states send in Carrubba and Gabel's model is worth considering carefully. In the model, states simply expend "effort." The authors suggest that effort can be understood as persuasive in nature. It is somewhat unclear how a well-constructed argument about why a state has not violated a regime rule would either be particularly costly to that state or persuasive to the other states or both. Legal argumentation might be profitably understood as cheap talk.

If effort can instead be understood as forms of payments to states or otherwise as direct benefits to state interests, then we will have to consider the possibility that the opposing briefs that governments file are designed to prompt targeted states to buy off their support. If this is possible, then the distribution of briefs offers defendant states a far from perfect sense of who really supports them. At its core, the Carrubba and Gabel argument depends on the costliness of these "signals." We agree with this position. The question is how to conceive of what would generate costly signaling. In our model, we will suggest that a natural costly signal is noncompliance with a court order.

4.1 AN INFORMATIONAL MODEL OF REGIME BREAKDOWN

We will consider a model that deals with a fundamental challenge of managing a regime compromise, which reflects key elements of the Stephenson and Fox (2011) model of pandering. Consider a political regime that consists of a leader, endowed with governing power, and a supporter on whom the leader depends.[1] We assume that the leader and the follower have come to some understanding about regime rules, which may include, for example, promises to limit terms of office, exercising extreme caution when considering a criminal investigation of a political rival, or promises to divide regime surplus in particular ways. The players know that the political context in which they operate sometimes requires the leader to take actions that are inconsistent with the general understanding of regime rules. In order to maintain the spirit of a regime compromise, leaders are sometimes called upon to take extraordinary actions, which in normal times would surely constitute a violation of regime rules. Indeed, if the political context does not warrant extraordinary policy measures, such measures may be used to shift the balance of power in the favor of the leader. Critically, the supporter cannot necessarily know that a leader who is taking an extraordinary action is doing so appropriately, i.e. as would be expected under the regime's rules. We first consider several properties of this regime in the absence of a court. We will then introduce a court and consider the possible differences that it makes.

4.1.1 *Baseline Model*

Following the setup in Stephenson and Fox (2011), we begin by assuming that a political context can be understood by the players to be "normal" or "extraordinary." Likewise, leaders can adopt "normal" or "extraordinary" policies, and supporters may respond "normally" or "extraordinarily." Specifically, let $X = \{n, x\}$ denote the set of possible descriptions of political contexts or actions taken by the leader or

[1] The leader may be thought of as a governing party or coalition in either a democratic or an autocratic context. The supporter may be conceptualized as whatever set of individuals on whom the leader depends for continued leadership. This may be thought of as a party, a group of individuals, or the leader's "winning coalition." The key point is that the leader has immediate and formal control over the instruments of governance.

supporter. We denote a political context $\omega \in X$. We assume that a political context is drawn from a Bernoulli distribution over X, which is known commonly to the players. We let π reflect the probability of an extraordinary context. We assume further that the leader observes ω and then proposes a policy response, $p \in X$, where $p = x$ reflects an extraordinary policy that might violate regime rules and $p = n$ reflects a policy that is clearly understood not to violate these rules. Given this information structure, the leader may be conceived of as one of two types, $t \in X$. We will refer to the leaders as the extraordinary and normal types. Observing p, the supporter responds to the policy, choosing an $r \in X$. We assume that $r = x$ induces a costly conflict of uncertain outcome with the leader whereas $r = n$ results in continued support of the leader per the regime rules. A mixed strategy for the leader, σ_l, assigns a probability distribution over X for each state, where $\sigma_l(\omega)$ indicates $Pr(p = x|\omega)$. Similarly, a mixed strategy for the supporter, σ_s, assigns a probability distribution over X for each policy they observes, and where $\sigma_s(p)$ indicates $Pr(r = x|p)$.

Preferences

The problem on which the model focuses is how to ensure that policy choices the leader makes are appropriate given the state of the world, while also minimizing conflict. To focus on that problem, we normalize the value of the regime agreement to 1. A failure to respond to an extraordinary political context reduces the value of the regime to both players. We scale the regime value by $\gamma \in (0, 1)$ in the event that the $\omega = x \neq p$. We assume that conflicts, should they emerge, are resolved probabilistically. Specifically, if $r = x$, the leader receives v, where $v \sim \mathcal{B}e(\alpha, \beta)$. In the event that $\omega = r = x \neq p$, the leader and supporter receive γv and $\gamma(1 - v)$, respectively. Finally, should $\omega = n = r \neq p$, and the normal leader has unnecessarily taken the extraordinary policy, we assume that the value of the regime to the leader (supporter) increases (decreases) by $k > 1$. This implies the following payoff function for the leader:

$$u_l = \begin{cases} 1 & \text{if } \omega = p \wedge r = n \\ 1 + k & \text{if } \omega = n = r \neq p \\ \gamma & \text{if } \omega = x \neq p = r \\ v & \text{if } r = x \wedge \neg(\omega = x \neq p) \\ \gamma v & \text{if } \omega = r = x \neq p. \end{cases}$$

Likewise, the payoff function for the supporter is given by

$$u_s = \begin{cases} 1 & \text{if } \omega = p \wedge r = n \\ 1 - k & \text{if } \omega = n = r \neq p \\ \gamma & \text{if } \omega = x \neq p = r \\ 1 - v & \text{if } r = x \wedge \neg(\omega = x \neq p) \\ \gamma(1 - v) & \text{if } \omega = r = x \neq p. \end{cases}$$

Analysis

Our solution concept is Perfect Bayesian Equilibrium (PBE). We assume that beliefs are derived via passive conjectures at information sets that are not reached.[2]

We begin by considering the possibility for a complete revelation of the political circumstances. First note that the supporter will react normally to the normal policy, no matter their beliefs. Independently of the political context, an extraordinary response to a normal policy only wastes resources since the leader has not attempted to shift the balance of power. In the worst case scenario, where the state warrants an extraordinary action but the leader acts normally (i.e. $\omega = x \neq p$), the supporter would only compound the problem (i.e. $\gamma(1 - \mathbb{E}(v)) < \gamma$).

The key question for the supporter is how to respond to an extraordinary policy. Suppose that the leader chooses a policy that is matched to the state ($p = \omega$). If this were true, the supporter would infer the leader's type upon observing the policy. Thus, upon observing the extraordinary policy, the supporter would accept the policy, selecting a normal reaction ($r = n$). This kind of reaction would provide the normal leader with a strong incentive to adopt an extraordinary policy, and thus the equilibrium would unravel.

Now suppose that each type selected a policy mismatched to the state. In this case, the supporter would again correctly infer the leader's type from the policy. Upon observing the extraordinary policy, they would know that they confronts a normal leader attempting to change the balance of power. For that reason, they would react extraordinarily (setting $r = x$), and that would incentivize the normal leader to adopt the normal policy. Thus, the baseline model is inconsistent with communication that fully reveals to the supporter the true state of the world.

Lemma 1 *There is no PBE in which the types fully separate.*

Political Opportunism and Political Failure

There are two types of equilibria in this model, one in which the leader types can be expected to take the same action, and another in which the extraordinary leader can be distinguished partially from the normal leader. Consider the first type of equilibrium. In an equilibrium in which both leaders adopt the extraordinary policy, the supporter's beliefs are defined via Bayes's rule when they observe the extraordinary policy ($p = x$). By passive conjectures, they hold the same beliefs when observing an unexpected normal policy. As the prior probability of an extraordinary political event increases, the supporter is naturally more likely to accept an extraordinary policy response.

[2] This means that if a player reaches an information set that should not be reached in equilibrium, the player does not update their prior beliefs beyond what has been updated prior to reaching this information set.

Definition 1 *Let $\bar{\pi} \equiv 1 - \frac{\alpha}{k(\alpha+\beta)}$ denote the prior probability of an extraordinary set of political circumstances above which the supporter will choose $r = n$ if they observe $p = x$ when they expects the leaders to adopt the same policy.*

When the probability that the political context is extraordinary is sufficiently high (when $\pi \geq \bar{\pi}$), the supporter will accept an extraordinary policy response, knowing that sometimes they will fall victim to opportunistic behavior by the normal leader – a leader whose extraordinary policy is ill suited to the state. As the consequences of an inappropriate use of the extraordinary policy become increasingly problematic (k increases), that is, for large shifts in the nature of the regime that follow from opportunistic leader behavior, it becomes increasingly difficult to sustain this kind of behavior. Still, if ever the supporter is expected to behave in this way, both leaders will select the extraordinary policy for all other values of the model's parameters. In contrast, for low values of π, the model is consistent with a pooling equilibrium in which both leaders simply adopt the normal policy, independent of the state, expecting the supporter to select $r = x$ if they observe the extraordinary policy. For this kind of profile of strategies to be part of a PBE, the extraordinary leader must be unwilling to engage in conflict, which requires that the consequences of failing to respond to extraordinary circumstances must be less severe than the political conflict that would ensue were they to move forward with an extraordinary policy (i.e. $\gamma \geq \mathbb{E}(v)$).

Proposition 1 *For $\pi \geq \bar{\pi}$, there exists a pooling PBE in which both leaders adopt $p = x$ and the supporter sets $r = n$ in response to all policies. For $\pi < \bar{\pi}$ and $\gamma \geq \mathbb{E}(v)$, there exists a pooling equilibrium in which both types adopt $p = n$ and the supporter sets $r = n$ if $p = n$ and $r = x$ if $p = x$. The supporter's beliefs are equal to their priors at all information sets.*

INTERPRETATION. These equilibria reflect two distinct and yet related problems of managing regime rules. The first, investigated carefully by Svolik (2012), involves deterring leaders from reneging on regime rules by taking advantage of uncertainties about the true nature of policy challenges. An equilibrium in which the leaders pool on the extraordinary policy involves such rule violations – they are successful in political contexts in which the likelihood that regime rules ought to be bent is relatively high. In such contexts, opportunistic leaders can take advantage of perceived crises to alter bargains that were previously necessary for compromise.

The second problem, addressed by Stephenson and Fox (2011), is that sometimes leaders with the best of intentions are deterred from taking extraordinary actions when such actions would be appropriate, i.e. political circumstances that call for extraordinary action are not responded to appropriately. This kind of policy failure emerges in the second equilibrium when it appears that political circumstances do not warrant extraordinary action, yet in reality they do. Leaders hoping to act in good faith can be deterred from doing so because of the very same uncertainties that can produce opportunistic behavior. Despite the fact that these equilibria present one of two political failures, critically, the players avoid conflict in both cases, albeit for different reasons.

Political Conflict

The second type of equilibrium will involve conflict between the players, at least on occasion. Here, the extraordinary leader always moves forward with the extraordinary policy. The normal leader only sometimes faithfully implements the normal policy; sometimes the normal leader implements the extraordinary policy. The supporter always accepts the normal policy, but when they observe the extraordinary policy, they sometimes respond in kind. These are the circumstances in which there is conflict. In this kind of equilibrium, the supporter must be selecting the extraordinary response at a sufficient rate to deter the normal leader from always attempting to take advantage of the supporter's uncertainty (i.e. always setting $p = x$); and, yet the normal leader cannot be too aggressive so that the supporter would always react extraordinarily (i.e. always setting $r = x$).

Definition 2 *Let* $\rho \equiv \frac{k}{k+1-\mathbb{E}(v)}$ *denote the value of* $\sigma_s(x)$ *such that the normal leader is indifferent between their two policies; and, let* $\lambda \equiv \frac{\pi}{(1-\pi)(1-\mathbb{E}(v)k^{-1})} - \frac{\pi}{(1-\pi)}$ *denote the value of* $\sigma_l(n)$ *such that the supporter is indifferent between their two responses, when the extraordinary type is expected to adopt* $p = x$.

It is useful to note that $\frac{1}{2} \leq \rho \leq 1$ and that $0 \leq \lambda \leq 1$ as long as $\pi < 1 - \frac{\alpha}{k(\alpha+\beta)}$, so that this kind of equilibrium requires that the prior probability that the state is extraordinary is sufficiently low (i.e. $\pi < \bar{\pi}$).

Proposition 2 *For* $\pi < \bar{\pi}$ *and* $\gamma < \mathbb{E}(v)$, *there exists a semi-separating equilibrium in which the players adopt the following strategies:*

$$\sigma_l(\omega) = \begin{cases} 1 & \text{if } \omega = x \\ \lambda & \text{if } \omega = n \end{cases}$$

$$\sigma_s(p) = \begin{cases} 0 & \text{if } p = n \\ \rho & \text{if } p = x. \end{cases}$$

The supporter believes $Pr(\omega = x | p = x) = \frac{\pi}{\pi+(1-\pi)\lambda}$ *and may have any beliefs having observed* $p = n$.

In this case, policy failure is avoided; however, it is exchanged for both allowing violations of regime rules and costly conflict on occasion.[3]

The probabilities of regime violations and conflict depend on the equilibrium rates with which normal leaders adopt extraordinary policies and supporters refuse to accept them. What is more, a third political problem emerges. Specifically, conflict, when it emerges, can reflect efforts to stop opportunism, but it can also reflect a fundamental miscalculation – where supporters react extraordinarily to a leader's good faith effort to solve a serious policy problem.

INTERPRETATION. Figure 4.1 summarizes features of the three equilibria in the baseline model. The left panel displays the probability with which the normal leader adopts the extraordinary policy in any equilibrium. When it is sufficiently likely that the state is extraordinary (above $\bar{\pi}$), the game's equilibrium will involve both leaders selecting the extraordinary policy (pooling on $p = x$), where the normal leader always takes advantage of the fortuitous situation. Below $\bar{\pi}$, equilibrium opportunism depends on the way in which the consequences to the extraordinary leader of failing to match the state relate to the expected outcome of a conflict. Should the consequences of a policy failure be insignificant relative to the expected outcome of a regime conflict (i.e. $\gamma > \mathbb{E}(v)$), both leaders will adopt the normal policy, resulting in a policy failure but one that avoids a costly conflict. However, should the consequences of policy failure be significant relative to the expected outcome of a regime conflict, then the equilibrium will be in mixed strategies. As Figure 4.1 suggests, the normal leader's probability of choosing the extraordinary policy rises in the prior probability that the state is extraordinary, reflecting the fact that it becomes easier to take advantage of the supporter as expectations become increasingly certain that the political circumstances do in fact warrant extraordinary action.

The right panel shows the equilibrium probability of conflict across our three cases. Notably, when a conflict is likely to be particularly costly (or when policy failures are insignificant), there will be no conflict in equilibrium. This is reflected by the gray curve, which tracks the probability of conflict in the pooling equilibria. When the policy failure consequences are significant (again relative to expected outcomes of a conflict), in contrast, the probability of conflict rises in the prior probability of extraordinary circumstances, but only up to $\bar{\pi}$, after which it drops to zero, because once people believe that the state of the world is truly extraordinary, supporters will accept extraordinary policies and normal leaders will take advantage of them. Thus, in the baseline model, the probability of conflict is both nonlinear in expectations about the seriousness of potential political crises as well as conditional on the consequences of failing to respond to extraordinary circumstances.

3 The same strategy profile can be part of a PBE if $\gamma \geq \mathbb{E}(v)$, as long as k is sufficiently small ($k < \frac{1-\gamma-\mathbb{E}(v)(1-\gamma)}{\gamma-\mathbb{E}(v)}$). To simplify the discussion, we will assume that k is larger than this threshold in cases where it would matter.

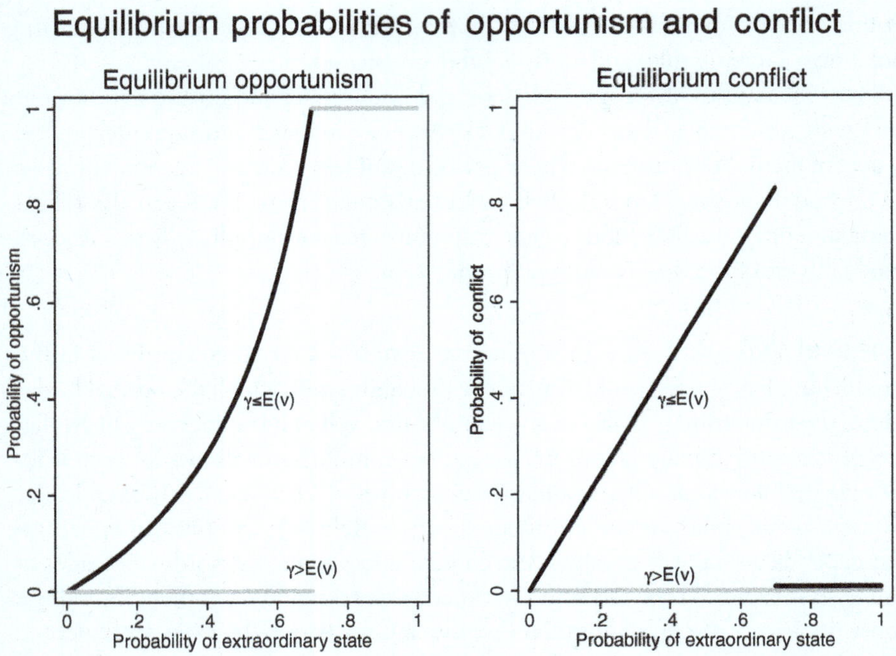

FIGURE 4.1 The left panel displays the equilibrium probability of opportunism in the model's three equilibria. The right panel shows the probability of regime conflict.

4.1.2 *Judicial Review Model*

We now consider a model in which a court endowed with judicial review powers is called upon to evaluate the policy produced by the leader. The model is sparse. For one, we assume that the policy is reviewed if enacted, setting aside concerns over who would have the incentive to challenge a policy in court, as well as questions of jurisdiction or standing, which might limit the ability of potentially aggrieved parties to sue. Likewise, a judicial decision will come in the form of a veto, setting aside concerns over rules that the court might set to govern future policy outcomes, as well as properties of rules, which might complicate the interpretation of the decision. Despite these simplifications, the model is designed to address the core ideas in work on courts and their effects on regime compromise. What is essential here is that the court can issue a decision that, formally at least, sets aside the policy adopted by the leader.

Timing and Information

In this version of the model, we continue to assume that a political context is first drawn from a Bernoulli distribution over X, and that the leader adopts a policy $p_1 \in X$. If $p_1 = n$, then the structure is identical to the baseline, i.e. the supporter chooses a reaction $r_1 \in X$. Instead, if $p_1 = x$, we assume that the court is called upon to issue a decision. The court selects a decision $d \in \{0, 1\}$, where 0 indicates a ruling finding that the policy does not violate regime rules and where 1 indicates the opposite. Should the court select 0, as in the baseline, the supporter then selects an $r_2 \in X$. Should the court select 1, the leader is called upon to play again, and may select $p_2 \in X$. We conceive of $p_2 = x$ as a policy reimplementing the extraordinary policy, the consequences of which we parameterize. Finally, the supporter selects an $r_3 \in X$ should the leader adopt $p_2 = x$.

A mixed behavioral strategy for the leader, σ_l, assigns a probability distribution over X for each state, and for all histories $(\omega, x, 1)$. Similarly, a mixed behavioral strategy for the supporter, σ_s, assigns a probability distribution over X for all histories (ω, n), $(\omega, x, 0)$, and $(\omega, x, 1, p_2)$.

Preferences

The supporter's preferences reflect those of the baseline. They wish the policy to match the state; they lose utility from opportunistic leadership behavior (reflected by k), from a policy failure (reflected by γ) and in the event of conflict $(1 - v)$, precisely as in the baseline. None of this is influenced by the court's decision, so that in particular, the supporter does not pay a cost for the litigation and does not care whether the leader adopts $p_i = n$ if $\omega = n$ in response to a court order or when first called upon to set the policy. We make a similar assumption about the leader, however, we also assume that should the leader defy a court order, they pay a cost $b > 0$. This cost may be interpreted in a variety of ways from the consequences of public protest, electoral losses, a decrease in international investment flowing from increased uncertainty about the inviolability of contracts, etc. (e.g. Vanberg, 2005). One natural source of variation in these costs derives from the ability to mobilize mass groups of people (or at least to be able to credibly mobilize such groups). Political societies that have deep and robust civil societies are more likely to have organizations that are capable of doing this kind of mobilization. Recent scholarship by Chilton and Versteeg (2020) have shown that constitutional rights protecting organizational interests (e.g. the right to collectively bargain or the right to practice religion) are more likely to be enforced because there are organizations capable of solving the kinds of coordination and collective action problems that make mass mobilization so difficult. The key point is that defying a court order may be more or less costly to the leader. We assume that in the event that $p_1 \neq p_2$, the leader may accept the court's decision without cost.

Our approach to the court's preferences reflects elements of the literature in comparative judicial politics. We will assume first that the court wishes to allow extraordinary policies only should the state of the world warrant it. Thus, we assume that the court's preferences track the supporter's identically. We do so in order to provide minimal autonomy from the government, which is necessary for any information to be influenced by the court, but the assumption also sets the stage for a court to play the role of political insurance. We also assume that, all else equal, the court would prefer to be obeyed, and thus assume that the court pays a cost $c > 0$ should the leader defy an order. We do not assume that the court receives a special signal about the true state of the world. Instead, the court will have to infer it as anyone else in society. The court's utility is characterized as follows:

$$u_c(p_i, r_j; \omega) = I_1 a - I_2 c$$

for $i = 1, 2$, $j = 1, 2, 3$; and, where I_1 is an indicator variable that takes the value of 1 when the court has set $d = 0$ if $\omega = p_1$ and 0 otherwise; and, where I_2 is an indicator variable that takes the value of 1 if $p_2 = x$ and 0 otherwise. Thus, a reflects the value of making a decision that matches the state and c the cost of being defied.

Analysis

As in the baseline model, the supporter will always react normally to the normal policy. We can restrict the leader's strategies as well. Note that the leader is indifferent between setting $p_1 = n$ and setting $p_1 = x$ and $p_2 = n$, whatever the supporter's strategy. For this reason, we will not consider strategies that involve the leader initially adopting the extraordinary policy, knowing that the court will strike it down, a decision that the leader will ultimately accept. We do this to reduce the number of cases to consider, but it is important to consider this choice from a substantive perspective. A strategy like this, i.e. in which the leader selects $p_1 = x$ and $p_2 = n$, could be party of a PBE. They would exist in precisely the same region of the parameter space consisting of pooling equilibria in which the leader types both adopt $p_1 = n$, what we are calling the "policy failure" cases. In substantive terms, these equilibria are reflected by politics in which presidents adopt policies, which are struck down by a court whose decision is respected.

As in the baseline, this version of the model is inconsistent with behavior that fully reveals the state of the world to the players who are uncertain about it. Suppose that the leader sets $p_i = \omega$. Upon observing $p_1 = x$, the court would uphold the policy and the supporter would accept it. This would incentivize the normal leader to set $p_1 = x$, as well. And, of course, if the leader set $p \neq \omega$, then upon observing $p_1 = x$, the court would infer that the normal leader had engaged in opportunism, strike down the policy, and the normal leader would accept the decision, knowing that the supporter would set $r_3 = x$ should the leader not back down.

Lemma 2 *There exists no fully separating equilibrium in the judicial review game.*

The equilibria in the judicial review game turn on the court's beliefs over the state, which are shared of course by the supporter. For sufficient confidence that the state is extraordinary, the court will declare the extraordinary policy to be an acceptable use of power.

Definition 3 *Let $\bar{\pi}_c \equiv \frac{a-c}{2a}$ denote the value of π above which the court will select $d = 0$ if the leader types are expected to adopt the same policy.*

This threshold depends on the cost the court perceives for being defied. As will be clear, any case in which $c > a$, and the court cares more about compliance than exercising its judgment sincerely, results in equilibria that reflect the baseline case precisely. Obviously a highly deferential court, one that behaves as if it were not part of the political system, will not influence behavior at all. The interesting cases involve those in which $a > c$, and thus the court might be willing to exercise its authority to declare policies invalid under regime rules.

Equilibria in the Judicial Review Game

The judicial review model contains three classes of equilibria, which reflect closely the results of the baseline model, as the following proposition suggests. We first state these conditions formally and then compare the results to the baseline, relying in part on Figure 4.2.

Proposition 3 *There are two types of pooling equilibria in the judicial review game, which can be divided into four sub-cases:*

Case 1a: For $\pi \geq max\{\bar{\pi}, \bar{\pi}_c\}$, there exists a pooling PBE in which both leaders adopt $p = x$, the court selects $d = 0$, and the supporter always sets $r = n$.

Case 1b: For $\bar{\pi} \leq \pi < \bar{\pi}_c$ and $b \leq min\{k, 1 - \gamma\}$, there exists a pooling PBE in which both leaders adopt $p = x$, the court selects $d = 1$, and the supporter always sets $r = n$.

Case 2a: For $\bar{\pi}_c \leq \pi < \bar{\pi}$ and $\gamma \geq \mathbb{E}(v)$, there exists a pooling PBE in which both leaders adopt $p = n$, the court selects $d = 0$, and the supporter selects $r = n$ if $p_i = n$; the supporter selects $r = x$ if $p_i = x$.

Case 2b: For $\pi < min\{\bar{\pi}, \bar{\pi}_c\}$ and $\gamma \geq \mathbb{E}(v) - b$, there exists a pooling PBE in which both leaders adopt $p = n$, the court selects $d = 1$, and the supporter selects $r = n$ if $p_i = n$; the supporter selects $r = x$ if $p_i = x$.

Beliefs for the court and supporters are equal to their priors at all information sets.

As in the baseline model, there are also mixed strategy equilibria in which the extraordinary leader adopts the extraordinary policy for sure yet the normal leader chooses the extraordinary policy with positive probability.

Proposition 4 *In a mixed strategy equilibrium of the judicial review game, the extraordinary leader always sets $p_i = x$ and the normal leader chooses $p_i = x$ with probability λ. The court sets $d = 0$ if either $a < c$ or if $a > c$ and $\lambda \leq \frac{a-c}{(1-\pi)(a+c)}$. It sets $d = 1$ otherwise. The supporter chooses $r = n$ if ever $p = n$, chooses $r = x$ with probability equal to ρ if the court sets $d = 0$; otherwise, the supporter sets the* *probability of* $r = x$ *to* $\rho_2 \equiv \frac{k-b}{k+1-\mathbb{E}(v)}$. *The supporter and the court believe that* $Pr(\omega = x \mid p = x) = \frac{\pi}{\pi+(1-\pi)\lambda}$. *The supporter may have any beliefs having observed* $p = n$.

Importantly, if ever the players adopt mixed strategies in equilibrium, the normal leader plays the exact same strategy as they did in the baseline. The reason is that if ever the supporter is called upon to react to an extraordinary policy – independently of the court's decision – their expected utility calculus is identical to the baseline model. Thus, to render the supporter indifferent, the normal leader adopts the same probability distribution over X. In contrast, the mixed strategy that the supporter adopts depends on the court's decision. Should the court uphold the policy in equilibrium, the supporter would adopt the same mixed strategy; however, should the court be expected to strike the policy down, the normal leader confronts an additional cost to opportunism. This is because they must defy the court order. For that reason, the supporter's equilibrium probability of an extraordinary action must drop in order to prevent the normal leader from simply adopting the normal policy. Thus we can state the following result.

Result 1 *In any mixed strategy equilibrium of the judicial review game, the probability of conflict is weakly lower than it is in the baseline game.*

INTERPRETATION. Figure 4.2 provides a visual summary of the key differences between the equilibria of the baseline and judicial review games. The x-axis reflects the prior probability that the state is extraordinary, whereas the y-axis reflects the consequences of a failure of the extraordinary leader to choose an appropriate policy. The top panel shows the results for the baseline model. The middle panel shows the results for the judicial review game, in a case where the costs to the court of being defied are relatively large. The bottom panel depicts the results of the judicial review game, but for relatively low costs of defiance.

The figure displays immediately the consequences of including judicial review in this interaction, even a form of judicial review that does not inject the interaction with additional information about the underlying state of the world. Consider the middle panel. Although the region of opportunism has not changed, because the court's threshold for upholding policies is relatively low, what has changed is the region where mixed strategy equilibria were possible. In their place we find pooling equilibria in which policy failures result. The addition of the court increases the cost of adopting the extraordinary policy. Clearly, if the costs of defying a court (b) are close to zero, then the constitutional model reduces to the baseline, as the lower threshold on the y-axis would converge on the higher threshold. If Chilton and Versteeg (2020) are correct, then this result highlights that without a strong organizational base to support the decisions of courts, independent judges will have no meaningful effect on regime survival. Similarly, as we discussed earlier

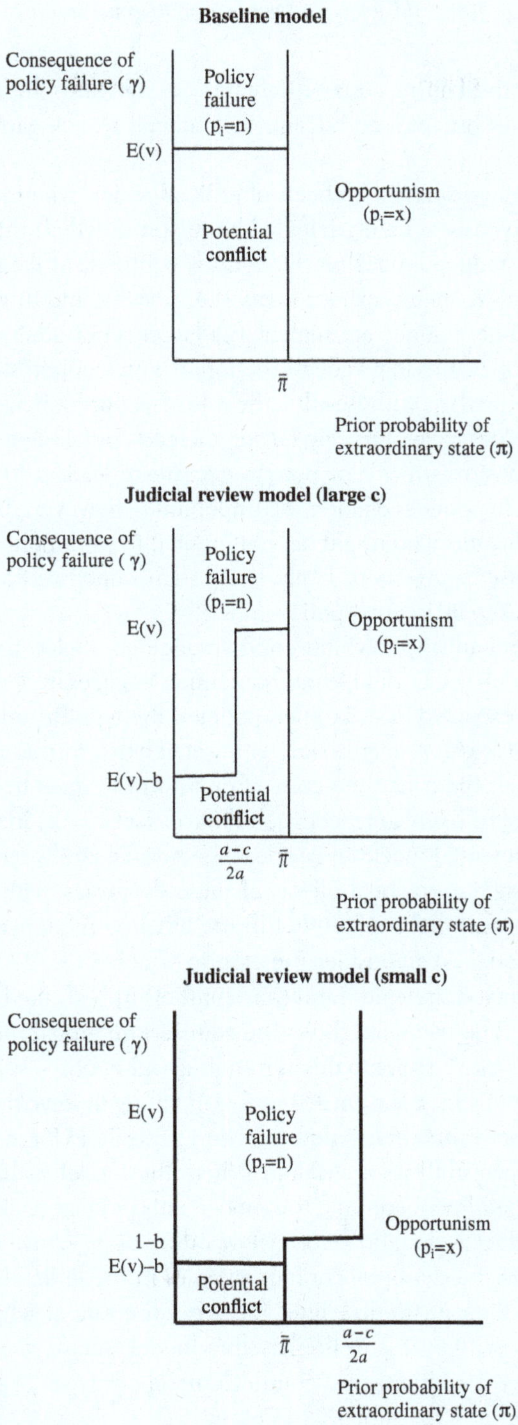

FIGURE 4.2 Classes of equilibria in the baseline and judicial review games. The top panel describes equilibria in the baseline model for varying levels of γ and π. The middle panel describes equilibria for the judicial review model for large values of c. The bottom panel describes equilibria for the judicial review game with small values of c.

in this section, if the court's costs of defiance (c) increase, the first threshold on the x-axis converges on zero, and again, the judicial review game reduces to the baseline.

The bottom panel displays the effects of judicial review when judges do not perceive considerable costs to being defied. The region in which mixed strategies are possible is further reduced, because the court is willing to strike policies at higher probabilities when the state is extraordinary (i.e. $\omega = x$), and thus the costs of pursuing the extraordinary policy are higher in a larger set of contexts. Similarly, the policy failure region begins to invade the region in which opportunism was possible.

Combining this analysis with Result 1, the role of a court in helping elites manage regime rules becomes clear. First, by raising the costs of taking extraordinary measures, courts endowed with review powers encourage leaders to be careful about how they respond to political challenges. Importantly, however, this effect comes at a price – namely leaders who might have attempted to solve policy challenges with extraordinary measures are more likely to let such opportunities go. This avoids conflict, but it does so by inviting policy failure.

The second mechanism by which courts reduce conflict is more subtle. In an equilibrium in which the normal leader sometimes engages in opportunistic behavior, if the court is expected to strike such policies, the equilibrium probability with which the supporter reacts aggressively is lower relative to the game without the court. The reason is that since the costs of opportunism have been increased, the supporter must be less likely to react extraordinarily (set $r = x$) in order to offset the normal leader's increased incentive to adopt the normal policy ($p = n$).

Figure 4.3 shows the practical effects of these dynamics. The left panel shows the equilibrium probabilities of conflict in the baseline model versus those in the judicial review model. We consider the case in which $\gamma < \mathbb{E}(v)$, where there is the possibility of mixed strategies (and thus conflict) in both the baseline and judicial review games. The left panel shows the equilibrium probabilities of conflict for $\mathbb{E}(v) - b < \gamma < \mathbb{E}(v)$. We refer to this as middling values of γ – substantively we are considering a case in which the consequences of failing to solve the policy crisis are reasonably high. For values of π below the court's threshold for upholding policies, the difference in probabilities is striking. Where the model without review shows an increasing probability of conflict, the model with judicial review shows that the probability of conflict is flat and zero for low values of π. Above that threshold, at roughly $\pi = .38$ in the example, conflict emerges in the judicial review game but it is always lower than in the baseline. Likewise, the rate at which the probability increases is lower than it is in the baseline model. Above $\bar{\pi}$ conflict is equally likely in both cases, i.e. there is no conflict, since both types of leaders adopt the extraordinary policy and the support accepts it.

Turning to the right panel, the results are nearly identical. When $\gamma < \mathbb{E}(v) - b$ and the consequences of failing to respond to a political crisis are highly significant conflict emerges with positive probability in both game types; however, the rate at

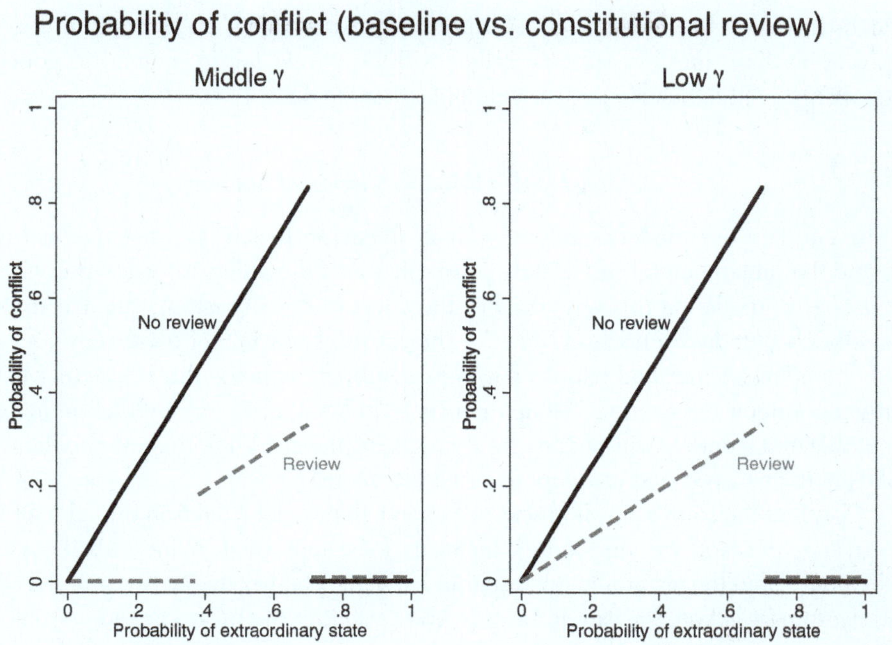

FIGURE 4.3 Equilibrium conflict probabilities in baseline and judicial review games. Solid black curves indicate probabilities in the baseline model whereas the dashed gray curves indicate probabilities in the judicial review game. The left panel shows the results for middling values of γ. The right panel shows results for high values of γ. In each panel, the probability of conflict in the judicial review game is never larger than it is in the baseline game, for all values of π.

which this probability increases remains lower in the judicial review game. We can thus state the following result.

Result 2 *The probability of conflict is weakly lower in the judicial review game than in the baseline game.*

Summary

The baseline model identified conditions under which we might expect opportunism, policy failure, and political conflict as elites' attempt to manage regime rules. The judicial review model suggests that conflict is less likely with judicial review carried out by a minimally independent court, even one that does not enjoy special informational advantages. To do so, courts first must be willing to use their authority, and they must accept that doing so will result in conflict with leading officials. Noncompliance must be a part of the process by which courts help groups manage regime compromises. Judicial review also is likely to reduce opportunism. However, both of these effects, decreases in conflict and opportunism, come at the expense of an increased likelihood of policy failures. By encouraging leaders to limit their power, tensions are relieved, yet leaders will sometimes fail to respond to policy challenges when their supporters would like them to do so.

4.1.3 *A Model with a Stronger Version of Autonomy*

The court in our model is autonomous in the sense that it does not necessarily share the preferences of the leader – it simply wants the policy to match the state. Of course, modeling this way attaches the court to the supporter, which is itself another way to lack autonomy. That is, the court asked whether there is evidence of compelling contextual reasons for an extraordinary policy – this is exactly what the supporter wants to know. Set up in this way, judicial review nevertheless reduces conflict, but it does so without powerfully resolving the elites' information problems. An alternative approach to autonomy might do more.

Consider the court's payoff function. Suppose that we let I_1 take on the value of 1 only if $p_1 = \omega$ and the court judges the means to be appropriate to the ends. That is, the court is no longer simply interested in knowing whether the facts warranted an extraordinary action. Instead, it wants to know whether the means are appropriate, say given the norms and traditions of a democratic society. Consider a policy in which the court does not find the means appropriate even if $\omega = x$. Here, the court would strike down the policy for all beliefs in the state, so long as $a > c$.

In this case, there exists a fully separating equilibrium, one in which *only the extraordinary leader sets* $p = x$. For this to work, the extraordinary leader must be prepared to defy the court, while the normal leader is not, so that $k \leq b < 1 - \gamma$. The costs of a backlash must not be too high so that the extraordinary leader would be willing to accept a policy failure; but they must not be low enough to induce the normal leader to act opportunistically.

In this equilibrium, the supporter would learn the true state of the world. The court would still be defied if $\omega = x$, but the benefit to society of defiance is clear communication of the elite's understandings of regime rules. Conflict would be avoided because of the accurate communication of the leader's true motives. The bottom line is that a court that is sufficiently independent from important political interests in society can powerfully resolve the regime's communication problems. Such a court would do so by exercising judgment, even knowing that its decisions are likely to be met with resistance or outright defiance.

4.2 DISCUSSION

We began this chapter by discussing how existing theoretical accounts envision a role for judges in the management of uncertainty about the meaning and application of regime rules. One kind of account, which considers judges as trustees of the regime, more or less assumes that problem away. Once we recognize that competing groups in society will never fully agree on the meaning of regime rules, the possibility of simply delegating the problem becomes attractive. Courts are often asked to resolve conflicts over constitutional meaning. As long as we believe that they are independent from political interests in society, we simply agree to accept their interpretations. A second argument, associated with the work of Clifford Carrubba and Matthew Gabel, directly addresses the problem. Their account highlights the ways in which judicial proceedings provide groups in a political system the ability to coordinate information about the collective understanding of regime rules as well as the ability of potential violators to signal their resolve. Our model builds on these accounts in a number of ways.

4.2.1 *Policy Failure and Opportunism Trade-Offs*

There is a sense in which the central problem to solve is relatively transparent. Uncertainty and misunderstandings about whether leaders are respecting regime rules can lead to political conflict. The problem to solve is conflict. Our analysis clarifies several aspects of this challenge. Consider a president who has received credible information that their political opponent, a leader of the opposition party, has violated a public corruption law. Suppose that the president moves forward with a public investigation. The most obvious aspect of the challenge concerns how to incentivize opposition party leaders to accept this kind of investigation, or at least to remain committed to protesting via legitimate democratic mechanisms. In so far as courts produce that result, they obviously risk opportunistic behavior on behalf of unscrupulous leaders. This is the first trade-off independent courts ask us to confront. A second aspect of the problem is that opposition parties might engage in conflict when leaders are doing exactly what they would like them to do. This would be true here if the leader under investigation is in fact guilty and opposition party members believe that corruption ought to be punished.

A third aspect of the problem is that leaders might fail to address policy challenges for fear of starting a regime conflict. Should the president pursue the corruption investigation and risk a regime conflict? A choice to move forward will naturally raise concerns that there are political motivations for the prosecution, and many presidents will elect not to prosecute. Yet should the opponent be guilty in fact, the president will have failed to exercise authority that the majority of opposition party members might have preferred. Thus, in so far as independent courts reduce political conflict, they invite a second trade-off between conflict and policy failure.

4.2.2 *When Can Courts Help the Parties Reveal Information?*

Under what conditions might courts exercising some kind of judicial review power help leaders reveal private information? In our model, courts change the nature of the communication between elites under three conditions. The first and most important condition is that judges must have preferences that are disconnected from both the leadership and the opposition in order to directly affect learning among the parties. This is a very particular kind of judicial independence. Simply rendering courts independent of the government is not enough for the judicial process we consider to help reveal information. The reason is courts of this type share preferences and information with opposition leaders. When it appears that the context in which leaders are making decisions are likely to warrant an extraordinary response, judges will defer to leadership. This is exactly the same decision that opposition party leaders would make were they sitting on the court. The key point is that without some special access to information and with preferences that match those of the opposition, judges do not influence the information that leaders reveal.

On the other hand, if judges have preferences that are disconnected in some way from both parties to the conflict, they can influence information transmission. If this is true, then there may be cases in which judges share opposition beliefs that the conditions are sufficiently likely to warrant an extraordinary measure and yet still believe that what the leader has done violates limits on authority. The example we consider is one in which judges might first ask if the context is such that an extraordinary power might be warranted. They then engage in a second line of questioning. They ask whether the particular means adopted are appropriate. They might find that the means are out of proportion to the problem being addressed. They might instead find that there were different means available, which could have been adopted. The key point is that if judges are willing to strike down a policy even when they perceive the context to be extraordinary, it is possible for leaders to credibly reveal their information. In this situation, leaders will be given an opportunity to signal their concerns. This will require noncompliance; and, so the second condition is that judges must be willing to accept noncompliance with their orders. Indeed, since noncompliance is essential to generate costly signaling, it is also important that judges be willing to be defied. The third condition is that leaders confronting extraordinary challenges must be willing to accept backlash for noncompliance and that leaders considering an opportunistic policy must be unwilling to accept such a backlash. In these circumstances, judicial review can improve communication about the rationales for taking actions that appear to violate regime rules.

It is worth asking whether this scenario is likely to emerge in many states during many years. In other words, where exactly are we to find judges whose preferences are disconnected from the central political cleavages of a state? Appointment processes commonly connect judges to particular political projects. Alternation of power can produce diverse judiciaries, but it is unclear how judges can ever be fully disconnected from the central cleavages that structure the politics of their states. And yet courts can influence regime stability even if they are unable to meaningfully influence communication among elites, a point to which we now turn.

4.2.3 *Can Courts Influence Regime Conflict If They Do Not Influence Information?*

We believe they can. Even in cases where courts do not materially influence the exchange of information, they influence regime conflict in two ways. The first way is by incentivizing leaders to be more prudent – to make fewer policy decisions that might raise opposition concerns than they would in the absence of independent courts. Levitsky and Ziblatt (2018) argue that leadership forbearance, or the commitment to not using all of the powers available to the majority, is a norm essential to managing potential regime conflicts. Independent courts incentivize forbearance in the form of more prudent policy-making. As we have argued, this effect comes with a cost – that some actions that should be taken will not be precisely because leaders are concerned about generating conflict. This effect has much in common with the concept of "autolimitation" (e.g. Engst, 2019; Vanberg, 1998). Law and courts scholars have described a "second face" of judicial power, in which legislators anticipate judicial reactions to policies, and thus craft bills with judicial review in mind. In this sense, our argument is that autolimitation is not merely about the power of courts but about the survival of democratic regimes. Indeed, the court in our model is not particularly powerful – it can always be ignored.

The second effect of independent courts is to make opposition party leaders less aggressive in their own policing of regime rules. Conditional on a leader taking an action that might plausibly be understood as a rule violation, opposition leaders will be less likely to respond outside the boundaries of normal democratic competition in the presence of independent courts.

In these two ways judicial processes lower the temperature of intra-elite conflict even if they do not influence the parties' ability to communicate. Uncertainties about the true rationales behind the use of power will remain. But commitments to democracy are nevertheless stronger with independent courts. Such courts help translate potential conflict in political society into interinstitutional conflict.

For this type of mechanism to work, judges must not be "single-minded pursuers of compliance," an assumption that seems to pervade much of the political science literature on judicial politics. While it is unlikely that judges prefer a world in which orders are routinely ignored, there is abundant evidence that judges understand that legal systems sometimes require flexibility. It is useful to recall that noncompliance need not manifest as a categorical refusal to implement a judicial order forever and under all circumstances. Some forms of noncompliance emerge in contexts where judges and administrators negotiate the best way for the state to fulfill its duties – a process that plays out over time. In these contexts, judges understand that their orders will not be implemented.

The Colombian Constitutional Court's effort to force the Colombian state to address a massive failure to protect victims of the internal conflict is particularly instructive in this regard (Cepeda, 2009). So too is the experience of international judges, especially judges on regional human rights courts (European Court of Human Rights or the Inter-American Court of Human Rights) where noncompliance is understood to be a massive problem. A participant at a Brandeis University conference of international jurists, commenting on the eventual implementation of decisions regarding gay rights, suggested, "There is wisdom in waiting, as events occur later, and decisions that are not enforced become enforced" (International Center for Ethics, Justice and Public Life, n.d.). Although the problems international judges confront are often thought to be distinct from those confronted by domestic judges, in many respects they are quite similar. In that similarity may lie useful insight into how legal systems might best wrestle with the tensions that follow from pursuing many rule of law values.

The bottom line is that some types of noncompliance with judicial orders can be part of a robust political system. Clearly, there are well-understood normative rationales for expecting leaders to comply with judicial orders. And broad disrespect for judicial authority could have negative consequences for a wide array of economic and political activities. That said, noncompliance can also be part of a process by which leaders communicate about their resolve and the seriousness of the policy problems they confront. This kind of communication can strengthen regimes.

APPENDIX 4.A PROOFS

BASELINE MODEL

Proof of Lemma 1. In text. ■

Proof of Proposition 1. Let $I(x)$ denote the information set for the supporter when observing $p = x$ and $I(n)$ the information set reached when observing $p = n$. If the players pool on the policy x, the supporter believes that $Pr(\omega = x|p) = \pi$, that $Pr(\omega = n|p) = 1 - \pi$ via Bayes's rule at $I(x)$ and passive conjectures at $I(n)$. As argued in the text, the supporter always selects n at $I(n)$. At $I(x)$, the expected utility of setting $r = x$ is $1 - \mathbb{E}(v)$ and the expected utility of setting $r = n$ is $1 - k(1 - \pi)$, and thus the supporter chooses n if $\pi \geq 1 - \frac{\alpha}{k(\alpha+\beta)} \equiv \bar{\pi}$. Should $\pi \geq \bar{\pi}$ and the players pool on x, the supporter will choose n, and if that is true, neither player can profit from choosing n. Should $\pi < \bar{\pi}$, pooling on x cannot be part of a PBE, since the supporter would set $r = x$, giving the normal leader an incentive to select $p = n$. Suppose that $\pi < \bar{\pi}$ and that the leaders both select n. At both information sets the supporter continues to hold their prior beliefs about the state, by Bayes's rule or passive conjectures. For the leader's strategy to be part of a PBE, the supporter must be setting $r = n$ at $I(x)$, which they do. Given this, the normal leader has no incentive to set $p = x$, since $1 - \mathbb{E}(v) < 1$. For the extraordinary type to select n, we require $\gamma \geq \mathbb{E}(v)$. ■

Proof of Proposition 2. In the proposed mixed strategy PBE, the supporter and the normal leader must be indifferent between selecting n and x. Consider the normal leader. Since the supporter always chooses n at $I(n)$, the expected utility of setting $p = n$ is 1, whereas the expected utility of $p = x$ is $\rho(\mathbb{E}(v)) + (1 - \rho)(1 + k)$. Thus we need $\rho^\star = \frac{k}{(k+1-\mathbb{E}(v))}$. Now consider the supporter. The expected utility of x is $1 - \mathbb{E}(v)$ and the expected utility of n is $Pr(t = x|p = x) + (1 - Pr(t = x|p = x))(1 - k)$. Thus, we need $Pr(t = x|p = x) = 1 - \frac{\mathbb{E}(v)}{k}$. In equilibrium $Pr(t = x|p = x) = \frac{\pi}{\pi+(1-\pi)\lambda}$, and so solving for λ and given $k > 1$, we have $\lambda^\star = \frac{\pi}{(1-\pi)(1-\frac{\mathbb{E}(v)}{k})} - \frac{\pi}{(1-\pi)}$. Since $1 - \frac{\mathbb{E}(v)}{k} > 0$, $\lambda^\star > 0$, and a little algebra shows that $\lambda^\star \leq 1$ as long as $\pi < 1 - \frac{\mathbb{E}(v)}{k}$.

The extraordinary leader receives γ should they choose $p = n$. The expected utility of choosing x is $\rho^{\star}(\mathbb{E}(v) + (1 - \rho^{\star})$ and thus the extraordinary leader prefers x to n as long as $\rho^{\star} \leq \frac{1-\gamma}{1-\mathbb{E}(v)}$. Should $\gamma < \mathbb{E}(v)$, this condition is always met since $\frac{1-\gamma}{1-\mathbb{E}(v)}$ would be greater than 1. If $\gamma \geq \mathbb{E}(v)$, the condition is met if $k \geq \frac{1-\gamma-\mathbb{E}(v)(1-\gamma)}{\gamma-\mathbb{E}(v)}$. ■

JUDICIAL REVIEW MODEL

Proof of Lemma 2. In text. ■

Proof of Proposition 3. If the players pool on the policy x, the supporter and court believe that $Pr(\omega = x|p) = \pi$, that $Pr(\omega = n|p) = 1 - \pi$ via Bayes's rule on the equilibrium path and via passive conjectures off path. As argued in the text, the supporter always selects n if $p - 1 = n$. Whatever the court decides, the supporter faces the same choice as in the baseline model in response to p_2. If $\pi \geq max\{\bar{\pi}, \bar{\pi_c}\}$, the court upholds the extraordinary policy, and neither leader has an incentive to adopt $p = n$. If $\bar{\pi} \leq \pi < \bar{\pi_c}$, the court would strike down the policy. Again, the supporter would confront the same choice calculus as in the baseline, and thus set $r = n$ no matter what the court has ruled. However, to sustain pooling, the leaders must defy the order. For this to be true, the backlash parameter must be sufficiently small, as argued in the text.

To sustain a PBE with pooling on the normal policy, it must be that the supporter would choose $r = x$ off the equilibrium path. If the court is expected to set $d = 0$, then the problem for the leaders is exactly as in the baseline, and we require $\gamma \geq \mathbb{E}(v)$. If instead, the court strikes the policy, the leaders would have to pay a further cost to implement x. Both leaders will adopt n so long as $\gamma \geq \mathbb{E}(v) - b$. ■

Proof of Result 1. In any mixed strategy equilibrium of both games, the $Pr(\text{conflict}) = \pi\rho + (1 - \pi)\rho\lambda$. In the judicial review game, ρ is strictly smaller than it is in the baseline game, since $b > 0$. ■

Proof of Result 2. The probability of conflict is precisely zero in the pooling equilibria of both games. There are values of the parameters such that there is a mixed strategy equilibrium in the baseline game when there are only pooling equilibria in the judicial review game. In every case in which mixed strategies are played for the same parameter values in the both games, the probability of conflict is weakly higher in the baseline game, because the supporter sets a higher probability of an extraordinary reaction while the normal leader sets the same probability of an extraordinary policy as they did in the baseline. ■

Proof of Proposition 4. Since the leaders only either choose $p_i = x$ or $p_i = n$, the question of what probability to play on each policy decision for the leader is captured by the same logic. As before, both the supporter and the normal leader must be indifferent between x and n. The supporter's calculus is identical to the baseline model. To see this, note that whatever the court decides in response to $p_1 = x$ the expected utility of x is $1 - \mathbb{E}(v)$ and the expected utility of n is $Pr(t = x|p = x) + (1 - Pr(t = x|p = x))(1 - k)$. For the leaders the calculus is slightly different. Since the supporter always chooses n at $I(n)$, the expected utility of setting $p = n$ is 1, whereas the expected utility of $p = x$ is $\rho(\mathbb{E}(v) - b) + (1 - \rho)(1 + k - b)$. Thus we need $\rho^{\star} = \frac{k-b}{(k+1-\mathbb{E}(v))}$. This quantity is greater than zero as long as $b < k$. ■

5

Imprudent Politics

"Is there any point to which you would wish to draw my attention?"
"To the curious incident of the dog in the night-time."
"The dog did nothing in the night-time."
"That was the curious incident."

The Adventure of Silver Blaze, Sir Arthur Conan Doyle

Our focus on prudence has important implications for how to evaluate our empirical claims. Judicial decisions that strike down laws and executive orders or which compel leaders to take (or refrain from taking) some type of action are readily observable. They make front page news. They are debated in scholarly circles. But if the second face of judicial power is the most important force through which democracies are protected, then evidence of its effects will not necessarily be found in court decisions. Evidence will be found in choices not taken, proposals never proposed, and conflicts that do not happen. Indeed, by the time a court is called upon to review a controversial decision of a state's leaders, it may be too late.

This chapter focuses on three types of outcomes: (1) extraordinary actions of leaders, (2) extraordinary responses of those out of power, and (3) democratic regime collapse. The primary effect of independent courts is to encourage leaders to less frequently make choices that raise allegations of regime rule violations. Importantly, this effect should be particularly strong when it is insufficiently likely that the state of the world warrants extraordinary actions on the part of leadership (in our model this would reflect a low value of π). The reason is that when the evidence any person can readily observe about the world strongly suggests that leaders confront a challenge that warrants an extraordinary response, extraordinary policy choices are much less likely to be perceived as unjustifiable violations of regime rules. Judges, including judges who are independent of the sitting government, are likely to draw similar conclusions; and for that reason, leaders will not believe that courts, independent or otherwise, will reflect impediments to their policy goals. Thus, when readily observable evidence suggests that exigent circumstances exist, independent courts are unlikely to be important. On the other hand, as it becomes less and less likely that an extraordinary action is warranted, the presence of independent courts matters. This suggests the following empirical implication.

> *Extraordinary Actions: Leaders should be less likely to take extraordinary actions in the presence of independent courts, as long as observable evidence about the rationale for an extraordinary action is not sufficiently compelling.*

Evaluating this kind of expectation requires that we identify types of leadership decisions that might reasonably reflect what we mean by "extraordinary actions." These should be decisions that are likely to raise suspicions that leaders are violating regime rules in an effort to aggrandize power. Ideally, we will also have variation in beliefs among people in a state about the circumstances that warrant extraordinary actions. In this chapter, we discuss three types of choices: (1) the choice to pursue electoral reform, (2) the choice to investigate political rivals, especially former leaders, and (3) the choice to declare a state of emergency following (a) natural disasters and (b) terrorist attacks.

Electoral reform can surely change the balance of power in a democracy by insulating leading coalitions from meaningful political accountability or by creating the opportunity to extend the tenure of a popular leader. This is most obvious in cases of the drawing of district boundaries and eliminating presidential term limits. The investigation of former leaders is sometimes warranted by the facts, but it is also sometimes a political tactic designed to simply eliminate a rival and increase the power of leadership. National emergencies typically confer new or special powers on current leaders, and so the decision to declare one is very closely related to the extraordinary action concept.

Importantly, these choices are typically carried out in very different political contexts, which we believe plausibly reflect variation in beliefs about the circumstances in which policy choices are made (i.e. π). Electoral reform proposals are not typically made in contexts where people are likely to perceive extraordinary circumstances. This is not to say that countries never undergo electoral reform in a context of political crisis. It is just that changing electoral rules is unlikely to be a policy responding to some special concern which only leaders are likely to understand. The investigation of political rivals, in contrast, typically involves slightly more uncertainty about circumstances. By either directly controlling the investigative arms of the state or by having influence through appointments, state leaders will likely have more information about the underlying facts that speak to the necessity of a criminal investigation. To be sure, uncertainty will vary. There will be clear evidence of malfeasance against some leaders suggesting extraordinary circumstances; however, there will be cases in which the facts are less clear. Finally, states of emergencies are very often called in contexts characterized by considerable evidence of exigent circumstances, though here too there can be uncertainty. We will consider the decision to declare states of emergencies following natural disasters and terrorist attacks. Our view is that the former can reflect more uncertainty about extraordinary circumstances than the latter, when many people in a state will believe that extraordinary responses are likely warranted.

The secondary effect of independent courts operates on opposition leaders. Specifically, the opposition should be less likely to engage in an extraconstitutional conflict over power in the presence of independent courts.[1] To evaluate this mechanism, we turn to coup and coup attempts.

Coups: Coup attempts should be less likely in the presence of independent courts.

Ultimately, our model has predictions for the survival of democratic regimes, which in our model is possible only if leaders and the opposition act in extraordinary ways. We will evaluate the following implication.

Democratic Breakdown: Democratic breakdown should be less likely in the presence of independent courts.

In addition to these implications we should also observe that coups and democratic breakdowns are less likely in the presence of features of a political system that incentivize judges to behave independently and features of the system that encourage leaders to comply with court orders. We will consider the consequences for democratic survival of government attacks on courts, which might be understood to significantly raise the costs of challenging the state (high c in our model). Courts might be less likely to veto government policies in settings where their judges' integrity is called out in public and where judges are removed for political reasons. We will also consider the consequences of a robust civil society. Robust civil society might be understood as the primary force through which leaders will perceive a significant public backlash for ignoring court orders (high b in our model). In such contexts, leaders will be more likely to confront organizations who have inherent interests in supporting courts or in seeing their decisions enforced (e.g. bar associations, human rights organizations, unions) (Chilton and Versteeg, 2020).

Finally, we will consider the consequences of noncompliance. One interpretation of expected noncompliance is that it raises the costs of vetoing a policy in our model (i.e. an increase in c), though since noncompliance merely leaves a decision unenforced, merely expecting noncompliance is likely to reflect far lower costs of vetoing government policies than would an expectation of efforts to attack judicial institutions directly. Indeed, as our model suggests, noncompliance can be a part of an equilibrium in which courts help stabilize democratic regimes. Thus, we we should not expect to observe that noncompliance with court orders destabilizes democratic states. The following summarizes these claims.

1 As before, this effect should be conditioned on beliefs about the state of the world. We have yet to identify an empirical test that allows us to test that prediction.

Judicial orders are broadly understood to not be self-enforcing, a challenge that is particularly pressing when the target of an order is the state itself (Becker and Feeley, 1973; Birkby, 1966). Critically, although there are many examples of noncompliance in settings not characterized by high levels of the rule of law (Ginsburg and Moustafa, 2008), courts are not always obeyed in rule of law states (Carrubba, Gabel, and Hankla, 2008; Vanberg, 2005). The Constitutional Bench of Costa Rica's Supreme Court confronts a variety of compliance challenges in its amparo jurisdiction (Staton, Gauri, and Cullell, 2015). The Netanyahu government's pattern of evading Israel's high court and administrative court decisions across a very wide set of issue areas is particularly notorious (Association for Civil Rights in Israel, 2010).

Perhaps of greatest concern, scholars have suggested that in order to avoid conflict and noncompliance, judges often engage in politically deferential patterns of decision-making, at least in particularly salient cases, which render the constraints they might place on governments practically nonbinding (e.g. Bill Chávez, Ferejohn, and Weingast, 2011; Carrubba, Gabel, and Hankla, 2008; Chilton and Versteeg, 2018; Rodríguez-Raga, 2011). Summarizing these challenges, USAID's Office of Democracy and Governance writes:

> [I]n several countries, governments have refused to comply with decisions of the constitutional court (e.g. Slovakia and Belarus) and substantially reduced the court's power (e.g. Kazakhstan and Russia). This illustrates the dilemma constitutional courts often face: Should they make the legally correct decision and face the prospect of non-compliance and attacks on their own powers, or should they make a decision that avoids controversy, protects them, and possibly enables them to have an impact in subsequent cases? Bold moves by constitutional courts can be instrumental in building democracy and respect for the courts themselves. However, the local political environment will determine the ability of the courts to exercise independent authority in these high stakes situations (Office of Democracy and Governance, 2002).

Judicial Attacks, Civil Society and Noncompliance: Coups and democratic breakdown should be more likely in the presence of attacks on the judiciary, less likely in the presence of a vibrant civil society, and no more or less likely when courts experience noncompliance with their orders in salient cases.[2]

[2] We might also consider the implications if the judiciary is independent both of the interests of the leadership and the opposition. This kind of court is capable of influencing the transmission of information from leadership to the opposition, a scenario discussed at the end of Chapter 4.

For this to work, the consequences for leaders of defying a court order have to be sufficiently severe to deter opportunism but insufficiently severe to ensure that the leader who truly observes extraordinary facts about the world can move forward. In the presence of this kind of court system, even extraordinary actions on the part of leaders will be understood as necessary given exigent circumstances. In such cases, the opposition will accept the leader's behavior because only leaders who perceive a genuine need to exercise authority unnecessary in normal circumstances would take extraordinary actions.

5.1 EXTRAORDINARY ACTIONS OF LEADERS

What are the types of leadership choices that might reflect what we have called "extraordinary actions" in Chapter 4? A key feature of these actions is that, while leaders might have a perfectly reasonable rationale for them, such actions have the possibility of altering the balance of power within the state. Every democracy is likely to have a particular set of actions that would raise significant questions among the opposition about the government's intentions. We believe that four leadership choices, in particular, that historically have raised concerns within many democracies offer insights into our expectations. In the sections that follow, we consider the choice to reform the electoral system, the choice to investigate (or to allow an investigation into) a political rival, the choice to declare a state of emergency, and the choice to attack the courts themselves.

5.1.1 *Electoral Reform*

The rules for translating votes in an election into seats in a legislature constitute the core institutions of representative democracy. List structures under proportional representation, district magnitude, electoral thresholds, and district boundaries in the context of proportional and majoritarian electoral systems all have powerful effects on the kinds of interests that are ultimately represented. For this reason, choices to reform electoral systems are always salient and often controversial.

In Latin America, the issue of reelection, and specifically the reelection of presidents, has been a salient issue since independence (Carey, 2003). It remains a major source of political tension in the modern era. Between 1988 and 2015, there were thirty-six attempts to either eliminate restrictions on presidential terms (e.g. Argentina (1994), Bolivia (2009), Colombia (2005)) or add new restrictions (e.g. Brazil (1988), Colombia (2015), Paraguay (1992)) (Corrales, 2016). Efforts to free presidents to run for successive terms can be profoundly destabilizing. Manuel Zelaya's likely pursuit for reelection was certainly the most immediate policy responsible for the coup in Honduras in 2009.[3]

Many electoral rules are left to secondary legislation and thus are commonly subject to judicial review; however, some electoral rules are entrenched in constitutions and are amended only via constitutional reform itself. Presidential reelection is one such example. Yet even here courts have been called upon to evaluate

We do not believe that we can fully distinguish in our data between independent courts of the first and second types. That said, we can unambiguously claim that this kind of independent court would powerfully reduce the incentives for coups as well as the rates of democratic regime breakdown. Similarly, an independent court of the second type should be less likely to exist when judges are routinely attacked. They are also increasingly likely to be found in states with strong civil societies. Thus, the core predictions we have described above hold for this kind of judicial independence.

3 We return to this case in our conclusion.

the constitutional validity of amendments to presidential terms. This has been accomplished often through the application of what has come to be known as the "unconstitutional constitutional amendment" doctrine (Landau, Roznai, and Dixon, 2019). The doctrine has been increasingly applied across the region. Its core idea is that there are some elements of a constitution, which are so fundamental to the structure of the state, that their amendment requires a fundamental reform of the constitution rather than a mere amendment. Changes to rules on presidential term limits have been challenged via this doctrine since 2005 in Colombia, Costa Rica, Nicaragua, Honduras, and Bolivia (Landau, Roznai, and Dixon, 2019).

Given the salience of the decision and the possibility for generating regime instability (e.g. Honduras), reform of presidential reelection rules would seem a particularly useful case to consider our empirical claims. Although there are not many existing studies, recent work is suggestive. Kouba (2016) studies a sample of all Latin American presidents from 1990 to 2013 who served a full term and were barred from reelection. Kouba finds that judicial independence (here measured with the original Linzer and Staton LJI scores) are strongly and negatively associated with successful attempts to remove term limits.

Calvo and Negretto (2019) study electoral reforms more broadly in Latin America, conducting an event history analysis of 112 major legislative and executive electoral reforms from the early 1980s to 2015. They find a strong and negative relationship between the V-Dem judicial constraints index and the hazard of observing a major electoral reform. They write "after ten years, close to 35% of countries with high judicial constraints engaged in major electoral reforms compared to almost 60% of countries with low judicial constraints" (p. 55). On the whole, the most recent work on the politics of electoral reform offers empirical support for the claim that judicial independence reduces the propensity of electoral reforms.

5.1.2 *Investigating Former Leaders*

Every concept of democracy contains within it a commitment to compete for power peacefully via the counting of ballots. In principle, political rivals in the opposition are allowed to mobilize free from undue constraints. Former leaders are permitted to live out their lives in peace should they so desire. The choice to investigate former leaders for simple malfeasance or worse is a choice not to be taken lightly. It is in a certain sense one of the most extraordinary actions a democratic leader can take, as it might fundamentally call into question their commitment to a basic tenet of democratic competition.

Of course, there are sometimes quite good reasons to investigate the former leaders of states. An overwhelming amount of evidence existed linking Augusto Pinochet to conspiracies to commit terror attacks, murder, torture, and embezzlement (Roht-Arriaza, 2009). Video evidence of Alberto Fujimori's secret-police chief and coconspirator Vladimiro Montesinos Torres bribing Supreme Court Justices, members of the National Elections Board, members of Congress, and television executives among others was broadcast to a horrified nation (McMillan and Zoido, 2004). It would have appeared quite likely that Fujimori was guilty of serious crimes. In the context of our model, these are surely cases in which the probability of an extraordinary set of circumstances would have been extremely high.

Yet, former leaders commonly call the legitimacy of these cases into question, arguing that investigations are politically motivated and designed to eliminate a political rival. Their claims are sometimes quite believable. The many investigations into former Ukrainian prime minister Yulia Tymoshenko were widely believed to be politically motivated and directed by then president Viktor Yanukovych (see extended discussion in Epperly, 2013). As Catherine Conaghan (2012, p. 653) writes,

> While it is clearly in the interest of the accused to represent prosecutions as a judicialised form of political persecution, this dark view is also supported by a considerable body of historical evidence. As Sznajder and Roniger convincingly show, Latin America has a long history of driving former presidents into exile, with legal charges serving as the basis for forcing this type of political exclusion.

While some, perhaps most, investigations of former leaders take place in the context of credible evidence of wrongdoing, things are not always clear. As Donna Bahry and Young Hum Kim (2021) write

> When malfeasance in the former administration is exposed, it can be difficult to establish the leader's personal involvement. The president-PM may have arranged illicit transactions such as embezzlement of government funds or biased deals on state contracts through intermediaries, rather than in person. Funds diverted from government coffers or received via bribes may have been laundered through multiple non-transparent channels. Orders from the president-PM to use extrajudicial force against civilians or to use illegal wiretaps may have been unwritten. Without an eyewitness who can provide details of the former leader's personal involvement, the evidence can be ambiguous; and even eyewitness accounts can be challenged. Given the ambiguities, an incumbent administration has some latitude in deciding whether to proceed with a case or not.

This ambiguity creates the kind of informational problem that can risk regime instability. Of course, court systems are important actors in these in contexts. Just as independent courts might serve to block or slow down politicized prosecutions, dependent court systems are highly useful tools. Thinking broadly about the use of prosecutions to undermine opposition political movements Maria Popova (2010, p. 1206) writes

> A subservient judiciary can severely undermine the opposition by prosecuting its financial backers for tax evasion or fraud, siding with municipal authorities to deny meeting permits for opposition rallies or prosecuting opposition activists on trumped up hooliganism or vandalism charges.

Existing scholarship on the role of independent courts in the prosecution of former political leaders is consistent with the predictions of our model. Epperly (2013) studies the post-tenure fate of state leaders from 1960 to 2004. Leveraging data from the Archigos Project (Goemans, Gleditsch, and Chiozza, 2009) and an earlier version of the Linzer and Staton LJI measure, Epperly finds a very strong and substantively meaningful positive relationship between the independence of a state's judiciary and the probability that its former leaders will go unpunished.

Research by Bahry and Kim (2021) is even more illuminating. The authors collected data on investigations of all former, democratically elected state leaders for states that became a democracy in 1970 or later, and for all years between 1970 and 2011. They further focus on states where the successor was also democratically elected and on investigations begun by the successor. They also find a strong and substantively meaningfully negative relationship between the Linzer and Staton LJI scores and the probability that a leader will be investigated for malfeasance after leaving office. Importantly, Bahry and Kim find that the effect of judicial independence is negative only when there is no "insider" providing evidence against the former incumbent. When there is such evidence, which is highly credible, judicial independence is not an important predictor of investigations. Independent courts matter when there is comparatively weaker evidence. This finding in particular is highly consistent with our model, in so far as we expect the primary impact of independent courts to be in cases where the probability that the state of the world is extraordinary is insufficiently high. In other words, we should be particularly likely to see an effect of judicial independence when the evidence against a former leader is far from overwhelming.

5.1.3 *States of Emergency*

A court's propensity to incentivize prudence can also be observed in an executive's willingness to declare a state of emergency. Such declarations are one of many tools that executives can use to respond to emergencies, such as natural disasters or domestic turmoil. Once enacted, emergency declarations temporarily reduce or remove certain checks on executive authority, providing the executive additional power to respond to an event. Importantly, however, these declarations also raise the prospect that an executive may engage in opportunism, attempting to alter fundamental regime rules under the cover of responsibly responding to a domestic event. The challenge for members of the opposition is to decipher an executive's intentions.

In the presence of such declarations, the opposition may hold different beliefs about whether some event, natural or political, is indeed extraordinary. As we note in our model in Chapter 4, the prior probability of the state of the world being extraordinary, π, can be conceived of mapping into an empirical distribution of events that are more or less likely to represent audience agreement about the event being extraordinary. When audiences have substantial agreement that an event is indeed extraordinary, or high π, then courts are likely to offer little incentive to be prudent. However, at medium levels of π, where there is greater disagreement over whether an event is indeed extraordinary, courts are better able to incentivize prudence.

Prior work offers supporting evidence that courts may indeed encourage prudence in such contexts. In a novel investigation, Bjørnskov and Voigt (2018) examine emergency declarations, for both natural disasters and political events, across all regimes, both autocracies and democracies, between 1976 and 2007. While not the main focus of their investigation, their analysis supports the claim that courts appear to incentivize prudence on emergency declarations. In the presence of independent courts, they find that executives are less likely to declare emergencies for natural disasters. However, this association does not extend to those emergencies declared for domestic political events (measured as domestic conflict from Banks).

In the following sections, we build on and extend the work of Bjørnskov and Voigt (2018), examining declared states of emergency to assess the degree to which judicial independence incentivizes democratically elected leaders to be prudent in their declarations. We employ a statistical strategy to assess how executive state of emergency declarations vary under separate contexts that we believe represent two levels of π, or the likelihood of being in an extraordinary state. We use natural disasters to assess state of emergency declarations under middling levels of π and the occurrence of terrorist acts to assess such declarations under high levels of π.

Judicial Independence, Emergency Declarations and Opportunism

Declaring a state of emergency (SOE) is a formal legal action taken by the government to expand its powers (Ramraj, 2008).[4] We follow Bjørnskov and Voigt (2018) and utilize data on emergency declarations from the original Hafner-Burton, Helfer, and Fariss (2011a) study. These data include all states of emergency from 1976 to 2007 and offer two separate codings for emergency declarations. The first codes *declared states of emergency*. A declared state of emergency exists if there is a "decree or order of the President or Prime Minister of the country, or a bill passed by the country's legislature" (Hafner-Burton, Helfer, and Fariss, 2011b, p. 2). To be coded as such, the state must publicly declare or announce an emergency. A country remains coded as being under the declared state until it is removed. The second codes *undeclared states of emergency* as the presence of some crisis that is of sufficient magnitude that it may threaten the country's population, political independence,

4 For our purposes, emergency declarations refer to procedures that find their basis in either statutory or constitutional foundation. *Extralegal* emergency declarations are conceptually distinct and indications of a putsch, or an effort by elements from within the regime to subvert democracy. We believe that citizens would have a relatively high level of confidence that a government declaring an emergency, when it has no legal foundation to do so, is unjustifiably attempting to alter the regime's rules and such an action would be better characterized as an attempted coup.

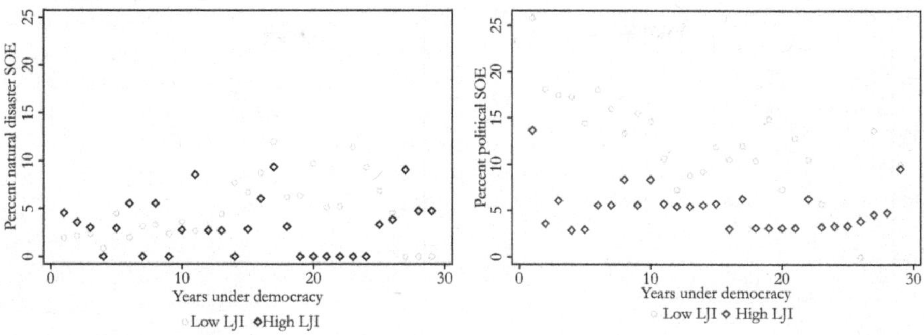

FIGURE 5.1 Plots of emergency declaration rates by democratic regime age and judicial independence. Democracies with high judicial independence are black diamonds, while gray circles represent low independence courts. Natural disaster emergency declarations are displayed in the left panel and political emergency declarations are displayed in the right panel.

or human rights institutions. Hafner-Burton, Helfer, and Fariss (2011a) offer three types of undeclared emergencies in their data: national political, natural disaster, and extraterritorial. To construct our dependent variable, we utilize information from these undeclared emergencies to sort the declared emergencies into two types.

We are interested in examining whether judicial independence incentivizes government prudence in declaring an emergency; accordingly, we wish to code declared emergencies as our dependent variable. We also are interested in assessing different levels of the likelihood that the state of the world is extraordinary. To accomplish this, we generate two dependent variables from the Hafner-Burton, Helfer, and Fariss (2011a) data that reflect different types of emergency declarations: *declared political declaration* and *declared natural disaster declaration*.[5]

Over the time period the data are available, 1976–2007, among democratic regimes there were 312 political emergencies declared compared to 129 natural disaster emergencies. Over the course of a democracy's lifetime, political emergency declarations average 5.83 per democratic-year, with a standard deviation of 10.69. Natural disaster declarations average 2.62 declarations per democratic-year, with a standard deviation of 11.29.

Our interest is in how these declarations covary with judicial independence. To begin, we consider the distribution of emergency declaration rates over democratic regime tenure split by high and low judicial independence.[6] Figure 5.1 displays

5 We generated *declared political declaration*, which is coded "1" when both *declaredsoe* and *nationalpoliticalsoe* are coded "1," and *declared natural disaster declaration*, which is coded "1" when both *declaredsoe* and *naturaldisastersoe* are coded "1." We ignore extraterritorial declarations. Such declarations are relatively rare, registering only 29 over the time period, and heavily populated by one state – Israel with 11.

6 High and low judicial independence represents a median split on LJI. High judicial independence democracies averaged an LJI of .894, while low judicial independence democracies averaged an LJI of .513.

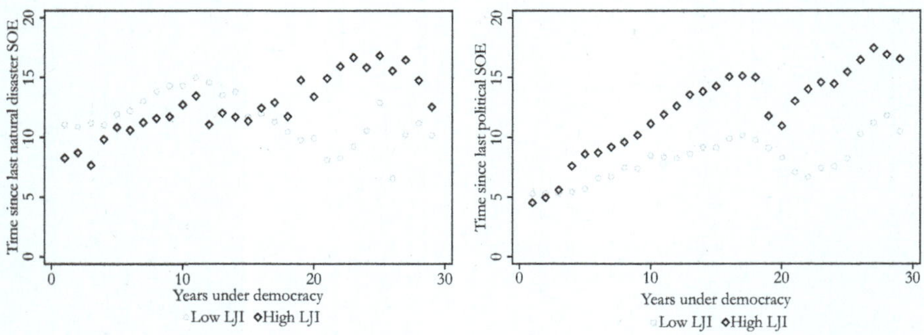

FIGURE 5.2 Plots of time since last emergency declaration by democratic regime age and judicial independence. Democracies with high judicial independence are black diamonds, while gray circles represent low independence courts. Natural disaster emergency declarations are displayed in the left panel and political emergency declarations are displayed in the right panel.

the rate of emergency declarations (in percentages) for a given year of a democratic regime's tenure for both high and low judicial independence. Natural disaster emergency declarations are displayed in the left panel and political emergency declarations are displayed in the right panel.

Figure 5.1 highlights several interesting features of emergency declarations. The left panel shows that at any given age in a democracy's lifetime, a small percentage of democratic regimes have declared emergencies for natural disasters, and there appears to be relatively no difference between the declaration rate between democracies with different levels of court independence. The right panel suggests that while emergency declarations are consistently low for democracies operating with independent courts, democratic regimes with less independent courts appear to have higher rates of declared political emergencies.

The differences over the first ten years of a democracy's life, thought to be the most vulnerable years in a democracy's tenure, are particularly noteworthy. For natural disaster declarations, the average rate of declarations over the first ten years of a democracy's life for low and high independence courts are 2.65 and 2.80, respectively. This difference widens dramatically when we consider political declarations. The average rate of declarations for political emergencies is 6.24 and 17.04 for low and high independence courts, respectively.

Another perspective is whether independent courts affect the average amount of time that passes since a democracy's last emergency declaration. If courts are incentivizing prudence, then we might expect to observe longer periods of time passing between emergency declarations. Figure 5.2 considers this possibility. The figure displays the time since the last emergency declaration (in years) over a democratic regime's tenure split by high and low independence courts. Natural disaster emergency declarations are displayed in the left panel and political emergency declarations are displayed in the right panel.

The panels reveal descriptive support for the expectation that courts may incentivize prudence. In both panels, democratic regimes with high independence courts are generally more resilient to repeated emergency declarations. The average amount of time between emergency declarations for high and low independent courts is quite similar early in a democracy's lifetime. This pattern can be seen on the left-hand side of the panels for both natural disasters and political emergencies. However, as democracies age (the right-hand side of the panels) high independence courts appear to incentivize prudence among democratic governments, generating longer wait times between declarations.

Of course, one cautionary note for both Figure 5.1 and Figure 5.2 is that neither controls for features of democracy that are well documented to ease the distributional tensions within a regime. Economic development, economic growth, and social homogeneity lower the stakes of the democratic game. As such, the apparent benefits of an independent court incentivizing prudence on emergency declarations may be spurious to these other features. Moreover, not all emergencies offer the same potential for political opportunism and conflict but rather depend upon whether the true state of the world is likely to demand an extraordinary action from the government.

In the following sections, we consider multivariate models of emergency declarations that examine two types of emergency declarations: natural disasters and terrorist acts. If these circumstances offer contexts for citizens to hold different beliefs as to the whether extraordinary actions are warranted, then we ought to see uneven court influence on incentivizing prudence across these contexts.

Natural Disasters and Opportunism: Middling π

To assess the presence of a domestic crisis that may reflect a middling level of π, we include an exogenous measure of natural disaster impact. Using data from the Emergency Events Data (EM-DATo)[7](Guha-Sapir, Hoyois, and Below, 2014), we construct an annual index of natural disasters. To ensure that our index is exogenous to the politics within a country, we include all natural disasters that are reasonably independent from human intervention[8] and we drop disasters that are potentially endogenous or not "natural" if they have a reasonable likelihood of being influenced by political choices.[9] We also consider different controls for natural disaster impact including: (1) a dichotomous measure of whether a natural disaster occurred, (2) the

7 The database is located at www.emdat.be.

8 We include the following natural disasters: ash fall, avalanche, coastal flood, cold wave, convective storm, drought, extratropical storm, flash flood, ground movement, heat wave, landslide, lava flow, locust, mudslide, pyroclastic flow, riverine flood, rockfall, severe winter conditions, subsidence, tropical cyclone, and tsunami.

9 We exclude the following disasters: air, bacterial disease, chemical spill, collapse, explosion, famine, fire, forest fire, gas leak, grasshopper, land fire (brush, bush, pasture), oil spill, other, parasitic disease, poisoning, radiation, rail, road, viral disease, and water.

number of deaths (1,000s) resulting from a natural disaster, and (3) the damage costs ($100,000s) associated with a natural disaster. We run separate models with each of these controls.

When we cross our dichotomous measure of natural disaster occurrence with our dichotomous indicators of natural disaster declarations, we see that of the 1,113 country-years that have experienced some type of a natural disaster, emergencies were declared in only 117 country-years. Emergency declarations also appear to be linked to the extent of economic destruction wrought by a given disaster more than the total number of lives lost. The average amount of economic damage associated with a natural disaster for which an emergency was declared was US $2,062,000 compared to US $777,000 for those in which an emergency was not declared. Emergency declarations do not appear to be driven by the total lives lost, however, with a statistically nonsignificant difference between 680 lives lost and an emergency declaration and 651 lives lost for those with no declaration.

We estimate the annual risk of a natural disaster emergency declaration as a function of judicial independence, three measures of natural disaster impact, and a set of controls. We employ a random effects cross-sectional, time series logit parameterization of the occurrence of a declaration. We report the associations of covariates in this model as odds ratios, which represent the relative change in the odds of an events occurring for a unit-change in a given independent variable. We report estimates that are clustered on country, yielding a consistent estimator in the presence of serial correlation or heteroskedasticity.

We also include a set of controls that are likely to be correlated with our key judicial variables and our outcome of interest, natural disaster emergency declaration. To control for economic development and growth, we use data from Fariss, Anders, and Markowitz (2020) to assess both annual GDP per capita (in thousands) and annual GDP growth. We also control for the effect of political institutions, including political competition and the robustness of civil society. We also include a variable to reflect the presence of domestic conflict in the form of civil war and control for the size of the country's population. We also include a counter and set of cubic splines to account for the serial dependence between observations.

Figure 5.3 reports the odds ratios for our measure of judicial independence (LJI) for three models, each controlling for a different measure of natural disaster impact. In each model, an independent judiciary is associated with a reduction in the odds of the government declaring an emergency, controlling for the presence or the severity of the disaster. Recall that LJI is measured on a scale of 0–1, so each odds ratio reports the estimated association of comparing the extremes of judicial independence. Of course, we do not have any country in our data with an LJI of 0. Therefore it is more useful to consider a change in LJI of .5, or two standard deviations.

The results suggest that when we control for the occurrence of a natural disaster (Model 1), enhanced judicial independence, corresponding to an increase in LJI

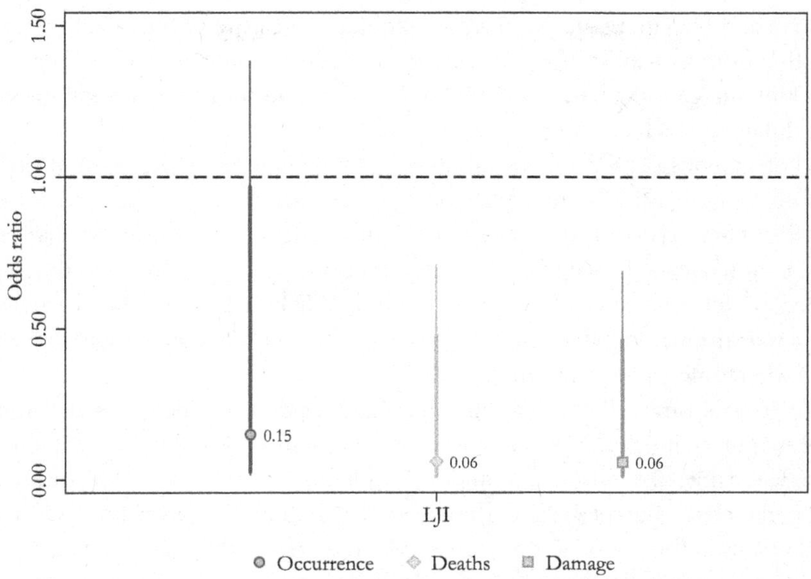

FIGURE 5.3 Odds ratios of LJI estimates on declarations of states of emergency for natural disasters: 1960–2007. Ratios less than 1 suggest a reduction in odds. Results reported for three different controls for extent of disaster: Occurrence (dichotomous), Deaths (1,000s), and Damage Cost (US $100,000s). Full models are reported in Appendix 5A. Two-tailed intervals for $p < .05$ and $p < .10$ are reported.

of .5, is associated with an approximate 61 percent reduction in the odds of an emergency declaration. Moreover, this association is relatively robust across the three models. Whether we operationalize natural disaster with its occurrence (Model 1), the number of deaths (Model 2), or the total damage in financial terms (Model 3), an independent judiciary incentivizes prudence in declaring natural disaster emergencies. Regarding the substantive size of these associations, for the sake of comparison, consider that the occurrence of a natural disaster increases the odds of a natural emergency declaration by nearly 800 percent. This suggests that the presence of an independent court has a nontrivial influence shaping government incentives.

Terrorism and Opportunism: High π

To assess the presence of a domestic crisis that is likely to reflect a high level of π, we use three different measures of violent domestic crises. First, we make use of two variables from the Global Terrorism Database (GTD) (2018). We include a simple dichotomous variable indicating the occurrence of a terrorist incident within a given calendar year. The GTD defines a terrorist attack as the "threatened or actual use of illegal force and violence by a non-state actor to attain a political, economic, religious, or social goal through fear, coercion, or intimidation"

(LaFree and Dugan, 2007). Second, we include a measure of total deaths (1,000s) resulting from a terrorist incident. Last, we include a weighted conflict index from the Domestic Conflict Event dataset (Banks, n.d.). This measure is an additive scale with different weights assigned to each item.[10]

When we consider the joint distribution of our dichotomous indicators of terrorist occurrence and political emergency declarations, we see that of the 1,150 country-years that have experienced a terrorist incident, emergencies were declared in 244 of these country-years. Emergency declarations also appear to be linked to the deaths related to a terrorist incident. The average amount of killed and wounded associated with a terrorist incident that saw an emergency declared was 250 compared to 39 for those where one was not declared.

We again estimate the annual risk of a natural political emergency declaration as a function of judicial independence, three measures of violent domestic disaster impact, and a set of controls. We employ a random effects cross-sectional, time series logit parameterization of the occurrence of a declaration. We report the associations of covariates in this model as odds ratios, which represent the relative change in the odds of an events occurring for a unit-change in a given independent variable. We report estimates that are clustered on country, yielding a consistent estimator in the presence of serial correlation or heteroskedasticity. We also include the same set of controls that we included in our analysis of natural disaster emergency declarations.

Figure 5.4 reports the odds ratios for our measure of judicial independence (LJI) for three models each controlling for a different measure of terrorist act impact. It is useful to consider a change in LJI of .5, or two standard deviations. This suggests that for the first model, controlling for the occurrence of a natural disaster, an increase in judicial independence, corresponding to a shift in LJI of .5, is associated with an approximate 61 percent reduction in the odds of an emergency declaration. For the sake of comparison, the occurrence of a natural disaster increases the odds of a natural emergency declaration by nearly 800 percent. Still, an independent judiciary does appear to stem the declaration of emergencies.

5.2 EXTRAORDINARY REACTIONS: COUPS

Our model also suggests that an opposition ought to be less likely to engage in an extraconstitutional conflict over power in the presence of judges that have incentives to behave independently. Recall from the beginning of the chapter that we have two sets of expectations regarding how independent courts might influence incentives to attempt a coup. First, they may do so directly by offering members of the opposition incentives to behave more prudently in situations that may call

10 The index (with weights in parentheses) includes Assassinations (25), Strikes (20), Guerrilla Terrorism/Guerrilla Warfare (100), Government Crises (20), Purges (20), Riots (25), Revolutions (150), and Anti-Government Demonstrations (10). The database is located at www.cntsdata.com.

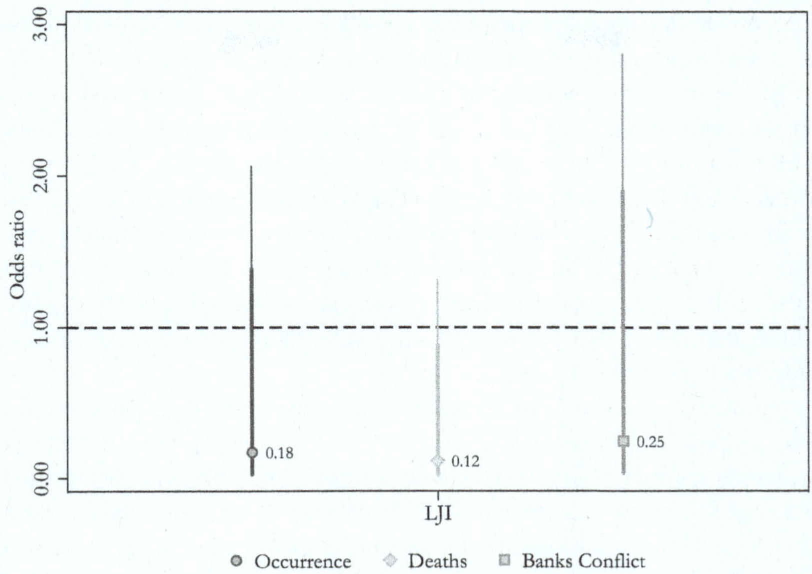

FIGURE 5.4 Odds ratios of LJI estimates on declarations of states of emergency for political emergencies: 1960–2007. Ratios less than 1 suggest a reduction in odds. Results reported for three different controls for extent of disaster: Occurrence (dichotomous), Deaths (1,000s), and Banks Conflict Index. Full models are reported in Appendix 5A. Two-tailed intervals for $p < .05$ and $p < .10$ are reported.

for extraordinary actions. Second, coups should be more likely in the presence of attacks on the judiciary, less likely in the presence of a vibrant civil society, and no more or less likely when courts experience noncompliance with their orders in salient cases. We will examine all of these expectations in turn.

We begin evaluating our propositions by selecting a set of democratic regimes for our analysis. We use the democratic regime event history dataset by Boix, Miller, and Rosato (2012) to classify the set of regimes within which an attempted coup may occur. Our data contain every democratic regime from 1900 to 2015. Using this definition of democratic episodes, we use the coups in the world dataset by Powell and Thyne (2011) to measure the onset of a successful or attempted coup, providing data from 1950 to 2015. An attempted coup is one that "includes illegal and overt attempts by the military or other elites within the state apparatus to unseat the sitting executive" (p. 252). A successful coup is one where, "the perpetrators of a coup seize and hold power for at least seven days" (p. 252). Given that our expectations are about an opposition's incentives to subvert the current government, we do not need to distinguish between successful vs. attempted coups. Accordingly, we code democratic regimes that experienced either an attempted coup or a successful coup as "1" and code others "0." In these data, we have 3,865 country-years of data, 104 of which experience at least one form of a coup.

We estimate the annual propensity of a coup as a function of judicial independence as well as measures of concepts our model suggests might influence coups. The first is a measure of robust civil society (measuring *b* in our model). As civil society becomes more robust, the cost of defying a court order should increase. One effect of this increase is that the rate at which the opposition will engage in an extraordinary act of protest decreases. This is because as *b* increases, the equilibrium rate of extraordinary responses must decrease in order to offset the decreasing incentives on the part of an opportunistic leader to take an extraordinary action.[11] We also include measures of judicial attacks and noncompliance, to capture the possibility that judges will behave less independently in these contexts. Finally we includes a set of control variables.

We employ a random effects cross-sectional, time-series logit parameterization of coup propensity. We report the associations of covariates in this model as odds ratios, which represent the relative change in the odds of an event occurring for a unit-change in a given independent variable. We report estimates that are clustered on country, yielding a consistent estimator in the presence of serial correlation or heteroskedasticity.

To measure judicial independence, we again use LJI. We use V-Dem data as indicators of our latent constructs on government beliefs about the perceived costs of defying the court and a court's perceptions of the expected costs for being defied. V-Dem's primary measures are derived from a Bayesian, graded item response model fit to categorical scores provided by thousands of international country experts (Coppedge et al., 2015a). We also use V-Dem data to measure judicial independence and noncompliance with judicial orders. To measure a court's perceived costs of defiance, we create a scale of V-Dem's *Government Attacks on Judiciary* and *Judicial Purges* variables, which results in a scale with a Cronbach Alpha of .81. To assess the potential costs that leaders perceive of defying court orders, we include V-Dem's *Civil Society* index to control for the role that civil society groups may play in mitigating institutional conflict. The V-Dem civil society index assesses the degree to which the government represses civil society, controls the entry and exit of civil society groups and the degree to which the public participates in civil society organizations (Bernhard et al., 2020). To measure judicial independence, we use our updated LJI, which includes V-Dem's *High Court Independence* and *Lower Court Independence* variables. Last, to measure government noncompliance with the court, we create a scale of V-Dem's *Compliance with High Court* and *Compliance with Lower Court* variables and reverse its polarity to assess noncompliance. This results in a scale with a Cronbach Alpha of .94. Each of these scales is standardized to ease interpretation.

11 See Proposition 4 in Chapter 4.

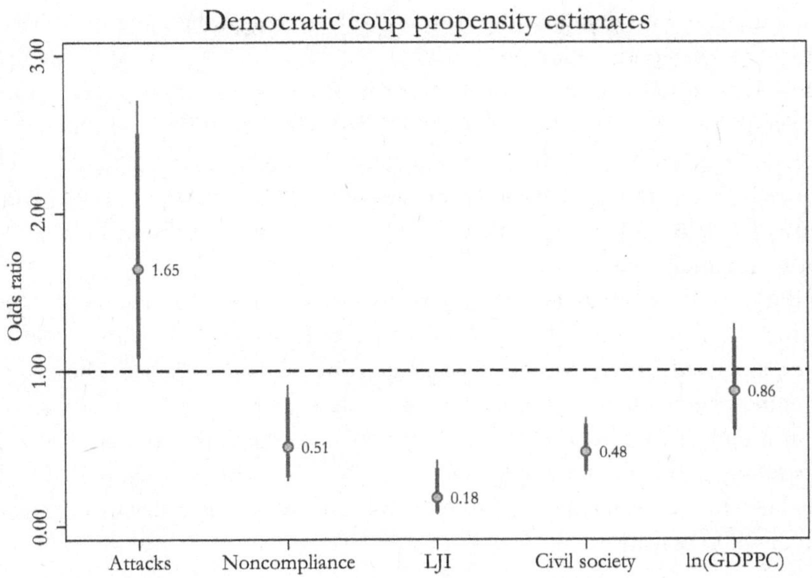

FIGURE 5.5 Odds ratios of estimates on coup propensity with democracies: 1950–2015. Ratios less than 1 suggest a reduction in odds. Full models are reported in Appendix 5A. Two-tailed intervals for $p < .05$ and $p < .10$ are reported.

We also include a set of controls that are likely to be correlated with our key judicial variables and our outcome of interest, political order. To control for economic development and growth, we use Madison's Historical Statistics (2003) to assess both annual GDP per capita (1,000s) and annual GDP growth. We also control for the effect of political institutions, including dummy variables reflecting whether the democratic regime employed a presidential or parliamentary system. Each of these dummy variables is compared to the base category of having a mixed system. We also include dummy variables that code whether the authoritarian government prior to the democratic episode was headed by the military, civilians, or a monarchy. Each of these dummy variables is compared to the base category of a country not having been independent prior to the transition.

The complete tables reporting the coefficients and model statistics for our analyses are included in Appendix 5A. The odds ratios of the key variables along with benchmark control variables are displayed in Figure 5.5.

The propensity for the occurrence of a coup is lower among democracies with independent courts. Democratic regimes that possess courts that are one standard deviation more independent than their counterparts are associated with an 82 percent reduction in the odds of a coup. This suggests that democratic regimes experience greater regime instability when their courts can provide incentives for prudence among potential challengers. Closely related to this, in the presence of government actions that raise the costs to the courts of challenging the state in the form of regular purge attempts or verbal attacks against the court, such judicial attacks reduce the likelihood that a court will veto government policies and provides incentives for oppositions to mount a coup. In the presence of such attacks (1 standard deviation higher), the odds of a coup increase by 65 percent. Judicial independence is a clear resource for democratic regimes to draw upon, but attempts to erode that independence can draw down that resource and diminish its ability to provide regime benefits.

Additionally we see that when governments perceive relatively higher costs of defying the court, assessed by our civil society variable, democratic regimes are better insulated from destructive political conflict. Democracies whose citizens are entrenched in nongovernmental organizational life, or one standard deviation above the mean, are associated with a 52 percent reduction in the odds of a coup. Importantly, judicial noncompliance is not associated with an attempt to overthrow a regime. In fact, noncompliance with judicial orders has a negative association with coup propensity.

5.3 THE SURVIVAL OF DEMOCRACY

Our model also suggests that the survival of democracy, perhaps the most extreme indicator of extraconstitutional conflict, ought to be enhanced in the presence of independent courts. Our analysis combines well-known data on democratic regimes with new data on comparative judicial politics. Specifically, we focus on a salient indicator of political instability – democratic regime collapse. We again use the democratic regime event history dataset by Boix, Miller, and Rosato (2012) to classify the onset and collapse of our democratic episodes. Our data contain every democratic regime between 1900 and 2015. Democratic regimes that break down prior to 2015 are coded as reversals, and those that experienced no breakdown by the end of our temporal window are coded as right-censored. Episodes that began prior to our temporal window are left-censored. Left censoring is adjusted for in the initial coding of the regime count variable. In these data, we have 5,224 country years of data, with 185 episodes of democracy, of which 88 end in breakdown. Missing data reduces our usable data to 181 episodes of democracy, of which 81 end in breakdown.

For every democratic state-year between 1900 and 2015 we make use of V-Dem's estimates of two types of attacks on the judiciary (Coppedge et al., 2015b). We again use LJI to assess judicial independence. To measure a court's perceived costs of defiance, we again use V-Dem's *Government Attacks on Judiciary* and *Judicial Purges* variables to create a judicial attack variable. To measure noncompliance with the judiciary, we again use a scale of V-Dem's *Compliance with High Court* and *Compliance with Lower Court* variables and reverse its polarity (so that higher numbers reflect "noncompliance." Finally, to assess the potential costs that leaders perceive of defying court orders, we again include V-Dem's *Civil Society* index to control for the role that civil society groups may play in mitigating institutional conflict. We standardize all of these variables for ease of interpretation.

We estimate the hazard of a democratic regime experiencing a collapse using fully parametric event history estimators. We employ a Weibull parameterization of the baseline hazard, which assumes a monotonic baseline hazard rate and possesses the proportional hazards property, where the effect of a covariate induces a change in the hazard that is proportional to baseline hazard and this change is presumed to be constant over time.[12] We estimate these models with a Gamma frailty parameter with standard errors clustered on country to account for unobserved heterogeneity.[13]

We also include a set of controls that are likely to be correlated with our key judicial variables and our outcome of interest, political order. To control for economic development and growth, we use Madison's Historical Statistics (2012) to assess both annual GDP per capita (1,000s) and annual GDP growth. We also control for the effect of political institutions, including dummy variables reflecting whether the democratic regime employed a presidential or parliamentary system. Each of these dummy variables is compared to the base category of having a mixed system. We also include dummy variables that code whether the authoritarian government prior to the democratic episode was headed by the military, civilians, or a monarchy. Each of these dummy variables is compared to the base category of a country not having been independent prior to the transition. We include two indicators of colonial legacy – a dummy variable indicating whether a country was never a colony and another indicating whether a country was a former British colony. Last, we include a control for the presence of other democracies in the region.

As we turn to the findings, it is worth pausing to consider interpretation. This is particularly important in light of the fact that we are fitting a statistical model to cross-national, country data, some of which is derived from a measurement model fit to the results of an international expert survey. Three natural concerns arise. The first is that modeling all of the possible sources of heterogeneity across states that is materially related to the political contexts in which judges operate is challenging. The second is that we should be skeptical that the V-Dem scores are measured without error, and it seems possible that like efforts to measure judicial independence cross-nationally, measurement error will not be random (Ríos-Figueroa and Staton, 2014). We address this issue in Appendix 5B of this chapter. Third, it seems possible theoretically that judicial attacks and noncompliance are endogenous to regime breakdown – that as regimes fall, judges attempting to hold the regime to

12 We also estimated Cox, Exponential, Log-Log, and Log-Normal parameterizations of the hazard. Using AIC and BIC criteria, examination of alternative models suggests that the Weibull offered the best fit to the data. (See Table A5 in this chapter's Appendix 5A.)

13 We also estimated an Inverse Gaussian frailty model, but seeing no gains resorted to the more common Gamma frailty (see Table A6 in this chapter's Appendix 5A). Conditional risk models stratified on democratic spell also suggest that our inferences are not sensitive to the multiple-failure nature of the data (see Table A7 in this chapter's Appendix 5A).

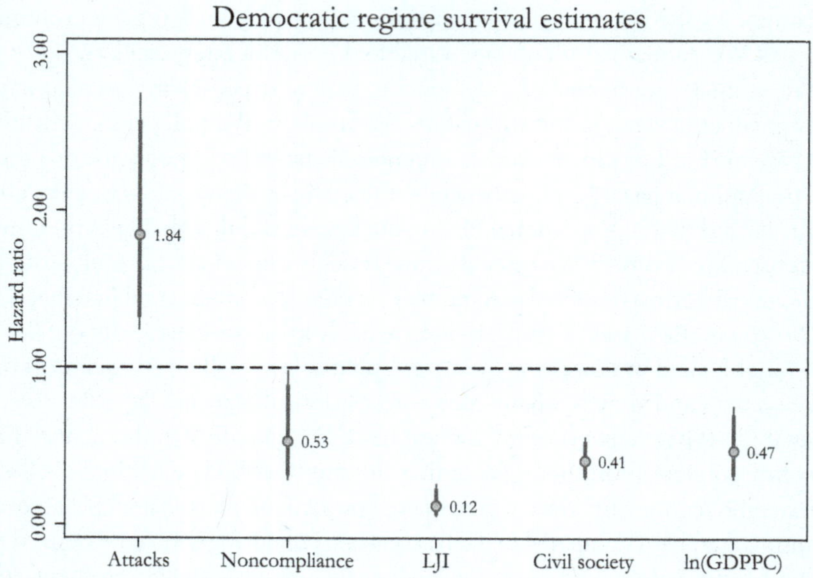

FIGURE 5.6 Hazard ratios of estimates on democratic regime survival: 1900–2015. Ratios less than 1 suggest a reduction in hazard of breakdown. Full models are reported in Appendix 5A. Two-tailed intervals for $p < .05$ and $p < .10$ are reported.

old rules will be ignored and ultimately attacked and purged. Our design, which includes a frailty parameter for each state, addresses the first concern in part. As we shortly discuss, we will consider the results of our models when we allow measurement error to propagate through our inferences, addressing the second concern. We do not have and do not believe that there is a strong candidate for an instrument for the two types of V-Dem judiciary measures (see discussion in Reenock, Staton, and Radean, 2013). We can, however, consider the issue of reverse causality from a theoretical perspective. As we will discuss, we believe that the findings are consistent with the argument we give and inconsistent with the most obvious alternative. Having said that, absent a strong identification strategy for the causal effect of judicial attacks/noncompliance on democratic breakdown, we prefer to interpret our findings as providing prima facie evidence of a possible causal connection that is understandable in light of our theory, rather than as strong evidence of causation.

Complete tables reporting the coefficients and model statistics for our analyses are included in Appendix 5.4. The coefficients of the key variables along with benchmark control variables are displayed in Figure 5.6. The frailty model estimates a frailty variance that is not statistically distinguishable from zero. Given our frailty model and the fact that effect sizes are conditional on the frailty, all substantive effects discussed in the following paragraphs report the effect at the start time of a typical democracy's risk exposure.

A democratic regime's ability to survive is enhanced by the presence of independent courts. Democratic regimes that possess independent courts have an

(1 standard deviation higher) 88 percent reduction in the odds of a regime breakdown. Taken together with our analysis of coups, the results from Figure 5.6 suggest that democratic regimes that do not have the resource of an independent judiciary are more likely to experience not only attempts to overthrow the regime but also conflict that eventually overwhelms democratic institutions and their very survival.

Our results also suggest that democratic regimes experience greater regime instability when their courts are regularly purged or verbally attacked for their decisions. Democracies experiencing a higher level of judicial attacks (1 standard deviation) are associated with a newly inaugurated regime's hazard of breakdown increasing by 84 percent. A change in judicial conflict on this scale is well within the bounds of our data and reflects a relative shift in interinstitutional conflict akin to moving from Costa Rica throughout most of the 1960s and 1970s to Guatemala during the same time period. However, when governments perceive relatively higher costs of defying the court, measured by our civil society variable, democratic regimes are better insulated from destructive political conflict. Democracies whose citizens are well involved in civic organizations, or one standard deviation above the mean, are associated with a 59 percent reduction in the hazard of regime collapse. Importantly, again we see that judicial noncompliance is not associated with a higher propensity for democratic breakdown.

To provide additional context for our findings, consider the following comparisons with the economic benchmarks in the figure. On average a US $1,000 increase in GDP per capita is associated with a 25.9 percent reduction in the hazard of a regime collapse.[14] A 10 percent contraction in the economy during the prior year is associated with a 177 percent increase in the hazard of regime collapse for newly inaugurated democracies. Each of these estimates are in line with expectations from prior work (Svolik, 2008) and suggest that the effects of our judicial context variables are substantively meaningful.[15]

5.3.1 *An Alternative Interpretation of Judicial Attacks*

We have presented our analyses of coups and democratic survival with an interpretation of government attacks on courts that view such attacks as an action that

14 These estimates are drawn from a model with nonlogged GDP for ease of interpretation.

15 We interpret our findings as associations that are in line with the expectations generated by our theoretical argument. However, we might consider our results in light of an alternative causal story – that judges are attacked, judges are ignored, and civil society is dismantled as regimes collapse. But such an alternative "reverse" causal account is not consistent with our findings. Our theoretical argument suggests that attacks against judges are problematic for regime survival but that noncompliance need not be. If the relationships that we are observing in our models are merely a consequence of regime breakdown, then why would breakdown force the state to purge the judiciary? If the regime is in the throws of a breakdown, why not simply ignore a court's decisions? Noncompliance in particular cases is not particularly costly and, as we have shown, this sort of noncompliance is routine. So, if it were the case that regime collapse is what induces interinstitutional conflict, we should see not only an increasing hazard for collapse in our model for judicial attacks, but for noncompliance as well. But, we do not. The reported results are more consistent with our account than this alternative.

potentially raises the costs of the court challenging the state (high c in our model) by possibly eroding independence. Under this interpretation, in the presence of government rebukes and judicial purges, courts would be less likely to veto government policies, undermining the court's role that we envision. A reasonable alternative interpretation of judicial attacks is that they are another example of a government pursuing extraordinary actions, similar in intent to government attempts at electoral reform discussed in Section 5.1.1.

Under this alternate interpretation, judicial attacks are manifestations of a government's attempt to respond to an extraordinary state of the world either faithfully or opportunistically. The opposition is in the familiar position of needing to determine whether the government's action is a reasonable response to the state of the world or an unreasonable violation of regime rules. The controversial decision that the court is called upon to consider is an attack against the court itself. Despite this, under the extraordinary action interpretation, our vision of the court retains its proposed function. As a result, sufficiently independent courts will incentivize prudence from both the government and the opposition. Independent courts ought to be targeted for attacks less frequently than those captured by the government. And this is what we observe in the data.

Recall Figure 1.1 from our introductory chapter that displayed a plot of judicial attacks on de facto judicial independence for 2015. That plot suggests that judiciaries are less likely to be the target of government attacks as independence increases. Less independent courts are more likely to find themselves targets of government interference. But if a court operates with less autonomy from the government, then why would a government need to attack it? Historically, less autonomous courts are targets of newly inaugurated political coalitions seeking to unseat court layovers from the previous coalition. Indeed, all political coalitions have an incentive to remove policy frustrating members of the court. But, in systems with a history of a strong independent court, the incentive to dismantle the court gives way to more prudent behavior. Of course, even among those courts that enjoy a relatively high level of independence, we see governments attempt to question the virtue of the courts. But these sorts of challenges occur at much lower levels, when courts are sufficiently independent.

5.4 CONCLUSION

Managing beliefs about the extent to which leaders are constrained is an important political challenge. We have argued that judiciaries can help address this challenge in a number of ways. They incentivize leaders to be careful about the possible solutions to policy challenges that they see, though in so doing they create the possibility that leaders fail to take decisive action when they should. In cases where leaders are willing to move forward with arguably questionable policies, courts can help translate conflict among political competitors into conflict within the institutions of the state. It is in this regard that independent courts help establish credible commitments and serve as insurance policies in the event of a power transfer.

In so far as judges influence regime survival on our account, they encounter a dilemma. Courts charged with holding leaders accountable to limits on their authority are asked in many systems to make decisions that may be institutionally and personally costly. In such settings, the incentives for strategic deference are particularly high; and yet, if courts are strategically deferential, they do not serve their state constraint function. We have considered how judges that confront such rule of law tensions might nevertheless contribute to regime stability.

We have found considerable evidence that regimes characterized by a latent propensity for significant interbranch conflict, where courts are openly critiqued and purged when possible, are particularly vulnerable to instability. We envision two types of consequences of this kind of politics. The first, on which we focus considerable theoretical attention, is that judges in such contexts will have particularly strong incentives to avoid political conflict. This type of dynamic is reflected in former Venezuela Supreme Court president Cecilia Sosa's comments as she stepped down from her post following the court's approval of the Chavez-led Constituent Assembly's assertion of emergency powers: "The court simply committed suicide to avoid being assassinated. But the result is the same. It is dead."[16] The second consequence, which would undermine judicial independence in a distinct way, is that courts in these contexts become simple tools of interparty competition (Pérez-Liñán and Castagnola, 2009), tools used to discredit opposition leaders or otherwise harass domestic competitors (e.g. Aydın, 2013; Popova, 2010). This kind of court may become embroiled in political controversy, but there is no serious sense in which its involvement will be understood as injecting independent judgment. In neither case will judges materially impact regime outcomes – indeed, they may be part of the process by which the regime collapses.

Yet we have also found that a latent propensity for noncompliance with important decisions is not particularly problematic for democratic regime survival. We do not claim that the routine defiance of courts with judicial review authority is to be promoted or itself necessarily without harm. We claim instead that noncompliance need not be a totally uncommon or particularly destructive element of a political system. In many cases, noncompliance will follow from an executive's judgment that the particular context in which the decision is issued simply cannot be prudently obeyed. In a speech to Congress explaining his refusal to release John Merryman from a Fort McHenry prison cell at the beginning of the US Civil War, Abraham Lincoln asked, "[A]re all the laws, but one, to go unexecuted, and the Government itself go to pieces, lest that one be violated? Even in such a case, would not the official oath be broken, if the Government should be overthrown, when it was

16 Top Venezuelan judge resigns, BBC News, Aug. 25, 1999, http://news.bbc.co.uk/1/hi/world/americas/429304.stm

believed that disregarding the single law, would tend to preserve it?" (Hutchinson, 2010). More than a century later, echoes of Lincoln's rationale are heard in the Israeli Interior Ministry's rationale for noncompliance. There simply are political contexts in which judicial orders cannot be implemented without significant risk to the system, in terms of budgets or national security interests.

Of course, these types of claims can very well mask goals that fundamentally undermine regime rules. The point is that courts that enjoy reasonably broad support, especially courts that are understood to be independent of major political competitors in a society raise the stakes of noncompliance, and by so doing help transfer information about the true motives of a leader. It is in this way that we understand the periodic forms of noncompliance in states with reasonably strong rule of law commitments like the United States, Costa Rica, Germany, or Israel. Rationales for noncompliance may be fabrications, but they are less likely to be perceived in that way by relevant actors than they are in contexts that do not possess such courts.

APPENDIX 5A

Tables

TABLE 5.A.1 *Declaration of state of emergencies for natural disasters and de facto judicial independence (democratic regimes)*

	Association between SOEs and de facto JI		
	Occurrence	Deaths (1,000s)	Damage (100,000s)
Natural disaster	2.2173***	0.0078	0.0048*
	(0.2864)	(0.0098)	(0.0026)
De facto judicial independence	−2.2941*	−3.2916**	−3.3260**
	(1.3346)	(1.4635)	(1.4713)
Civil War	−0.1726	−0.2645	−0.2659
	(0.2440)	(0.2653)	(0.2645)
ln(GDPPC)	−0.0019	0.1246	0.1045
	(0.2392)	(0.2837)	(0.2837)
GDP growth	0.0872*	0.0954**	0.0972**
	(0.0459)	(0.0441)	(0.0445)
Civil society	−0.0175	0.0921	0.1031
	(0.2530)	(0.2975)	(0.2990)
Party competition	0.0344	0.0816	0.0830
	(0.1610)	(0.1869)	(0.1870)
Population	−0.0000	0.0000	0.0000
	(0.0000)	(0.0000)	(0.0000)
Constant	−3.4634**	−3.0579	−2.9116
	(1.6701)	(2.1071)	(2.1125)
lnsig2u	0.9386**	0.7954*	0.8078*
	0.4063	0.4403	0.4499
Log-likelihood	−312.1746	−330.2912	−329.6813
AIC	656.3492	692.5823	691.3626
BIC	743.5319	779.7650	778.5452
Random effects	YES	YES	YES
Autocorrelation robust	YES	YES	YES

TABLE 5.A.1 *(continued)*

	Association between SOEs and de facto JI		
	Occurrence	Deaths (1,000s)	Damage (100,000s)
Heteroskedasticity robust	YES	YES	YES
Number of observations	2,171	2,171	2,171
Years covered	1900–2015	1900–2015	1900–2015

Note: Standard errors are clustered on country-episodes. Two-tailed tests of statistical significance are displayed: $^{*}p < .05$, $^{**}p < .01$.

TABLE 5.A.2 *Declaration of state of emergencies for political emergencies and de facto judicial independence (democratic regimes)*

	Association between SOEs and de facto JI		
	Terror (Occurrence)	Terror (Deaths/ Wounded (1,000s))	Banks Conflict Index
Domestic acts	0.6396**	0.0009**	0.0003**
	(0.2883)	(0.0004)	(0.0001)
De facto judicial independence	−1.4975	−1.8759	−1.1202
	(1.4707)	(1.4494)	(1.4245)
Civil War	0.1385	0.1663	0.1162
	(0.1755)	(0.1790)	(0.1650)
ln(GDPPC)	−0.0787	−0.0203	−0.0154
	(0.2517)	(0.2482)	(0.2487)
GDP growth	−0.0512*	−0.0551*	−0.0486*
	(0.0297)	(0.0301)	(0.0272)
Civil society	−0.4042	−0.4228	−0.4778
	(0.3378)	(0.3513)	(0.3443)
Party competition	0.0135	0.0282	0.0963
	(0.2123)	(0.2157)	(0.2179)
Population	−0.0000	−0.0000	−0.0000
	(0.0000)	(0.0000)	(0.0000)
Constant	−0.2058	−0.2295	−1.0268
	(1.6045)	(1.6213)	(1.7306)
lnsig2u	0.9386**	0.7954*	0.8078*
	0.4063	0.4403	0.4499
Log-likelihood	−312.1746	−330.2912	−329.6813
AIC	656.3492	692.5823	691.3626
BIC	743.5319	779.7650	778.5452
Random effects	YES	YES	YES
Autocorrelation robust	YES	YES	YES
Heteroskedasticity robust	YES	YES	YES
Number of observations	2,171	2,171	2,171
Years covered	1900–2015	1900–2015	1900–2015

Note: Standard errors are clustered on country-episodes. Two-tailed tests of statistical significance are displayed: $^{*}p < .05$, $^{**}p < .01$.

TABLE 5.A.3 *Propensity of a successful or attempted coup by features of the judicial system (democratic regimes)*

	Propensity of successful or attempted coup
Judicial attacks	1.648*
	(0.42)
Judicial noncompliance	0.512*
	(0.15)
LJI	0.177**
	(0.08)
Civil society	0.477**
	(0.09)
ln(GDPPC)	0.863
	(0.18)
Growth	0.917**
	(0.03)
Executive form (parliamentary)	1.735
	(0.93)
Executive form (presidential)	1.492
	(0.74)
Previous autocratic regime (military)	3.931*
	(2.37)
Previous autocratic regime (civilian)	0.989
	(0.66)
Previous autocratic regime (monarchy)	1.000
	(.)
Time since last coup	1.042
	(0.10)
Cubic spline1	1.001
	(0.00)
Cubic spline2	0.999
	(0.00)
Cubic spline3	1.001*
	(0.00)
Constant	0.004**
	(0.01)
lnsig2u	1.217
	(0.63)
Log-likelihood	−317.260
Random effects	YES

TABLE 5.A.3 *(continued)*

	Propensity of successful or attempted coup
Autocorrelation robust	YES
Heteroskedasticity robust	YES
Number of observations	3,789
Years covered	1900–2015

Note: Standard errors are clustered on country-episodes. Two-tailed tests of statistical significance are displayed: $^{*}p < .05$, $^{**}p < .01$.

TABLE 5.A.4 *Hazard of democratic regime breakdown by features of the judicial system (democratic regimes)*

	Hazard of democratic regime breakdown
Judicial attacks	1.842**
	(0.37)
Judicial noncompliance	0.529*
	(0.17)
LJI	0.122**
	(0.05)
Civil society	0.408**
	(0.07)
ln(GDPPC)	0.474**
	(0.11)
Growth	0.903**
	(0.03)
ln(population)	1.004
	(0.16)
Executive form (parliamentary)	0.698
	(0.40)
Executive form (presidential)	0.523
	(0.29)
Previous autocratic regime (military)	0.772
	(0.53)
Previous autocratic regime (civilian)	0.808
	(0.53)
Previous autocratic regime (monarchy)	0.212*
	(0.18)
Constant	0.060
	(0.17)
Duration parameter	2.103**
	(0.17)

TABLE 5.A.4 *(continued)*

	Hazard of democratic regime breakdown
Frailty parameter	1.589
	(0.58)
Log-likelihood	−100.501
Random effects	YES
Autocorrelation robust	YES
Heteroskedasticity robust	YES
Number of observations	4,743
Years covered	1900–2015

Note: Standard errors are clustered on country-episodes. Two-tailed tests of statistical significance are displayed: $^{*}p < .05$, $^{**}p < .01$.

TABLE 5.A.5 *Democratic breakdown models by alternate baseline hazards*

	baseline hazard parameterizations				
	Exponential	Weibull	Log-log	Log-normal	Cox
Judicial attacks	0.638**	0.761*	0.747*	0.780*	1.543*
	(0.10)	(0.08)	(0.09)	(0.09)	(0.26)
Judicial noncompliance	1.573*	1.337	1.559*	1.586*	0.610*
	(0.34)	(0.21)	(0.35)	(0.30)	(0.14)
LJI	3.077**	2.452**	2.650**	2.812**	0.258**
	(0.70)	(0.41)	(0.61)	(0.56)	(0.07)
Civil society	1.889**	1.523**	1.566**	1.667**	0.512**
	(0.20)	(0.13)	(0.16)	(0.16)	(0.07)
ln(GDPPC)	1.281	1.307**	1.360**	1.294*	0.727
	(0.19)	(0.13)	(0.16)	(0.14)	(0.14)
Growth	1.067*	1.044*	1.059**	1.061**	0.923**
	(0.03)	(0.02)	(0.02)	(0.02)	(0.03)
ln(population)	0.897	0.967	0.976	0.988	1.086
	(0.09)	(0.07)	(0.08)	(0.07)	(0.12)
Executive form (parliamentary)	1.202	1.163	1.072	1.129	0.819
	(0.42)	(0.29)	(0.35)	(0.34)	(0.35)
Executive form (presidential)	1.554	1.530	1.439	1.358	0.574
	(0.50)	(0.36)	(0.41)	(0.36)	(0.23)
Previous autocratic regime (military)	0.745	0.701	0.755	0.842	1.500
	(0.31)	(0.20)	(0.26)	(0.26)	(0.67)
Previous autocratic regime (civilian)	1.209	0.948	1.068	1.165	0.953
	(0.51)	(0.27)	(0.38)	(0.37)	(0.45)
Previous autocratic regime (monarchy)	1.114	1.251	1.868	1.757	0.761
	(0.47)	(0.35)	(0.71)	(0.64)	(0.34)

TABLE 5.A.5 *(continued)*

	baseline hazard parameterizations				
	Exponential	Weibull	Log-log	Log-normal	Cox
Constant	133.834* (264.71)	19.851* (29.54)	8.727 (14.40)	9.856 (14.14)	
Weibull shape parameter		1.629** (0.14)			
Log-log scale parameter			0.438** (0.04)		
Log-normal sigma				0.774** (0.05)	
Log-likelihood	−120.920	−108.149	−115.987	−113.450	−289.016
AIC	267.840	244.299	259.975	254.900	602.031
BIC	351.878	334.801	350.477	345.402	679.604
Random effects	YES	YES	YES	YES	YES
Autocorrelation robust	YES	YES	YES	YES	YES
Heteroskedasticity robust	YES	YES	YES	YES	YES
Number of observations	4,743	4,743	4,743	4,743	4,743
Years covered	1900–2015	1900–2015	1900–2015	1900–2015	1900–2015

Note: Standard errors are clustered on country-episodes. Two-tailed tests of statistical significance are displayed: $^{*}p < .05$, $^{**}p < .01$.

TABLE 5.A.6 *Democratic breakdown models by alternate frailty specifications*

	Frailty specifications	
	Gamma	Inverse Gaussian
Judicial attacks	1.605* (0.33)	2.216* (0.71)
Judicial noncompliance	0.596 (0.18)	0.388* (0.18)
LJI	0.220** (0.07)	0.060** (0.03)
Civil society	0.494** (0.06)	0.260** (0.06)
ln(GDPPC)	0.641* (0.12)	0.465* (0.16)
Growth	0.927* (0.03)	0.866* (0.05)

TABLE 5.A.6 *(continued)*

	Frailty specifications	
	Gamma	Inverse Gaussian
ln(population)	1.055	1.080
	(0.12)	(0.22)
Executive form (parliamentary)	0.793	0.608
	(0.34)	(0.47)
Executive form (presidential)	0.499	0.307
	(0.21)	(0.25)
Previous autocratic regime (military)	1.760	2.515
	(0.87)	(2.24)
Previous autocratic regime (civilian)	1.052	0.974
	(0.55)	(0.86)
Previous autocratic regime (monarchy)	0.647	0.461
	(0.35)	(0.39)
Constant	0.007*	0.003
	(0.02)	(0.01)
Duration parameter	1.666**	3.042**
	(0.15)	(0.37)
Frailty parameter	0.032	37.755**
	(0.08)	(36.38)
Log-likelihood	−108.085	−106.960
AIC	246.170	243.921
BIC	343.137	340.887
Random effects	YES	YES
Autocorrelation robust	YES	YES
Heteroskedasticity robust	YES	YES
Number of observations	4,743	4,743
Years covered	1900–2015	1900–2015

Note: Standard errors are clustered on country-episodes. Two-tailed tests of statistical significance are displayed: $^{*}p < .05$, $^{**}p < .01$.

TABLE 5.A.7 *Sensitivity to repeated entry*

	Stratified/Conditional risk models	
	Cox	Weibull
Judicial attacks	1.5959*	1.5732*
	(0.3252)	(0.2989)
Judicial noncompliance	0.6651	0.6405
	(0.1595)	(0.1574)
LJI	0.2860**	0.2338**
	(0.0923)	(0.0654)

TABLE 5.A.7 *(continued)*

	Stratified/Conditional risk models	
	Cox	Weibull
Civil society	0.5163**	0.5043**
	(0.0665)	(0.0587)
ln(GDPPC)	0.7511	0.6180**
	(0.1512)	(0.1112)
Growth	0.9164*	0.9312*
	(0.0326)	(0.0302)
ln(population)	1.0878	1.0486
	(0.1137)	(0.1198)
Executive form (parliamentary)	0.9333	0.8253
	(0.4358)	(0.3828)
Executive form (presidential)	0.6191	0.4869
	(0.2608)	(0.1959)
Previous autocratic regime (military)	1.7385	1.8014
	(0.9261)	(1.0233)
Previous autocratic regime (civilian)	1.0823	1.1181
	(0.5644)	(0.5659)
Previous autocratic regime (monarchy)	0.7245	0.6800
	(0.3601)	(0.3121)
Democratic spell=1		1.0000
		(.)
Democratic spell=2		1.1664
		(0.8409)
Democratic spell=3		0.1099
		(0.1731)
Democratic spell=4		8.2614**
		(5.7790)
Democratic spell=5		0.0002**
		(0.0004)
Constant		0.0109
		(0.0253)
Weibull shape parameter		
Democratic spell=1		1.0000
		(.)
Democratic spell=2		1.0048
		(0.1393)
Democratic spell=3		1.4594
		(0.2972)
Democratic spell=4		0.6567
		(0.1472)
Democratic spell=5		0.0000**
		(0.0000)
Constant		1.6281**
		(0.1548)

TABLE 5.A.7 *(continued)*

	Stratified/Conditional risk models	
	Cox	Weibull
Log-likelihood	−215.2172	−105.6128
AIC	454.4344	253.2257
BIC	532.0075	388.9786
Random effects	YES	YES
Autocorrelation robust	YES	YES
Heteroskedasticity robust	YES	YES
Number of observations	4,743	4,743
Years covered	1900–2015	1900–2015

Note: Standard errors are clustered on country-episodes. Two-tailed tests of statistical significance are displayed: $^{*}p < .05$, $^{**}p < .01$.

APPENDIX 5B

Sensitivity to Measurement Error

Our analysis has assumed no measurement error in the V-Dem point estimates of our key variables. Importantly, the measurement approach in V-Dem assumes that there will be error. The measurement model addresses it and we make it very easy for future users to account for it in their applications. The values of the V-Dem measures we have used so far are means from the posterior distribution of the relevant latent variable for each state-year. Importantly, we also have access to 2000 samples from the posterior distribution of each parameter in V-Dem's measurement model, including of course the latent variable itself.

To allow measurement error to propagate through the model we adopt an iterative Monte Carlo procedure known as the "method of composition," as discussed in Tanner (1996) and used previously by Treier and Jackman (2008) and Pemstein, Meserve, and Melton (2010). The method follows three steps.

Step 1: For each state-year of each V-Dem variable, draw a sample from its posterior distribution. Combine the results of this step (new V-Dem variables that now incorporate measurement error) with the data described above.

Step 2: Fit the event history model described above, saving estimated parameters as well as the variance–covariance matrix.

Step 3: Draw one sample of each coefficient in the model from the multivariate normal density of the coefficients with the mean vector and variance–covariance matrix set to the estimates in Step 2.

These steps are iterated 2,000 times. The estimates at each iteration can be considered samples from the posterior distributions of each of the model's parameters. Figure 5.B.1 plots the posterior distributions for each of the key V-Dem variables in our study derived via the method of composition. Measurement error in the V-Dem variables contributes to the uncertainty of our coefficient estimates – country-level experts differ in their assessments of judicial context with respect to judicial attacks, judicial noncompliance and civil society. However, these sources of measurement

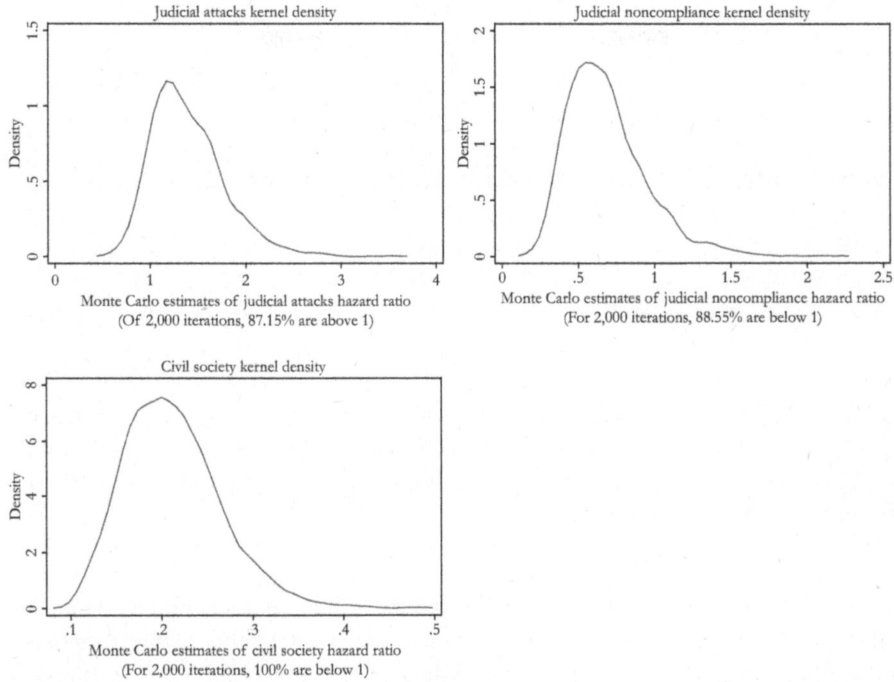

FIGURE 5.B.1 Monte Carlo analysis allowing for measurement error in V-Dem variables. Panels display kernel density plots of V-Dem indicator posteriors for judicial attacks (left panel), judicial noncompliance (center panel) and civil society (right panel), respectively.

error do not substantially alter the inferences that we reported above. We can see from Figure 5.B.1 that the error-adjusted estimates of the coefficients for judicial attacks, judicial noncompliance, and civil society are quite similar, albeit muted, compared to our original estimates. Judicial attacks are associated with regimes with greater hazards of breakdown, while democracies with robust civil societies are associated with lower hazards of democratic collapse and judicial noncompliance is not necessarily problematic for democratic regime survival.

6

Will Courts Be Bulwarks of Democracy in the United States?

I ask my judicial colleagues to continue their efforts to promote public confidence in the judiciary, both through their rulings and through civic outreach. We should celebrate our strong and independent judiciary, a key source of national unity and stability. But we should also remember that justice is not inevitable.

Chief Justice John Roberts 2019

When Anthony Romero claims that the federal courts of the United States are bulwarks of democracy, he envisions them as active protectors of the American constitutional system. Set against the backdrop of Executive Order 13769, Romero was concerned with the judiciary's checking function, declaring, "And when President Trump enacts law or executive orders that are unconstitutional and illegal, the courts are there to defend everyone's rights." This, too, is Kim Scheppele's vision of European constitutional courts as defenders of democratic principles. Courts defend democracies through findings of unconstitutionality, especially so when their decisions are grounded in a jurisprudence that evaluates government actions with respect to the substantive rights that give meaning to a democratic system.

Our model captures this kind of active behavior;[1] and we surely believe that active courts can hold political leaders within the legal limits on their authority through decisions that strike down laws or executive actions or otherwise set aside government actions. Yet, our argument highlights a related but distinct force through which courts influence democratic regime survival. Courts stabilize democracy by incentivizing prudence on behalf of both political leaders and the opposition.

Independent courts encourage leaders to eschew policies that are likely to raise concerns about potential violations of regime rules. They encourage opposition leaders to avoid extraordinary responses to policy choices that might appear to lie

[1] The equilibrium that we title "Policy Failure" is one which even the government that receives the extraordinary signal chooses the normal policy. As we discussed in the text, the parameter values that sustain this equilibrium are consistent with another equilibrium, in which both types of governments initially pursue the extraordinary policy, but following a judicial decision against this policy, they accept it and adopt the normal policy moving forward.

outside of the boundaries of democratic compromises. While we do not deny that courts might defend democracy through their checking function, we believe that the more important force lies with the second face of judicial power and the ways in which judiciaries encourage political elites to take paths less subject to claims of illegitimacy and less likely to result in conflict. To put it in the terms of Levitsky and Ziblatt, courts encourage forbearance on the part of leaders and patience on the part of the opposition.

This chapter considers the United States case. The goal of our discussion is to illustrate how the model can be used to think through the ways in which the courts of a particular state might stabilize its democracy. There are surely examples of judicial decisions in the history of the United States that seem to illustrate how a court could defend democracy through the active use of its powers. *United States* v. *Nixon*, whereby the Supreme Court required then president Richard Nixon to deliver tape recordings of his private conversations to a federal district court in the context of the Watergate investigation, is a tempting example. In late 2020, in the wake of the presidential campaign, it was common for opinion leaders to consider the democratic implications of dozens of court decisions from around the country ruling against Donald Trump's claims of electoral fraud. Writing in *The Hill*, Brent Budowsky put it bluntly, arguing that a Supreme Court order finding that the attorney general of Texas did not have standing to sue four states alleging violations of federal electoral law,[2] had ended an "attempted legal coup d'etat" by Donald Trump.[3] Yet, for every democracy-defending decision, we can point to other decisions of US courts that seem to undermine democracy under typical concepts. Notorious decisions like *Plessy* v. *Ferguson* and *Korematsu* v. *United States* come immediately to mind. We remain open to the idea that courts can defend democracy through their checking power as well as the idea that courts can attack democracy both by failing to check power and in some cases by doing so.[4]

On our account, if US courts have helped stabilize US democracy, it is because they have over their history incentivized more prudent choices among political leaders than would have been made with a far less independent set of courts. Clearly, at the end of 2020, at the end of the Donald Trump administration, it is tempting to question whether political leaders in the United States over the past four years have been prudent in the way that we highlight. In thinking about the answer to

2 The defendant states, Georgia, Pennsylvania, Wisconsin, and Michigan, were all states in which the Democratic candidate Joseph Biden won the popular vote by relatively small margins. The lawsuit asked the Supreme Court to set aside the electoral votes of these states unless their state legislatures appointed independent slates of electors.

3 "SCOTUS will save America from Trump's attacks on democracy," Brent Budowsky, *The Hill* Online, December 11, 2020.

4 The Supreme Court's campaign finance jurisprudence, including its decision in *Citizens United* v. *FEC*, are regarded (on the left especially) as fundamentally antidemocratic. The mechanism through which the court did its alleged damage involves the invalidation of regulation, i.e. the use of its checking powers.

this question it is critical that we pose the counterfactuals clearly. We must imagine the kind of politics we would have observed had the judiciary of the United States during this period been either (a) far less independent than it was or (b) far more so. To help frame the answer to this question, we believe it is useful to first consider the US case with respect to the conditions we have identified as necessary for a judiciary defense of democracy: (1) minimal conditions for democratic compromise, (2) minimal judicial independence, (3) judges willing to risk noncompliance, and (4) meaningful costs to politicians for noncompliance.

The US case is a particularly useful one to consider because it is exactly the kind of state where it is plausible to at least consider a role for courts in regime survival. As we discussed in Chapter 2, our argument connects naturally to Przeworski's (2005) model of democratic regime survival. To review, in this model, political parties represent social classes, which have diametrically opposed interests with respect to the redistribution of resources. The key idea of the model is that parties will find it easier to commit to democratic elections when they compete within the context of great state wealth. This is because it is easier to satisfy the interests of both the upper and lower classes with relatively low rates of redistribution when states are wealthy than when they are poor. The parties police themselves in this model, so that if ever a party in power produces a level of redistribution below (or above) what is necessary to prevent conflict, party leaders know. In so far as courts can be used to monitor these understandings, judicial independence should be increasingly important to democratic regime survival as the level of development of a state increases. This is because it will be in wealthy states where democracy is possible if only the competitors have a process for managing their uncertainty over potential violations of regime rules.

Reenock, Staton, and Radean (2013) find a strong connection between judicial independence and democratic regime survival when states are wealthy. Here we replicate the study on a broader dataset, making use of new measures. We reestimate our democratic survival models from Chapter 5, but this time, we do so conditioning the effect of judicial independence on economic development. We expect that any benefits reaped by democratic regimes in possession of independent courts ought to be greater at higher levels of economic development. Or conversely, at higher levels of economic development, democratic regimes will find it increasingly more challenging to endure with less independent courts.

The marginal association between a decrease in a court's independence and the mean expected duration of a democratic regime are displayed in Figure 6.1. For democracies at low levels of democracy, where mutual commitments to democratic competition are arguably more difficult to sustain, the benefits of an independent court would appear to be modest. Reductions in judicial independence are unlikely to deliver meaningful benefits on policing the democratic bargain. Yet at higher levels of economic development, where parties are more likely to commit to democratic competition, judicial independence is more important. Indeed, at higher

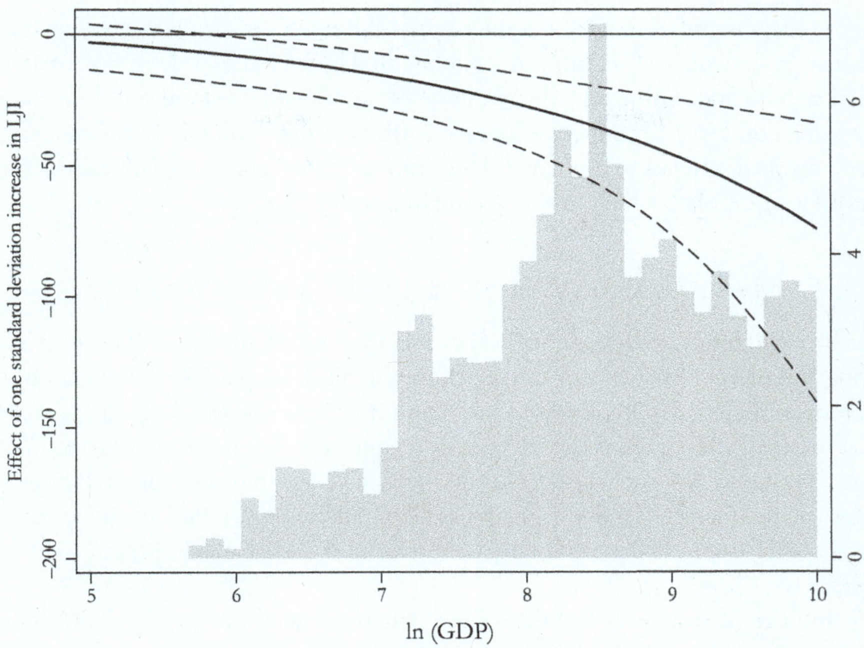

FIGURE 6.1 Mean expected duration of democratic regimes: 1900–2015. Marginal difference between regimes with a one standard deviation reduction in LJI displayed. Full models are reported in Appendix 5A. Two-tailed intervals for $p < .05$ are reported between dashed lines.

levels of development, e.g. between 7 and 9 ln(GDP) in the figure, democracies that have an LJI score one standard deviation between the mean, are expected to register substantially shorter lifetimes.

International aid projects aimed at judicial independence have looked to build independent courts in developing states. There are many reasons to support this kind of effort. Many of these efforts have been led by US NGOs and US federal agencies. Still, it is important to recognize that independent courts are doing work in developed states and that they need support as well. Indeed, from the perspective of stabilizing democracy, defending assaults on their independence may be more important than it is in developing states.

We divide the remainder of the chapter into two parts. In the first, we argue that the United States is a country that likely satisfies our conditions. In the second, we consider several caveats, which follow from well-known stresses on the United States system evident in the early twenty-first century and especially so in the context of the 2020 pandemic and presidential election. In some respects, the crisis induced by the coronavirus is hardly novel in terms of the past three years of the Trump administration. American politics were turbulent between 2017 and 2020, with several crises raising questions about the ability of American political institutions to provide meaningful oversight over the actions of the US president; the connection between free media and an informed public; the United States' role in the international system; and, ultimately, the ability of the American electoral system to offer representation to vast numbers of people in the country. Notably these concerns have provoked scholars to evaluate the robustness of the American political regime (Levitsky and Ziblatt, 2018; Ginsburg and Huq, 2018).

6.1 THE CASE FOR US COURTS AS BULWARKS

The first condition is that political elites must be minimally committed to competing for power via free and fair elections. It must be possible for competing interests in society to compromise such that losing power in the short run is more attractive than risking the consequences of regime collapse. If this is not true, then courts, no matter their independence, are quite unlikely to serve as important protectors of democracy. If elites are not fundamentally committed to democracy, courts are far more likely to be targets of reform aimed at making them tools of repression.

A number of structural features of the American state encourage democratic compromise, most notably its level of development. Perhaps the most well-known empirical relationship in the study of political regimes is the positive association between economic development and democracy (Lipset, 1959; Przeworski et al., 2000). The level of development in the United States is a powerful political stabilizer. Although natural resources are plentiful, the United States also possesses a diverse economy which limits its exposure to risks associated with the types of fixed assets that make inequality particularly problematic for democracy. Asset mobility acts as a sort of brake on redistributive demands (Boix, 2003). Gaining control of the US state for the purpose of predating on the resources of its citizens would not be particularly fruitful, as US citizens could move their assets relatively easily.

Institutional structures that are thought to promote instability are also largely absent. The United States is a presidential system; however, it features two political parties. The kind of political gridlocks associated with the combination of presidentialism and multipartism characterized by the Latin American experience in the twentieth century have been far less prevalent (e.g. Mainwaring, 1993; Linz, 1990). Of course, scholars have questioned whether "the difficult combination" is actually threatening to democratic survival (e.g. Bernhard, Reenock, and Nordstrom, 2003; Pereira and Melo, 2012; Power and Gasiorowski, 1997). Cheibub (2007) argues that what appeared to be a causal link between regime instability, presidents, and multiple parties was confounded by the failure to account for a long history of military involvement in politics. Yet even here the United States would appear to be relatively insulated. The country has a long history of civilian control of the military. Despite its current voluntary service model, the military remains a diverse institution along gender, race, and social class.[5] Even its officers are primarily drawn from its reserve officer training program, distributed across thousands of institutions of higher learning. This diversity in training and emphasis on professionalism ought to be insulating. Officers raised with professional norms that emphasize political neutrality ought to accept their subordination to elected civilians.[6] All of this suggests that, generally speaking, the US political system is one in which fundamental compromises among political elites should be relatively easily to sustain.

In most respects, it also would seem obvious the United States possesses the kind of independent judiciary that our model envisions. Law and politics scholarship has provided compelling theoretical models and empirical evidence in support of the claim that judges are not fully independent of political forces. Judicial decision-making in the United States does appear to be sensitive to political constraints. The separation of powers system gives Congress and the president control over both judicial resources, from their budgets to jurisdiction, and the implementation of their decisions. Scholars argue that when the stakes are clear and significant, American judges will take into account the preferences of external actors (Carrubba and Zorn, 2010; Clark, 2010; Epstein and Knight, 1998; Martin, 2006). That said, there is also consensus that, generally speaking, American courts enjoy a significant degree of independence from sitting governments and the real power necessary to check state actions in many cases.

This independence has been won over time via the combination of supermajoritarian appointment norms and frequent political turnover. Newspaper reports during the Trump administration raised concerns about a federal judiciary that was becoming increasingly staffed by Republican-affiliated judges with connections to the Federalist Society. Yet by the end of the Trump administration, the federal courts remained balanced in partisan terms. By the middle of 2020, roughly 50 percent of the judges serving below the level of the Supreme Court were nominated by a Democratic president; Obama appointees represented about 40 percent of the total. Although Republican appointees made up the majority in seven circuits, the majorities were very small on a number of circuits.

International judicial independence scores reflect this reality. The United States judiciary placed at or above the eighty-second percentile in every year from 1900 to 2015. American judges are still welcomed into countries throughout the world in order to give seminars and lectures of building and maintaining judicial independence. At least relative to the distribution of world judiciaries, the American federal judiciary stands out for its professionalism, competence, and autonomy. This is to

5 See www.cfr.org/article/demographics-us-military.

6 The relationship between the US military and the US president was no doubt stressed during the Trump administration. The president became involved in matters of military justice and the removal of naval officers in ways that were considered nontraditional at the time. Yet, we do not believe that there is sufficient evidence to claim that civil–military relations are fundamentally broken in the United States.

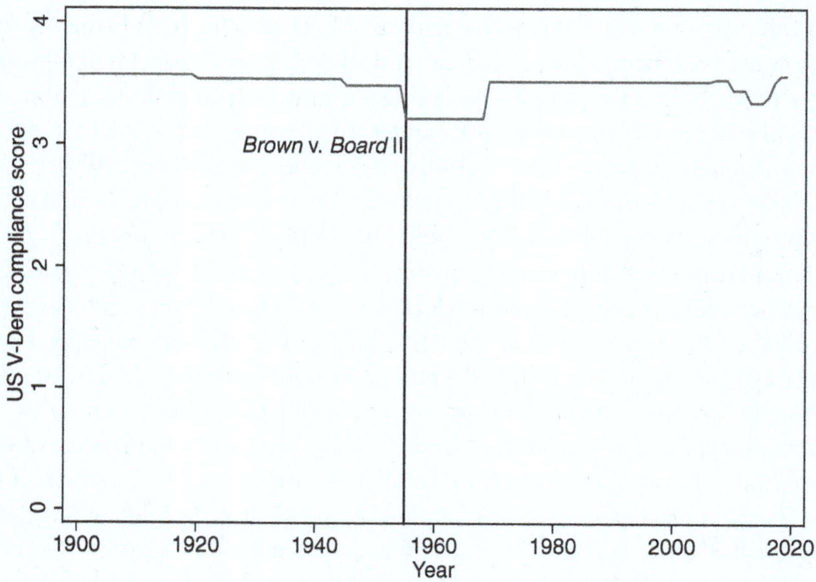

FIGURE 6.2 Noncompliance with US Supreme Court decisions over time

say that there is very much is a judiciary whose independence is worth defending in the United States.

The third condition we identify is that judges must be willing to risk noncompliance. Strategic models of judging often assume that, all else equal, courts would like to avoid noncompliance (Carrubba, 2005; Staton and Vanberg, 2008). That said, we also know that noncompliance is far from an uncommon feature of American judicial politics (Spriggs, 1996, 1997). Figure 6.1 plots the V-Dem compliance with high court scores for the United States from 1900 to 2018. Although the Supreme Court's record of compliance is clearly strong, there have been notable exceptions. The series picks up widespread forms of noncompliance with Warren Court decisions in the context of school prayer and desegregation. It also suggests that US judges are willing to issue bold decisions, which are politically unpopular, risking noncompliance.

The Eighth Circuit's recent reaction to a decision of the Board of Immigration Appeals (BIA) illustrates the point further. The Eighth Circuit had reviewed an appeal of a BIA decision finding that an immigration court judge lacked the authority to provide a waiver necessary for the Department of Homeland Security to consider the application for a U-Visa of a Mexican national.[7] The court remanded

7 The U visa provides a pathway for admission to the United States of an alien who has been a victim of a crime and provided material assistance to the state in prosecuting the perpetrator. See www.uscis.gov/humanitarian/victims-human-trafficking-and-other-crimes/victims-criminal-activity-u-nonimmigrant-status.

the matter to the BIA with instructions to consider two legal questions that it had yet to consider, and which would be necessary in order to sustain the judgment that the immigration court judge lacked the claimed authority. Writing for the court in a petition reviewing the BIA's decision, Judge Frank Easterbrook describes the case as follows.

> What happened next beggars belief. The Board of Immigration Appeals wrote, on the basis of a footnote in a letter the Attorney General issued after our opinion, that our decision is incorrect. Instead of addressing the issues we specified, the Board repeated a theme of its prior decision that the Secretary has the sole power to issue U visas and therefore should have the sole power to decide whether to waive inadmissibility. The Board did not rely on any statute, regulation, or reorganization plan transferring the waiver power ... We have never before encountered defiance of a remand order, and we hope never to see it again. Members of the Board must count themselves lucky that Baez-Sanchez has not asked us to hold them in contempt, with all the consequences that possibility entails ... Once we reached a conclusion, both the Constitution and the statute required the Board to implement it.

This is the kind of clear and direct writing and decision-making that we typically expect from American federal judges. Of all of the conditions on our list, the presence of brave judges who are willing to exercise their powers is the most likely one to be met.

The final condition we identify concerns how costly it is for political officials to defy an order of a federal court, including the Supreme Court of the United States. It would appear relatively straightforward that overt noncompliance with a decision of the Supreme Court would be significant. The Supreme Court continues to be viewed favorably by a majority of Americans. According to a nationally representative Gallup Poll in September 2019, 54 percent of respondents expressed approval for the Supreme Court's "handling of its job." Only 42 percent disapproved.[8] Scholars have also argued that the Supreme Court continues to enjoy considerable legitimacy, understood through Easton's concept of diffuse support, even if there are short run fluctuations in public opinion regarding the job that it is doing (Nelson and Gibson, 2017).

Figure 6.3 displays the status of civil society in the United States over time. If a robust civil society is a resource that can be drawn down in the defense of democratic institutions (Bernhard et al., 2020), then the United States appears to be in a favorable position. Participation in civil society organizations is strong and the legal profession is especially committed to advocating on behalf of courts, their judges, and judicial independence. So, in many ways, this condition is very likely to be met as well.

8 https://news.gallup.com/poll/4732/supreme-court.aspx.

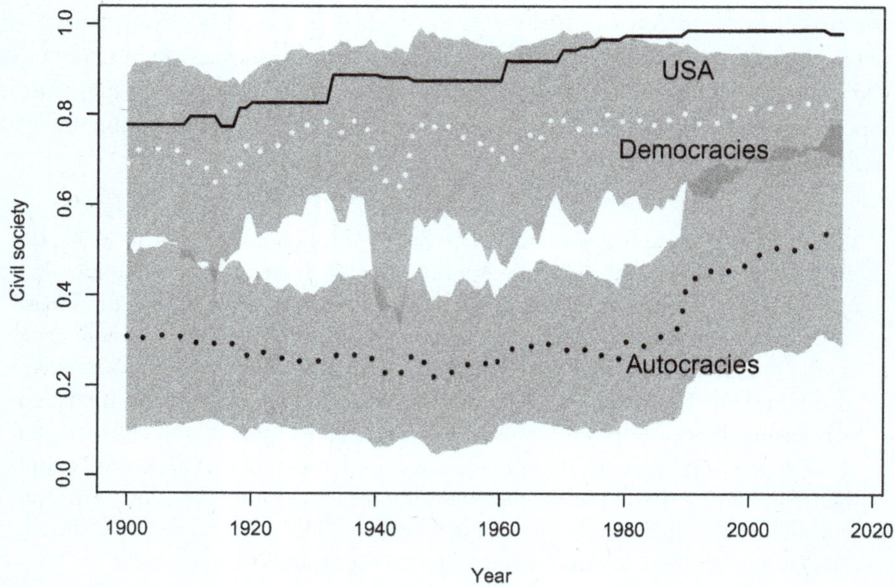

FIGURE 6.3 Civil society (1900–2018): V-Dem-based civil society scores for the United States are plotted using the solid black line. The white-dotted series reflects the average of attacks scores for democratic regimes; the black-dotted series shows the same information for autocracies.

To summarize, there are many reasons to suspect that the courts of the United States are likely to play the kind of role we have envisioned. Elites are likely to benefit from an effective monitoring system. American judges are both sufficiently independent of American governments and willing to risk noncompliance in the course of carrying out their duties. Political leaders surely will perceive nontrivial costs for defying a court order. These features of the US state sustain a context in which courts can promote prudence.

6.2 CAVEATS

Although the US case would appear to be one in which the conditions we lay out are likely to be met, we nevertheless wish to highlight a few caveats. Most obviously, income inequality has been on the rise in the United States for nearly forty years. Compared to absolute wealth, Acemoglu and Robinson (2006) argue that income inequality is more likely to be the catalyst that exposes democracy to either political erosion or collapse. Indeed, greater income inequality drives satisfaction with democracy among electoral winners and losers (Han and Chang, 2016). Moreover, wealth may exacerbate inequality's threat to democracy (Houle, 2009). Uneven income distributions in the face of higher economic development are more readily recognized and deemed unacceptable by citizens, leading to heightened risk of breakdown (Reenock, Bernhard, and Nordstrom, 2007). Thus, not all structural conditions that promote elite compromise point toward a stable US political system.

Of perhaps more immediate concern, scholars have raised questions about whether old commitments to democracy in the United States are as strong as they once were. Levitsky and Ziblatt point to breakdowns in related norms of "forbearance" and "mutual tolerance." Mark Tushnet points to the increasing appeal to "constitutional hardball," or the use of constitutional procedures to violate preexisting norms. Ginsburg and Huq point to "populism" in the form of Tea Party Republicans, though the campaign of Bernie Sanders shares many of the features of a populist movement from the left. Levitsky and Ziblatt write,

> If, twenty-five years ago, someone had described to you a country in which candidates threatened to lock up their rivals, political opponents accused the government of stealing the election or establishing a dictatorship, and parties used their legislative majorities to impeach presidents and steal supreme court seats, you might have thought of Ecuador or Romania. You probably would not have thought of the United States. (167)

The fact that seventeen Republican attorneys general joined the attorney general of Texas's 2020 lawsuit against the states of Georgia, Pennsylvania, Wisconsin, and Michigan seeking to overturn their presidential election results raised a question about the commitment of the Republican Party to elections as a means of transferring power. That the suit was supported by 126 Republican members of Congress, including some members from the very states whose systems were called into question, indicates the seriousness of the question. In mid-December, North Carolina state senator Bob Steinburg called on President Trump to declare a national emergency and invoke the Insurrection Act.[9] Virginia state senator Amanda Chase called on President Trump to declare martial law.[10] That elected representatives at multiple levels of government are willing to call for a president to simply ignore the results of a federal election is suggestive that core commitments to democracy are strained.

6.2.1 *Judicial Appointments*

Of particular importance for our discussion is the fact that many of the alleged violations of forbearance and mutual toleration have involved the judiciary itself. Although the judiciary has always been a location of partisan conflict, by the beginning of the twentieth century, strong norms of appointments existed, which incentivized cooperation and moderation. Most obviously, the Senate's sixty-vote

9 "North Carolina GOP lawmaker urges Trump to suspend civil liberties to keep power: 'Invoke the Insurrection Act'," Katie Shepherd, *Washington Post* Online, December 16, 2020.

10 "Republican contender for Va. governor says Trump should declare martial law," Laura Vozella, *Washington Post* Online, December 15, 2020.

majority necessary to close debate provided the minority party with a key role in the nomination process even if a single party held the presidency and the Senate. Minorities infrequently relied on the filibuster to stop appointments, because the threat alone was sufficient to ensure that presidents sent to the Senate judges who would be considered acceptable to the minority. Beginning during the administration of George W. Bush, in the wake of the highly controversial end to the 2000 presidential campaign, Senate Democrats began using the filibuster to stop the presidents' judicial nominees. When Senate Republicans used the same strategy to stop Barack Obama's nominations, Senate Democrats ended the practice of the filibuster for lower court appointments. The Senate ultimately ended the practice of the filibuster for even Supreme Court nominations in order to end debate on Justice Neil Gorsuch, who received his appointment only after Senate Republicans refused to act on President Obama's nomination of Merrick Garland for over a year. The same Senate majority that argued that the Garland nomination could not move forward in an election year appointed Justice Amy Barrett weeks after the death of Justice Ruth Bader Ginsburg and one week prior to the federal elections.

The effective end of the "blue slip" also points to a breakdown in old norms of appointment. By tradition, senators were empowered to stop committee action on nominations to courts in their home states. Although the specific approach to the blue slip has varied over time, in 2020 the practice is largely advisory.[11] The end of the filibuster and the traditional blue slip practice means that the Republicans are now able to fill the judiciary with nominees who never would have been supported by the Democratic minority under previous rules. There is no reason to believe that a future Democratic president, with a future Democratic Senate majority will behave differently. Consequently, federal judicial appointments are now governed by purely majoritarian rules at best.

6.2.2 *Attacks on the US Judiciary*

Parties always attempt to shape the ideological nature of the federal courts. We should expect a politically oriented appointments process. Of greater concern are recent attacks on sitting federal court judges. Using our measure of judicial attacks derived from V-Dem scores, Figure 6.4 displays trends in attacks on courts from 1900 to 2017. To provide global context, we calculated the mean and standard deviation of court attacks for democracies and autocracies across each year. By looking at the trend lines and the overlap of the standard deviations for autocracies and democracies, a "third wave of autocratization" is evident. The substantial distinction between regime types exists for the twentieth century, but starting around 2005, the level of court attacks of the two regime types converge until 2017 where they are nearly indistinguishable.

11 www.nytimes.com/2017/09/13/us/politics/mcconnell-federal-judges-trump.html.

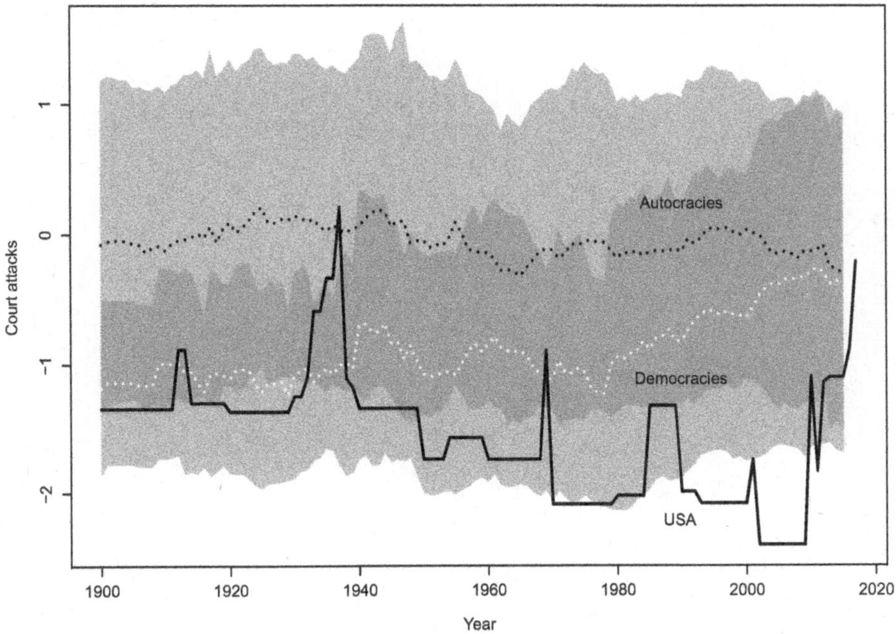

FIGURE 6.4 Attacks on courts (1900–2018): V-Dem-based judicial attacks scores for the United States are plotted using the solid black line. The white-dotted series reflects the average of attacks scores for democratic regimes; the black-dotted series shows the same information for autocracies.

Turning toward the US case, historically the United States has ranged widely on the intensity of court attacks. Across all states in the time frame, the United States ranges from a low in the early 2000s where it ranks in the third percentile of all state-years to a high in the early 1940s at the sixty-sixth percentile. The peak in attacks in the United States occurred during the Franklin D. Roosevelt (FDR) administration, when he clashed with the court over executive overreach, and released several statements, fomenting public dissatisfaction with the court. Conflict with the courts manifested as a result of promises and attempts to take greater executive action to reduce unemployment and employ other New Deal policies. It is perhaps no coincidence that the attacks coincided with what some historians argue is the closest the United States has come to a democratic breakdown in recent history. Stoked by the fears of wealthy business people, "The Business Plot" sought to recruit military to consider a coup.

Since FDR, attacks on the courts remained low. A nadir was reached during the Bush administration post-9/11, court attacks have since climbed such that attacks on the judiciary in the United States are worse than that of the average democracy. Court attacks have recently spiked, returning to levels previously observed under FDR. The administration of Donald Trump has returned the United States to a state of court attacks exceeding that of the average autocracy.

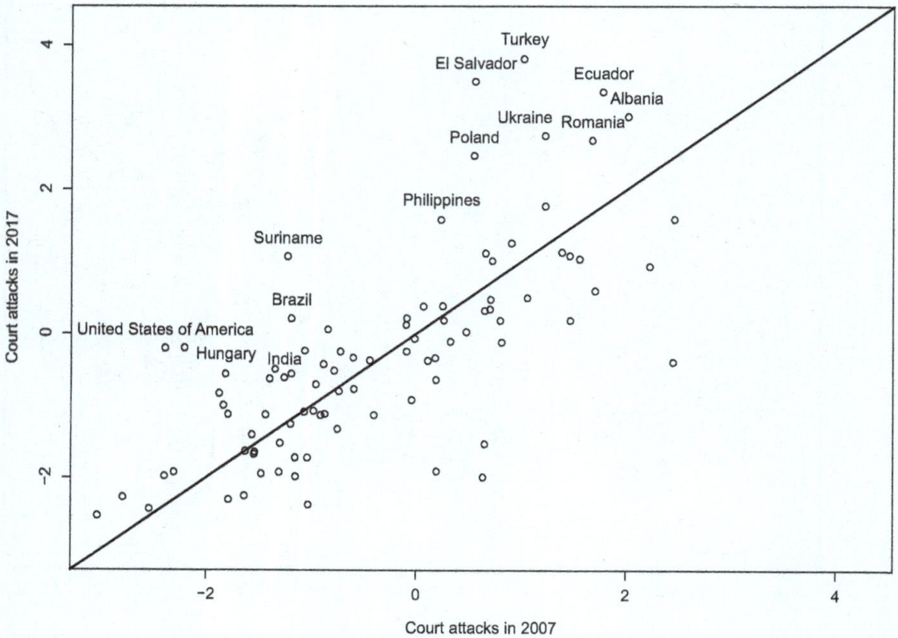

FIGURE 6.5 Change in judicial attacks over time: A plot of the V-Dem-based judicial attacks scores in 2017 on the same scores in 2007. States that lie above the diagonal are those whose attacks scores increased over ten years.

In Figure 6.5, we provide additional global context for what we are seeing in the United States. The figure plots the judicial attacks scores for countries in 2017 on those scores in 2007. Points above the forty-five-degree line are democracies where court attacks have increased from one decade prior. Some of the largest increases in court attacks occur in Turkey and El Salvador. Other notable states that are seeing attacks lie in Eastern Europe: in Albania, Hungary, Poland, Romania, and Ukraine. Note that while some of these are poor states, many exceed wealth thresholds for development.

Observe the left-hand side of Figure 6.5. These are democracies that had lower levels of court attacks roughly a decade ago. Of this subgroup, the democracies that have increased court attacks the most are Brazil, Hungary, India, Suriname, and notably, the United States. The United States appears to be seeing a medium number of attacks in the global context, but of the states in the lower quartile of attacks in 2007, it has experienced the greatest increase!

Given the increase in verbal attacks that we document, it is worth considering these attacks in greater detail. Public statements on the judiciary in the United States most often have taken the form of official White House statements and official speeches. President Trump is unique in that his administration released a wealth of statements on a multitude of topics via social media. Between his inauguration

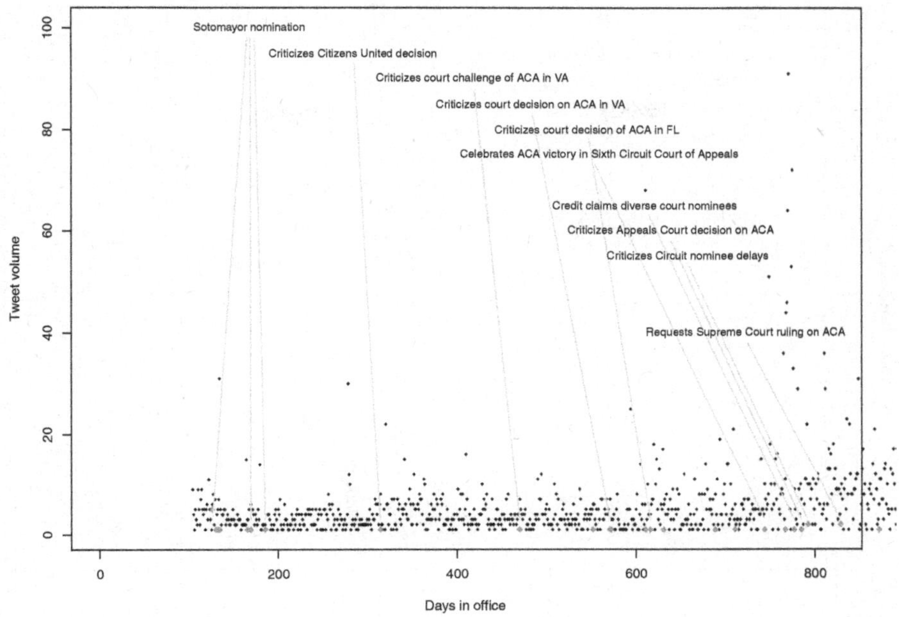

FIGURE 6.6 Obama tweets: A count of tweets by Baraǩ Obama over time. Tweets concerning the judiciary are highlighted.

on January 20, 2017, and May 19, 2019, Mr. Trump had tweeted 8,839 times. In an attempt to analyze this corpus of tweets for statements regarding the courts, we coded dummy variables for every instance that the president used "jud," "scotus," and "circuit." This yields a corpus of 259 times that the president mentioned the courts in his Twitter feed.[12]

Given the recency of the use of social media by a president, the best available comparison to President Trump's mentioning of the courts is that of President Obama. During the corresponding time frame in the Obama administration, the White House and the POTUS account tweeted 2,561 times, with 21 tweets concerning the courts.

Figure 6.6 and Figure 6.7 show the content, timing, and volume of tweets of the first 800 days in office of presidents Obama and Trump.

The Obama administration seldom commented on the courts. Barack Obama invoked the institution largely to credit claim for the court nominees and to publicize the nomination of Justice Sotomayor. Obama's negative tweets rarely involved criticism of the court. Rather, these statements target the obstruction of Congress in considering his nominations. Occasionally the administration would go so far as

[12] The coding procedure yielded five false positives where Trump uses these terms to discuss issues unrelated to his stance on the court such as personal lawsuits, a feud with fashion mogul Anna Wintour, and a shooting that happened to take place in a courthouse.

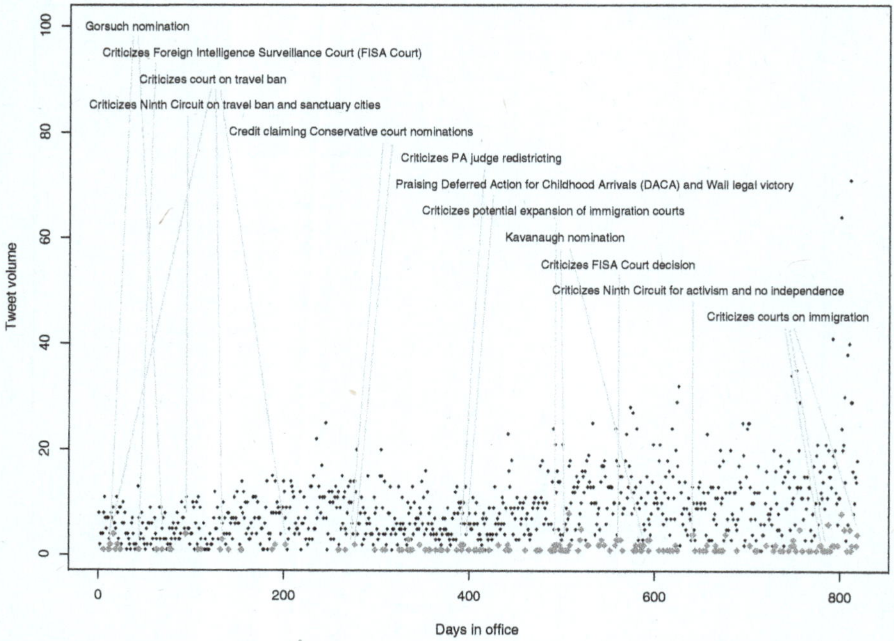

FIGURE 6.7 Trump tweets: A count of tweets by Donald Trump over time. Tweets concerning the judiciary are highlighted.

to criticize court rulings on keystone legislation such as the Affordable Care Act (ACA), suggesting they had hoped for a different outcome or to announce that they intend to pursue the matter in a higher court. No statements from the administration use language that imply the court is political, corrupt, or inept.

The Trump administration, however, was quite willing to invoke this language. The administration attacked the quality of court decisions by referring to them as "terrible" and "ridiculous" (Twitter, April 26, 2017). Notoriously, following district court judge James L. Robart's opinion temporarily blocking the original Trump Muslim travel ban, President Trump referred to Robart as a "so-called" judge. Figure 6.8 shows the tweet.

In saying, "Justice Roberts can say what he wants but the 9th Circuit is a complete & total disaster" (Twitter, November 22, 2018), the president called into question the opinion of the chief justice. Additionally, the Trump administration's attacks on the courts often made reference to putting the security of the country at risk. "Just cannot believe a judge would put our country in such peril. If something happens blame him and court system. People pouring in. Bad!" (Twitter, February 5, 2017). This is often done in the context of court decisions that do not favor Trump's policies on immigration.

Beyond attacking individuals, the Trump administration also referred to the institution as a whole: "In any event we are EXTREME VETTING people coming into

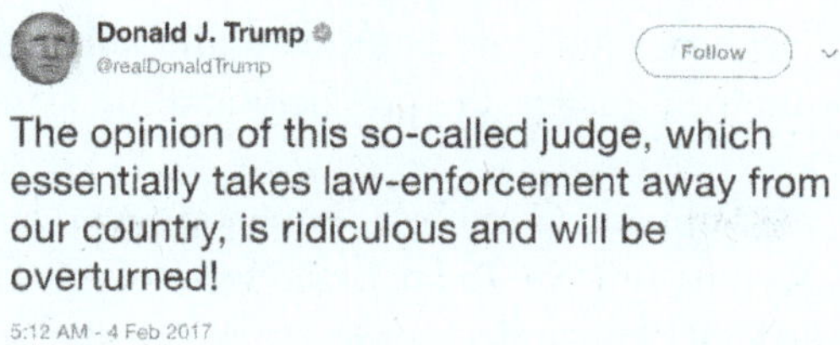

FIGURE 6.8 So-called judge: Text of Donald Trump's tweet concerning a federal judge's temporary restraining order on the enforcement of the executive order known as the travel ban.

the US in order to help keep our country safe. The courts are slow and political!" In other instances Trump referred to the Ninth Circuit as "broken" and "unfair" (Twitter, January 10, 2018), undermining the functionality and impartiality that confidence in the courts relies upon. He was also quick to refer to the courts as engaging in "judicial activism" (Twitter, November 21, 2018) in their rulings surrounding sanctuary cities and the circumstances under which migrants can apply for asylum.

It is clear that the rules governing judicial appointments have changed. It is also clear that Donald Trump engages in aggressive verbal attacks on US judges with whom he disagrees. In light of the empirical relationships we demonstrated in Chapter 5, these are surely alarming facts.

These facts suggest one of two interpretations. The first is that we are observing the behavior of elites who have abandoned their commitments to democratic competition. Although legal in nature, the Republican Party and the president of the United States were engaging in a slow but steady process aimed at eliminating the possibility of losing power. The second interpretation, which we think is more likely, is that the Republican Party and the president of the United States were carrying out a straightforward form of constitutional hardball, designed to create a federal judiciary that shares its views of economic regulation and democratic institutions, including electoral boundaries and rules that influence voter turnout. Under this interpretation, we are not necessarily observing direct efforts to fully eliminate democratic political competition. The Republican Party is still very much committed to fighting elections; it wants to lock in its ideological commitments and its current electoral advantages under existing rules.

Unfortunately, both interpretations are problematic from the perspective of the survival of US democracy and specifically from the perspective of a positive judicial influence on democracy. The best case scenario is that the country has been set off down a path of politicization of the judiciary. This has both obvious and more subtle effects on the remaining conditions for courts to influence democracy.

6.2.3 *The Supreme Court as a Republican Agent*

An argument that the federal judiciary of the United States is merely an arm of the Republican Party or the current president of the United States is very far from compelling. It is unclear how a judiciary as diverse as the American one could serve this purpose. As an empirical matter, the president and his agents commonly lose in federal court.[13]

Less clear is how the Supreme Court was coming to be understood in the early twenty-first century. Writing in *USA Today* in the wake of a Supreme Court decision that reversed a federal court judge's order extending the period for absentee balloting in Wisconsin's primary, Kurt Bardella put the problem as follows:

> For anyone hoping the Supreme Court will assert its role as the third branch of government, it has delayed hearing cases, including three lawsuits involving Trump's tax returns and financial dealings. And yet, somehow, the Supreme Court managed to reverse a federal judge's order to extend absentee voting by a week in Wisconsin's 2020 primary. The result was that voters had to choose between their health and their civic duty.
>
> The court's refusal to move forward with cases that impact the president, coupled with its willingness to interfere with the Wisconsin election, foreshadows a very dangerous path as we look ahead to the November elections. In essence, the court's conservative majority is just another political instrument for Trump to wield.[14]

Decisions of the Supreme Court by the end of 2020 were in tension with Bardella's account, but we do not need to take a position on whether he offered the correct view of the Supreme Court at the time. What matters is how current political leaders would have seen matters. If the court is broadly understood to share the interests of Republican executives, then it follows that the court should be broadly understood to oppose the interests of Democratic executives. There are two direct implications from our model if this idea fairly represented politics at the end of the Trump administration. The first is that Republican executives would have been more likely to engage in the kind of aggressive policy-making at the boundaries of their constitutional powers. The second is that Democratic executives will be less likely to do so. Another way of putting this is that Republican executives were better positioned to respond to true emergencies and yet they were also better positioned to aggrandize power opportunistically.

The Pew Research Center has documented an increasingly polarized view of the Supreme Court. In July 2019, there was a twenty-six-point gap between Republicans and Democrats' favorable views of the Supreme Court (76 to 49). Likewise, the share of liberal democrats who have a favorable view of the court dropped to a historic low of 40 percent.[15] It is not surprising that as polarization has increased,

13 See www.law.com/nationallawjournal/2019/12/27/trumps-2019-court-tab-all-the-major-losses-and-a-few-big-wins/.

14 www.usatoday.com/story/opinion/2020/04/09/trump-removes-inspectors-general-blatant-corruption-column/2973535001/.

15 See discussion in www.pewresearch.org/fact-tank/2019/08/07/partisan-gap-widens-in-views-of-the-supreme-court/.

views of national institutions have also polarized. But if the court comes to be viewed as "just another part" of the American political landscape, it is unclear that it will be able to draw on its legitimacy indefinitely.

A more alarming long-term issue concerns the information about the Supreme Court to which Americans are increasingly exposed. Legitimacy theorists suggest that the Supreme Court's legitimacy is constructed over time, both through an educational system that promotes an idealized view of the judiciary in American politics and via continuing favorable media coverage. Recent work by Bass (2018) has demonstrated that since roughly the year 2000, media coverage of the Supreme Court has become increasingly politicized and sensationalized. Where typical news stories about the court focused on jurisprudential points, stories in the modern era have increasingly placed the Supreme Court directly into a political discussion. This has been particularly true of coverage on cable news and blogs. If favorable media coverage that focuses on aspects of the "myth of legality" (the idea that American judges make decisions in fundamentally apolitical ways) is critical to the Supreme Court's sustained legitimacy, changes in its media coverage may have profound negative consequences.

6.3 WHERE THE AMERICAN JUDICIARY STANDS AND WHAT THIS MEANS

In this chapter, we have considered the claim that the American judiciary will be a bulwark of American democracy. There are many reasons to believe that the courts in the United States are well positioned to help insulate the state from breakdown. The federal judiciary is minimally independent, its judges are brave, noncompliance with court orders is costly, and the structural and institutional conditions for democratic compromise are generally met. That said, we have also highlighted a few caveats. Verbal attacks on federal judges are as high as they were during the 1930s. The Supreme Court's conservative majority may incentivize riskier behavior on behalf of Republican executives. Public opinion about the court is polarized, and there are reasons to worry that a polarized media environment is no longer possible to sustain a favorable long-term and positive image, which itself may reduce the costs of compliance.

It is helpful to develop these last points by considering the series of increasingly aggressive behavior we have observed from Republican elected officials at the end of 2020. Thinking about these cases from the perspective of the model suggests a series of counterfactuals. Suppose that instead of the current Supreme Court, it was packed with nine (or say five) close affiliates of Donald Trump. In such a case, would the secretary of state of Georgia have defended his state's electoral process? Would the president of the United States have been more likely to declare a national emergency? And then consider what would have happened if Merrick Garland had been appointed and Ruth Bader Ginsburg had retired during the Obama administration. Would we have observed the original travel ban? If the courts of the United States continue to be perceived as reflecting one party or the other, we should also expect to observe increasingly risky behavior on the part of power holders.

We are not in a position to give a definitive answer to these questions grounded in precise social science, but we can certainly speculate. We believe it is important to recognize that Republican officials who had real policy-making power over US elections (e.g. secretaries of state, governors, and lower-ranking electoral officers) handled the 2020 election results in ways that we would surely characterize as "normal." Elections were held, votes were recounted, and results were certified. The Electoral College met. If the Supreme Court was radically different and it appeared that a policy pathway existed that would have required defying court orders potentially some from the US Supreme Court, we suspect that there might have been different outcomes in Georgia or Arizona or Michigan.

In this discussion, we have placed considerable focus on the end of 2020, where the Supreme Court's majority shared interests with the Republican President. It is worth considering what happened following the transition to a Democratic administration. In terms of our argument, concerns about a lack of sufficient independence between the president and the Supreme Court flipped when Joseph Biden was inaugurated. Now, there is not a question about whether the Conservative majority is sufficiently independent of the Democratic president.

Yet, a series of different questions emerged. If the Democratic Party could, would it take the opportunity to increase the size of the court at least in order to address the perceived illegitimate appointment of Neil Gorsuch? How would that be viewed by Republicans in the opposition? This potential path of politicization has a very plausible end point: it may well take the costs of noncompliance with court orders to zero for some presidents, and if that happens, the democracy enhancing effect of independent courts will go to zero with it.

The breakdown of the Honduran democracy at the beginning of the twenty-first century provides a cautionary tale. In March of 2009, Manuel Zelaya, president of Honduras, instructed the National Statistics Institute (Instituto Nacional de Estadística, INE) to prepare a nonbinding referendum in which Hondurans would be asked to reveal an opinion about the possibility of holding a constituent assembly. Zelaya had been moving toward the political left for several years, filling his cabinet with progressive members of the Liberal Party and building relationships with Hugo Chávez and Daniel Ortega. These moves alienated both the major political parties of the country as well as economic elites and the military (Ruhl, 2010).

The proposed referendum was widely understood to be part of an effort to eliminate Honduras's constitutional prohibition on presidential reelection. Article 239 of the Constitution of Honduras not only prohibits reelection but makes even an indirect effort to advocate for the amendment of the article grounds for immediate loss of one's public office followed by a ten-year ban on holding any public function. When Zelaya's efforts were struck down by electoral and administrative courts, the president continued undeterred.[16] On June 26, 2009, the Honduran Supreme Court found that the president had failed to comply with the administrative order and ordered his arrest to answer charges against him. The military carried out this order, but instead of bringing Zelaya to answer questions before a court, it carried out a coup, flying Zelaya to exile in Costa Rica.

Honduran courts are very far from independent in the strong sense of the concept, i.e. in the sense that Honduran judges are unconnected to any particular political interest or party in the state. They also enjoy very low public support. Only 29 percent of respondents in the 2008 Honduras Latinobarometer sample provided a positive evaluation of the judiciary's work. In the case of Zelaya, the Supreme Court stood with forces opposed to the president, including the center and right wings of the Liberal Party. Zelaya would have expected some opposition from the courts, but given the low esteem with which the courts are held in Honduras, coupled with his efforts to build a new mass coalition, it is doubtable that the president would have necessarily expected much of a public backlash from ignoring a court order.

There is certainly a colorable argument that the court's decision aimed to protect a fairly important element of the Honduran constitution. This is the kind of active use of a court's power that we might like to point to as illustrating how courts defend democracies. The episode nevertheless illustrates how an active attempt to defend principles may not succeed. The counterfactual we would like to consider is whether Zelaya would have pushed forward with his proposal if the Honduran judiciary enjoyed strong public support and was not understood to be strongly connected to his rivals.

If political elites in the United States are not careful, if they insist on politicizing the courts, they may very well eliminate a very useful source of democratic stability by freeing American presidents to more frequently engage in behavior on the boundary of regime rules.

16 "Juzgado ordena a FF AA no participar en encuesta," *La Prensa* Online, June 19, 2009, www.laprensa.hn/honduras/531803-97/juzgado-ordena-a-ff-aa-no-participar-en-encuesta.

7

Conclusion

Remember Democracy never lasts long. It soon wastes exhausts and murders itself. There never was a Democracy yet, that did not commit suicide.

John Adams 1814

Presently, democracy is under assault worldwide. Newly inaugurated democracies are registering shorter lifetimes, and even well-established regimes are backsliding on critical features of liberal democracy (Levitsky and Way, 2010; Lührmann and Lindberg, 2019). Moreover, illiberal threats to democracy have spared no region of the world. Symptoms of democratic decline exist on nearly every continent, with indicators of regime health flashing yellow. Across the globe, scholars, practitioners, and international NGOs have all sounded warnings. The overriding question facing the international democratic community is how to shore up current democracies against further slippage. Specifically, what institutions, if any, might help democracies endure?

7.1 HOW COURTS MAY DEFEND DEMOCRACY

In this book, we have considered how one institution, the courts, might play a role in promoting democratic regime survival. To do so, we have built upon insights from scholars writing within two traditions: the literatures on democratic regimes and judicial politics. We have attempted to argue that each of these traditions offers a valuable starting point into the inquiry on how courts may help stabilize regimes.

We built our argument on insights from the democratic regimes' literature to understand the role that institutions play in easing the democratic compromise. The standard view of democracy as a self-enforcing equilibrium between contending political forces underscores conducive structural conditions, such as high levels of income, as critical to easing bargaining dilemmas. This view minimizes the role of institutions. Perhaps the most extreme expression of this view is that other than declaring the winners and losers of elections, institutions need play no role in securing the democratic equilibrium, economic development is sufficient (Przeworski et al., 2000; Przeworski, 2005). Still, others allow a role for specific democracy-preserving institutions if they enhance the power of the elite, providing added weight to elite preferences (Acemoglu, Johnson, and Robinson, 2001). If, under certain conditions, citizens may opt to employ institutions such as party systems or presidentialism as commitment devices to afford greater weight to elite preferences, then prospects for consolidated democracy may be strengthened. We have taken a slightly different tack here.

Building on our earlier work, we have argued that institutions under democracy can play a role in policing the democratic compromise (Reenock, Staton, and Radean, 2013). By relaxing assumptions in prior work regarding collective action and coordination, we have argued that institutions are useful at resolving a problem that immediately arises when groups transfer power peacefully by election – the implementation and maintenance of the democratic bargain. We argued that one institution in particular, independent courts, can help by addressing (1) monitoring problems that follow from the nature of democratic policy-making and (2) challenges of social coordination that are essential to the process by which observed violations of limits on state authority are remedied. We have argued that, when the underlying conditions for democratic compromise have been met, the courts help leaders establish credible promises to respect rights, thereby avoiding unnecessary conflict.

We also built our argument on insights from the literature on judicial politics that highlight independent courts as a product of democracy itself. Scholars have suggested that independent courts are desirable under conditions of high political competition. They are "insurance policies" against losses of power. We agree that incentives to create and sustain independent courts are strongest under conditions of high political competition. We have argued that part of the way in which courts offer insurance is by creating a mechanism that helps opposition groups monitor current leaders. But more importantly, we suggest that the system itself lowers incentives among current leaders to engage in behavior that arguably violates fundamental regime rules.

To serve this kind of role, judges encounter a dilemma. Courts charged with holding leaders accountable to limits on their authority are asked in many systems to make decisions that may be institutionally and personally costly. In such settings, the incentives for strategic deference are particularly high; and yet, if courts are strategically deferential, they do not serve their state constraint function. We have considered how judges that confront such tensions might nevertheless contribute to regime stability.

In the end, we have offered an account that merges insights across these literatures with our own to explain how independent courts can assist democratic survival. Our account provides an explanation for why elites might wish to provide independent judicial systems, illustrates how independent courts help reinforce democratic commitments by both solving informational problems and incentivizing prudent policy-making, and identifies what is required of a political system for this mutually reinforcing relationship to work. In short, courts help provide incentives for leaders and the opposition to be prudent, and thus lower the stakes of holding power.

Of course, independent courts are not a universal remedy for democratic shortcomings. Our results suggest that a court's ability to provide benefits for democratic regimes is circumscribed by underlying structural conditions as well as sociocultural features that embolden judges and provide them space within which to function as we propose. We discuss these conditions in the next section.

7.2 COURTS AS DEFENDERS OF DEMOCRACY: IMPORTANT IMPLICATIONS

Like others before us, we find that judicial independence is broadly promoting of democratic regime survival. Managing beliefs about the extent to which leaders are constrained is an important political challenge. We have argued that independent judiciaries help address this challenge in a number of ways. They incentivize leaders to be careful about the possible solutions to policy challenges that they see, though in so doing they create the possibility that leaders fail to take decisive action when they should. In cases where leaders are willing to move forward with arguably questionable policies, independent courts help translate conflict among political competitors into conflict within the institutions of the state. It is in this regard that independent courts help establish credible commitments and serve as insurance policies if power is transferred. There are, however, important implications that follow from our argument.

7.2.1 *Courts Cannot Police Nonexistent Bargains*

A critical lesson of our earlier work and one that we wish to emphasize again here is that courts will only be useful in so far as competing groups wish to sustain democratic cooperation (Reenock, Staton, and Radean, 2013). If fundamental structural conditions for democracy are not met or are tenuous, then courts will find it quite challenging to function as a tool for reinforcing democratic commitments. Simply put, courts do not lock in commitments to democracy; they help resolve monitoring problems inherent in the democratic arrangement. But the basis of that arrangement must exist for courts to play a democracy-preserving role.

To be clear, we are not claiming that independent courts bestow no benefits upon either newly inaugurated democracies or those with delicate democratic commitments. Independent courts contribute to broader rule of law assurances, leading to greater incentives for domestic and international investment (Voigt, Gutmann, and Feld, 2015) and reduced corruption (Ríos-Figueroa, 2012). All of these potential outcomes may indirectly ease distributional conflict through economic growth and development (Acemoglu, Johnson, and Robinson, 2001; Haggard and Tiede, 2011). Moreover, public commitments to democracy may be shaped in part by citizen evaluations of judicial independence (Gibson and Nelson, 2014). Despite these potential indirect paths, we nevertheless caution against concluding that courts are bulwarks for democracy under all conditions. If underlying commitments are sufficiently weak, independent courts will be unable to enhance directly a democratic regime's likelihood to survive.

7.2.2 *Courts Cannot Police Bargains That Have Already Broken Down*

An additional lesson of our book is that the primary power of the court lies in incentivizing prudence among political leaders. A powerful court is one that can encourage other actors to forego certain behaviors. This notion of power is one that evokes earlier work in political science on the "second face of power" or what Bachrach and Baratz called the "restrictive face of power" (Bachrach and Baratz, 1962, p. 952). In highlighting one actor's ability to exert power over another they note:

> But whatever the case, the central point to be made is the same: to the extent that a person or group-consciously or unconsciously creates or reinforces barriers to the public airing of policy conflicts, that person or group has power. (p. 949)

In other words, in addition to a court's ability to set aside government actions, another avenue of a court's power can be found in its ability to incentivize leaders to *never take up* certain actions or policies. The court function that we imagine is one that incentivizes leaders to resist advancing questionable policies. An important implication of our argument for the question of evaluating Anthony Romero's claim that courts serve as bulwarks of democracy is that when courts are called upon to defend democracy in the face of an aggressive executive, it may already be too late. In this respect, the view of courts as an effective external check on government authority has already broken down.

While judicial independence is a particularly helpful resource for democratic interests to draw upon, it is also one that can experiences rapid breakdowns. One element of the current worldwide erosion of liberal democracy is concerted attacks against independent courts. We have found considerable evidence that regimes characterized by a latent propensity for significant interbranch conflict, where courts are openly critiqued, purged, and packed when possible are particularly vulnerable to instability. We envision two types of consequences of this kind of politics. The first, on which we focus considerable theoretical attention, is that judges in such contexts will have particularly strong incentives to avoid political conflict. This type of dynamic is reflected in former Venezuela Supreme Court president Cecilia Sosa's comments as she stepped down from her post following the court's approval of the Chávez-led Constituent Assembly's assertion of emergency powers: "The court simply committed suicide to avoid being assassinated. But the result is the same. It is dead."[1]

1 "Top Venezuelan judge resigns," BBC News, August 25, 1999, http://news.bbc.co.uk/l/hi/world/americas/429304.stm.

The second consequence, which would undermine judicial independence in a distinct way, is that courts in these contexts become simple tools of interparty competition (Pérez-Liñán and Castagnola, 2009), tools used to discredit opposition leaders or otherwise harass domestic competitors (e.g. Aydın, 2013; Popova, 2010). This kind of court may become embroiled in political controversy, but there is no serious sense in which its involvement will be understood as injecting independent judgment. In neither case will judges materially impact regime outcomes – indeed, they may be part of the process by which the regime collapses.

7.2.3 *Noncompliance, Courts, and Democracy?*

We have also found that a latent propensity for noncompliance with important decisions is not particularly problematic for democratic regime survival. We do not claim that the routine defiance of courts with constitutional review authority is to be promoted or itself necessarily without harm. We claim instead that noncompliance need not be a totally uncommon or particularly destructive element of a political system. In many cases, noncompliance will follow from an executive's judgment that the particular context in which the decision is issued simply cannot be prudently obeyed. In a speech to Congress explaining his refusal to release John Merryman from a Fort McHenry prison cell at the beginning of the US Civil War, Abraham Lincoln asked, "[A]re all the laws, but one, to go unexecuted, and the Government itself go to pieces, lest that one be violated? Even in such a case, would not the official oath be broken, if the Government should be overthrown, when it was believed that disregarding the single law, would tend to preserve it?"[2]

Of course, these types of claims may very well mask goals that fundamentally undermine regime rules. The point is that courts that enjoy reasonably broad support, especially courts that are understood to be independent of major political competitors in a society, raise the stakes of noncompliance, and by so doing, help transfer information about the true motives of a leader. It is in this way that we understand the periodic forms of noncompliance in states with reasonably strong rule of law commitments like the United States, Costa Rica, Germany, or Israel.

In the end, for this type of mechanism to work, judges must not be "single-minded pursuers of compliance," an assumption that is commonly made in the political science literature on judicial politics. While it is unlikely that judges prefer a world in which orders are routinely ignored, there is abundant evidence that judges understand that legal systems sometimes require flexibility.

7.3 OPEN QUESTIONS

An open question is: how might reformers go about constructing judicial independence? Our work here has little to say on precise reform proposals to nurture judicial

[2] Abraham Lincoln, Message to Congress in Special Session, July 4, 1861.

independence. Our analyses from Chapter 3 provide evidence that political competition supplies elites incentives to support judicial independence. However, the path to constructing independent courts, to the extent that such institutional engineering is possible, is fraught with challenges. Our analyses also suggest that the provision of de jure institutions, while perhaps a necessary condition for independent courts, is likely not a sufficient one. There does not appear to be a magical combination of formal rules alone that renders courts independent. Therefore even reformers with the purest intentions are likely to fall short of "constructing" independent courts through formal institutional design alone.

In addition to formal institutions, many scholars of judicial politics have argued that courts rely, in part, on large reservoirs of public support to enhance their judicial independence. To enhance a court's independence, any reform initiative likely must include a plan to build up the public's confidence in the judiciary. But how do citizens establish their priors and update their beliefs about the courts? Gibson and Nelson (2014) offer a summary of whether and how judicial decisions can change public opinion. In brief, they suggest that democratic values strongly relate to individual assessment of court legitimacy. Moreover, the public's reaction to judicial decisions may hinge on important societal actors' attempts to frame the public's interpretation. The media's, elites', and citizens' own preexisting attitudes all serve as lenses through which citizens view and evaluate judicial acts. While more research on these mechanisms is required, political elites may very well have legitimacy-enhancing effects on citizen attitudes toward the courts and, by extension, judicial independence.

Whatever the origins of their autonomy, our work suggests that independent courts can be bulwarks of democracy. But, their ability to perform this function manifests in their capacity to incentivize political elites to be more judicious in their words, more mindful of their actions, and more cautious in their responses to crises – or, in other words, to be more prudent.

Bibliography

Acemoglu, Daron, and James A. Robinson. 2006. *Economic Origins of Dictatorship and Democracy*. New York: Cambridge University Press.

Acemoglu, Daron, Simon Johnson, and James A. Robinson. 2001. "The Colonial Origins of Comparative Development: An Empirical Investigation." *American Economic Review* 91(5):1369–1401.

Alter, Karen J. 2008. "Agents or Trustees? International Courts in Their Political Context." *European Journal of International Relations* 14(1):33–63.

Apodaca, Clair. 2004. "The Rule of Law and Human Rights." *Judicature* 87(6):292–299.

Association for Civil Rights in Israel. 2010. "Government Institutions." In *Project Democracy: Fighting for the Ground Rules*. https://law.acri.org.il/he/wp-content/uploads/2011/08/democ-chap3-en.pdf

Aydın, Aylin. 2013. "Judicial Independence across Democratic Regimes: Understanding the Varying Impact of Political Competition." *Law and Society Review* 47(1):105–134.

Bachrach, Peter, and Morton S. Baratz. 1962. "Two Faces of Power." *American Political Science Review* 56(4):947–952.

Bahry, Donna, and Young Hum Kim. 2021. "Executive Turnover and the Investigation of Former Leaders in New Democracies." *Political Research Quarterly* 74(1): 199–211.

Banks, Arthur S., and Kenneth A. Wilson. n.d. "Cross-National Time-Series Data Archive. Databanks International." www.cntsdata.com

Barak, Aharon. 2002. "A Judge on Judging: The Role of a Supreme Court in a Democracy." *Harvard Law Review* 116(16):19–162.

Bass, Leeann. 2018. Covering the Court: The Impact of a Modern Era of Journalism. PhD diss., Emory University Atlanta.

Becker, Theodore Lewis, and Malcolm Feeley. 1973. *The Impact of Supreme Court Decisions: Empirical Studies*. 2nd ed. New York: Oxford University Press.

Bernhard, Michael, Allen Hicken, Christopher Reenock, and Staffan I. Lindberg. 2020. "Parties, Civil Society, and the Deterrence of Democratic Defection." *Studies in Comparative International Development* 55(1):1–26.

Bernhard, Michael, Christopher Reenock, and Timothy Nordstrom. 2003. "Economic Performance and Survival in New Democracies: Is There a Honeymoon Effect?" *Comparative Political Studies* 36(4):404–431.

Bill Chávez, Rebecca, John A. Ferejohn, and Barry A. Weingast. 2011. "A Theory of the Politically Independent Judiciary: A Comparative Study of the United States and Argentina." In *Courts in Latin America*, ed. Gretchen Helmke and Julio Ríos-Figueroa. New York: Cambridge University Press, pp. 219–247.

Birkby, Robert H. 1966. "The Supreme Court and the Bible Belt: Tennessee Reaction to the 'Schempp' Decision." *Midwest Journal of Political Science* 10(3):304–319.

Bjørnskov, Christian, and Stefan Voigt. 2018. "The Architecture of Emergency Constitutions." *International Journal of Constitutional Law* 16(1):101–127.

Boix, Carles. 2003. *Democracy and Redistribution*. New York: Cambridge University Press.

Boix, Carles, Michael Miller, and Sebastian Rosato. 2012. "A Complete Data Set of Political Regimes, 1800–2007." *Comparative Political Studies* 20(10):1–32.

Brinks, Daniel M., and Abby Blass. 2018. *The DNA of Constitutional Justice in Latin America: Politics, Governance, and Judicial Design*. New York: Cambridge University Press.

Bull, Jesse, and Joel Watson. 2004. "Evidence Disclosure and Verifiability." *Journal of Economic Theory* 118(1):1–31.

Calvo, Ernesto, and Gabriel Negretto. 2019. "When (Electoral) Opportunity Knocks: Weak Institutions, Political Shocks, and Electoral Reforms in Latin America." In *The Politics of Institutional Weakness in Latin America*, ed. Daniel M. Brinks, Steven Levitsky, and Ma Victoria Murillo. New York: Cambridge University Press, pp. 41–60.

Cameron, Maxwell A. 1998. "Self-Coups: Peru, Guatemala, and Russia." *Journal of Democracy* 9(1):125–139.

Cane, Peter. 2004. "Understanding Judicial Review and Its Impact." In *Judicial Review and Bureaucratic Impact: International and Interdisciplinary Perspectives*, ed. Marc Hertogh and Simon Halliday. Cambridge: Cambridge University Press, pp. 15–42.

Carey, John M. 2003. "The Reelection Debate in Latin America." *Latin American Politics and Society* 45(1):119–133.

Carrubba, Clifford J. 2005. "Courts and Compliance in International Regulatory Regimes." *Journal of Politics* 67(3):669–689.

Carrubba, Clifford J., and Matthew J. Gabel. 2014. *International Courts and the Performance of International Agreements: A General Theory with Evidence from the European Union*. New York: Cambridge University Press.

Carrubba, Clifford J., and Christopher Zorn. 2010. "Executive Discretion, Judicial Decision Making, and Separation of Powers in the United States." *Journal of Politics* 72(3): 812–824.

Carrubba, Clifford J., Matthew Gabel, and Charles Hankla. 2008. "Judicial Behavior under Political Constraints: Evidence from the European Court of Justice." *American Political Science Review* 102(4):435–452.

Castagnola, Andrea, and Aníbal Pérez-Liñán. 2011. *The Rise (and Fall) of Judicial Review*. Cambridge: Cambridge University Press, p. 278.

Cepeda-Espinosa, Manuel José. 2004. "Judicial Activism in a Violent Context: The Origin, Role, and Impact of the Colombian Constitutional Court." *Washington University Global Studies Law Review* 3:537–687.

2009. "The Constitutional Protection of IDPs in Colombia." In *Judicial Protection of Internally Displaced Persons: The Colombian Experience*, ed. Rodolfo Arango Rivadeneira. Washington DC: Brookings Institute – University of Bern Project on Internal Displacement, pp. 1–48.

Cheibub, José Antonio. 2007. *Presidentialism, Parliamentarism, and Democracy*. Cambridge: Cambridge University Press.

Chilton, Adam S., and Mila Versteeg. 2018. "Courts' Limited Ability to Protect Constitutional Rights." *University of Chicago Law Review* 85(2):293–336.

2020. *How Constitutional Rights Matter*. New York: Oxford University Press.

Cingranelli, David L., and David L. Richards. 2008. "The Cingranelli-Richards (CIRI) Human Rights Dataset." www.humanrightsdata.org.

Clark, Tom S. 2010. *The Limits of Judicial Independence*. New York: Cambridge University Press.

Clark, Tom S., and Jonathan P. Kastellec. 2013. "The Supreme Court and Percolation in the Lower Courts: An Optimal Stopping Model." *Journal of Politics* 75(1):150–168.

Clark, Tom S., and Jeffrey K. Staton. 2015. "An Informational Model of Constitutional Jurisdiction." *Journal of Politics* 77(3):589–607.

Conaghan, Catherine M. 2012. "Prosecuting Presidents: The Politics within Ecuador's Corruption Cases." *Journal of Latin American Studies* 44(4):649–678.

Coppedge, Michael, John Gerring, David Altman, Michael Bernhard, Steven Fish, Allen Hicken, Matthew Kroenig, Staffan I. Lindberg, Kelly McMann, Pamela Paxton, Jeffrey K. Staton, Holli A. Semetko, Svend-Erik Skaaning, Jeffrey Staton, and Jan Teorell. 2011. "Conceptualizing and Measuring Democracy: A New Approach." *Perspectives on Politics* 9(2):247–267.

Coppedge, Michael, John Gerring, Carl Henrik Knutsen, Staffan I. Lindberg, Svend-Erik Skaaning, Jan Teorell, David Altman, Michael Bernhard, Agnes Cornell, M. Steven Fish, Haakon Gjerløw, Adam Glynn, Allen Hicken, Joshua Krusell, Anna Lührmann, Kyle L. Marquardt, Kelly McMann, Valeriya Mechkova, Moa Olin, Pamela Paxton, Daniel Pemstein, Brigitte Seim, Rachel Sigman, Jeffrey Staton, Aksel Sundtröm, Eitan Tzelgov, Luca Uberti, Yi-ting Wang, Tore Wig, and Daniel Ziblatt. 2018. "V-Dem Codebook v8." *Varieties of Democracy (V-Dem) Project.*

Coppedge, Michael, John Gerring, Staffan I. Lindberg, Svend-Erik Skaaning, Jan Teorell, David Altman, Michael Bernhard, M. Steven Fish, Adam Glynn, Allen Hicken, Carl Henrik Knutsen, Joshua Krusell, Anna Lührmann, Kyle L. Marquardt, Kelly McMann, Valeriya Mechkova, Moa Olin, Pamela Paxton, Daniel Pemstein, Josefine Pernes, Constanza Sanhueza Petrarca, Johannes von Römer, Laura Saxer, Brigitte Seim, Rachel Sigman, Jeffrey Staton, Natalia Stepanova, and Steven Wilson. 2017. "V-Dem Country-Year/Country-Date Dataset v7.1."

Coppedge, Michael, John Gerring, Staffan I. Lindberg, Jan Teorell, David Altman, Michael Bernhard, M. Steven Fish, Adam Glynn, Allen Hicken, Carl Henrik Knutsen, Kelly McMann, Daniel Pemstein, Megan Reif, Svend-Erik Skaaning, Jeffrey Staton, Eitan Tzelgov, Yi-ting Wang, and Brigitte Zimmerman. 2015a. *Varieties of Democracy: Methodology v4*. 4th ed. Varieties of Democracy Institute, Department of Political Science, University of Gothenburg. Varieties of Democracy Project.

2015b. *Varieties of Democracy: Codebook v4*. 4th ed. Varieties of Demoracy Institute, Department of Political Science, University of Gothenburg. Varieties of Democracy Project.

Corrales, Javier. 2016. "Can Anyone Stop the President? Power Asymmetries and Term Limits in Latin America, 1984–2016." *Latin American Politics and Society* 58(2):3–25.

Elkins, Zachary, Tom Ginsburg, and James Melton. 2009. *The Endurance of National Constitutions*. Cambridge University Press.

2014. "The Content of Authoritarian Constitutions." In *Constitutions in Authoritarian Regimes*, ed. Tom Ginsburg and Alberto Simpser. Cambridge Press, pp. 141–164.

Elkins, Zachary, Tom Ginsburg, James Melton, Robert Shaffer, Juan F. Sequeda, and Daniel P. Miranker. 2014. "Constitute: The World's Constitutions to Read, Search, and Compare." *Journal of Web Semantics* 27:10–18.

Engst, Benjamin. 2019. *The Two Faces of Judicial Power: The Dynamics of Judicial-Political Bargaining*. Cham Switzerland: Palgrave Macmillan.

Epperly, Brad. 2013. "The Provision of Insurance? Judicial Independence and the Post-Tenure Fate of Leaders." *Journal of Law and Courts* 1(2):247–278.

2019. *The Political Foundations of Judicial Independence in Dictatorship and Democracy*. Oxford University Press.

Epstein, Lee, and Jack Knight. 1998. *The Choices Justices Make*. Washington DC: CQ Press.

Fariss, Christopher J., Therese Anders, and Jonathan N. Markowitz. 2020. "New Estimates of Over 500 Years of Historic GDP and Population Data." Unpublished manuscript.

Feld, Lars P., and Stefan Voigt. 2003. "Economic Growth and Judicial Independence: Cross-Country Evidence Using a New Set of Indicators." *European Journal of Political Economy* 19(3):497–527.

Finkel, Jodi S. 2008. *Judicial Reform as Political Insurance: Argentina, Peru, and Mexico in the 1990s*. South Bend, IN: University of Notre Dame Press.

Friedman, Barry. 2002. "The Birth of an Academic Obsession: The History of the Counter-Majoritarian Difficulty, Part Five." *Yale Law Journal* 112(2):153–259.

Gallie, W. B. 1956. "Essentially.Contested Concepts." *Proceedings of the Aristotelian Society* 51:167–198.

Gibson, James L., and Michael J. Nelson. 2014. "The Legitimacy of the US Supreme Court: Conventional Wisdoms and Recent Challenges Thereto." *Annual Review of Law and Social Science* 10:201–219.

Ginsburg, Tom. 2003. *Judicial Review in New Democracies: Constitutional Courts in Asian Cases*. New York: Cambridge University Press.

Ginsburg, Tom, and Aziz Z. Huq. 2018. *How to Save a Constitutional Democracy*. University of Chicago Press.

Ginsburg, Tom, and Tamir Moustafa. 2008. *Rule by Law: The Politics of Courts in Authoritarian Regimes*. Cambridge University Press.

Ginsburg, Tom, and Mila Versteeg. 2013. "Why Do Countries Adopt Constitutional Review?" *Journal of Law, Economics, and Organization* 30(3):587–622.

Goemans, Henk E., Kristian Skrede Gleditsch, and Giacomo Chiozza. 2009. "Introducing Archigos: A Dataset of Political Leaders." *Journal of Peace Research* 46(2): 269–283.

Gross, Oren. 2011. Constitutions and Emergency Regimes. In *Comparative Constitutional Law*, ed. Tom Ginsburg and Rosalind Dixon. Research Handbooks in Comparative Law. Cheltenham, UK: Edward Elgar Publishing, pp. 334–355.

Guha-Sapir, Debarati, Philippe Hoyois, and Regina Below. 2014. Annual Disaster Statistical Review: Numbers and Trends 2013. Technical report.

Hafner-Burton, Emilie M., Laurence R. Helfer, and Christopher J. Fariss. 2011a. "Emergency and Escape: Explaining Derogations from Human Rights Treaties." *International Organization* 65(4):673–707.

2011b. "States of Emergency Codebook." Provided by authors.

Haggard, Stephan and Lydia Tiede. 2011. "The Rule of Law and Economic Growth: Where Are We?" *World Development* 39(5):673–685.

Han, Sung Min, and Eric C. C. Chang. 2016. "Economic Inequality, Winner-Loser Gap, and Satisfaction with Democracy." *Electoral Studies* 44:85–97.

Hanssen, F. Andrew. 2004. "Is There a Politically Optimal Level of Judicial Independence?" *American Economic Review* 94(3):712–729.

Hayo, Bernd, and Stefan Voigt. 2007. "Explaining De Facto Judicial Independence." *International Review of Law and Economics* 27(3):269–290.

Helmke, Gretchen. 2005. *Courts under Constraints*. Cambridge University Press.

2010. "The Origins of Institutional Crises in Latin America." *American Journal of Political Science* 54(3):737–750.

Houle, Christian. 2009. "Inequality and Democracy: Why Inequality Harms Consolidation but Does Not Affect Democratization." *World Politics* 61(4):589–622.

Huneeus, Alexandra. 2010. "Judging from a Guilty Conscience: The Chilean Judiciary's Human Rights Turn." *Law and Social Inquiry* 35(1):99–135.

Hutchinson, Dennis J. 2010. "Lincoln the Dictator." *South Dakota Law Review* 55:284–298.

Iacus, Stefano, Gary King, Matthew Blackwell, and Giuseppe Porro. 2009. "CEM: Coarsened Exact Matching in Stata." *Stata Journal* 9:524–546.

International Center for Ethics, Justice and Public Life. n.d. "The International Rule of Law: Coordination and Collaboration in Global Justice."

Jackson, Vicki, and Mark Tushnet. 2006. *Comparative Constitutional Law*. 2nd ed. New York: Foundation Press.

Keith, Linda Camp. 2002. "Judicial Independence and Human Rights Protection around the World." *Judicature* 85(4):195–200.

Kouba, Karel. 2016. "Party Institutionalization and the Removal of Presidential Term Limits in Latin America." *Revista de Ciencia Política* 36(2):433–457.

Kuran, Timur. 1991. "The East European Revolution of 1989: Is It Surprising That We Were Surprised?" *American Economic Review* 81(2):121–125.

LaFree, Gary, and Laura Dugan. 2007. "Introducing the Global Terrorism Database." *Terrorism and Political Violence* 19(2):181–204.

Landau, David, Yaniv Roznai, and Rosalind Dixon. 2019. "Term Limits and the Unconstitutional Constitutional Amendment Doctrine: Lessons from Latin America." In *The Politics of Presidential Term Limits, ed.* Alexander Baturo and Robert Elgie. Oxford University Press, pp. 53–74.

La Porta, Rafael, Florencio López de Silanes, Cristian Pop-Eleches, and Andrei Shleifer. 2004. "Judicial Checks and Balances." *Journal of Political Economy* 112(2):445–470.

Law, David S., and Mila Versteeg. 2013. "Sham Constitutions." *California Law Review* 101:863–952.

Levitsky, Steven, and Lucan A. Way. 2010. *Competitive Authoritarianism: Hybrid Regimes after the Cold War*. Cambridge University Press.

Levitsky, Steven, and Daniel Ziblatt. 2018. *How Democracies Die*. New York: Broadway Books.

Linz, Juan J. 1990. "The Perils of Presidentialism." *Journal of Democracy* 1(1):51–69.

Linz, Juan J., and Alfred C. Stepan. 1996. *Problems of Democratic Consolidation*. Baltimore, MD: Johns Hopkins University Press.

Linzer, Drew A., and Jeffrey K. Staton. 2011. "A Measurement Model for Synthesizing Multiple Comparative Indicators: The Case of Judicial Independence." Presented at the annual meeting of the American Political Science Association, Seattle, Washington, September 1–4.

2015. "A Global Measure of Judicial Independence, 1948–2012." *Journal of Law and Courts* 3(2):223–256.

Lipset, Seymour M. 1959. "Some Social Requisites of Democracy: Economic Development and Political Legitimacy." *American Political Science Review* 53(1):69–105.

Lührmann, Anna, and Staffan I. Lindberg. 2019. "A Third Wave of Autocratization Is Here: What Is New About It?" *Democratization* 26(7):1095–1113.

Mainwaring, Scott. 1993. "Presidentialism, Multipartism, and Democracy: The Difficult Combination." *Comparative Political Studies* 26(2):198–228.

Marshall, Monty, Ted Robert Gurr, Christian Davenport, and Keith Jaggers. 2002. "Polity IV, 1800–1999: Comments on Munck and Verkuilen." *Comparative Political Studies* 35(1):40–45.

Martin, Andrew D. 2006. "Statutory Battles and Constitutional Wars: Congress and the Supreme Court." In *Institutional Games and the US Supreme Court*, ed. James R. Rogers, Roy P. Flemming, and Jon R. Bond. Charlottesville: University of Virginia Press, pp. 23–43.

McMillan, John, and Pablo Zoido. 2004. "How to Subvert Democracy: Montesinos in Peru." *Journal of Economic Perspectives* 18(4):69–92.

Melton, James, and Tom Ginsburg. 2014. "Does De Jure Judicial Independence Really Matter? A Reevaluation of Explanations for Judicial Independence." *Journal of Law and Courts* 2(2):187–217.

Miaschi, John. 2017. "Countries with Uncodified Constitutions." www.worldatlas.com/articles/countries-with-uncodified-constitutions.html

Miklaucic, Michael. 2002. "Guidance for Promoting Judicial Independence and Impartiality," rev. ed. Technical report. US Agency for International Development.

Nelson, Michael J., and James L. Gibson. 2017. "US Supreme Court Legitimacy: Unanswered Questions and an Agenda for Future Research". In *Routledge Handbook of Judicial Behavior*, ed. Robert M Howard and Kirk A Randazzo. London: Routledge, pp. 132–150.

Office of Democracy and Governance. 2002. "Guidance for Promoting Judicial Independence and Impartiality," rev. ed.

Pemstein, Daniel, Stephen A. Meserve, and James Melton. 2010. "Democratic Compromise: A Latent Variable Analysis of Ten Measures of Regime Type." *Political Analysis* 18(4):426–449.

Pereira, Carlos, and Marcus André Melo. 2012. "The Surprising Success of Multiparty Presidentialism." *Journal of Democracy* 23(3):156–170.

Pérez-Liñán, Aníbal, and Andrea Castagnola. 2009. "Presidential Control of High Courts in Latin America: A Long-Term View (1904–2006)." *Journal of Politics in Latin America* 1(2):87–114.

Political Risk Group. 2004. *The International Country Risk Guide, Part II*. New York: PRS Group. www.columbia.edu/acis/eds/dgate/pdf/C3743.icrgextract_busguide04.pdf

Popova, Maria. 2010. "Political Competition as an Obstacle to Judicial Independence: Evidence from Russia and Ukraine." *Comparative Political Studies* 43(10): 1202–1229.

Powell, Jonathan M., and Clayton L. Thyne. 2011. "Global Instances of Coups from 1950 to 2010: A New Dataset." *Journal of Peace Research* 48(2):249–259.

Power, Timothy J., and Mark J. Gasiorowski. 1997. "Institutional Design and Democratic Consolidation in the Third World." *Comparative Political Studies* 30(2):123–155.

Przeworski, Adam. 2003. "Minimalist Conception of Democracy: A Defense." In *The Democracy Sourcebook*, ed. Robert A Dahl, Ian Shapiro, and José Antônio Cheibub. Cambridge, MA: MIT Press, pp. 12–17.

2005. "Democracy as an Equilibrium." *Public Choice* 123(3):253–273.

Przeworski, Adam, Michael Alvarez, José Antonio Cheibub, and Fernando Limongi. 2000. *Democracy and Development: Political Institutions and Well-Being in the World, 1950–1990*. New York: Cambridge University Press.

Ramraj, Victor V. 2008. *Emergencies and the Limits of Legality*. Cambridge University Press.

Raz, Joseph. 1997. "The Rule of Law and Its Virtue." *Law Quarterly Review* 93:195–202.

Reenock, Christopher, Michael Bernhard, and Timothy Nordstrom. 2007. "Regressive Socioeconomic Distribution and Democratic Survival." *International Studies Quarterly* 51:677–699.

Reenock, Christopher, Jeffrey K. Staton, and Marius Radean. 2013. "Legal Institutions and Democratic Survival." *Journal of Politics* 75(2):491–505.

Ríos-Figueroa, Julio. 2012. "Justice System Institutions and Corruption Control: Evidence from Latin America." *Justice System Journal* 33(2):195–214.

2016. *Constitutional Courts as Mediators: Armed Conflict, Civil-Military Relations, and the Rule of Law in Latin America*. Cambridge University Press.

Ríos-Figueroa, Julio, and Jeffrey K Staton. 2014. "An Evaluation of Cross-National Measures of Judicial Independence." *Journal of Law, Economics, and Organization* 30(1):104–137.

Rodríguez-Raga, Juan Carlos. 2011. "Strategic Deference in the Colombian Constitutional Court." In *Courts in Latin America*, ed. Gretchen Helmke and Julio Ríos Figueroa. Cambridge University Press.

Rogers, James R. 2001. "Information and Judicial Review: A Signaling Game of Legislative-Judicial Interaction." *American Journal of Political Science* 45(1):84–99.

Roht-Arriaza, Naomi. 2009. "The Multiple Prosecutions of Augusto Pinochet." In *Prosecuting Heads of State*, ed. Ellen L. Lutz and Caitlin Reiger. Cambridge University Press, pp. 77–94.

Roznai, Yaniv. 2013. "Unconstitutional Constitutional Amendments: The Migration and Success of a Constitutional Idea." *American Journal of Comparative Law* 61(3):657–720.

Ruhl, Mark. 2010. "Honduras Unravels." *Journal of Democracy* 21(2):93–107.

Scheppele, Kim Lane. 2005. "Democracy by Judiciary. Or, Why Courts Can Be More Democratic Than Parliaments." In *Rethinking the Rule of Law after Communism* ed. Adam Czarnota, Martin Krygier, and Wojciech Sadurski. Budapest: Central European University Press, pp. 25–60.

Schumpeter, Joseph A. 1942. *Capitalism, Socialism and Democracy*. New York: Harper & Brothers.

Schwartz, Herman. 2000. *The Struggle for Constitutional Justice in Post-Communist Europe*. University of Chicago Press.

Shapiro, Martin M. 1981. *Courts: A Comparative and Political Analysis*. University of Chicago Press.

Sikkink, Kathryn. 2011. *The Justice Cascade: How Human Rights Prosecutions Are Changing World Politics (The Norton Series in World Politics)*. New York: W. W. Norton.

Spriggs, James F. 1996. "The Supreme Court and Federal Administrative Agencies: A Resource-Based Theory and Analysis of Judicial Impact." *American Journal of Political Science* 40(4):1122–1151.

1997. "Explaining Federal Bureaucratic Compliance with Supreme Court Opinions." *Political Research Quarterly* 50(3):567–593.

Staton, Jeffrey K., and Will H. Moore. 2011. "Judicial Power in Domestic and International Politics." *International Organization* 65(3):553–587.

Staton, Jeffrey K., and Georg Vanberg. 2008. "The Value of Vagueness: Delegation, Defiance, and Judicial Opinions." *American Journal of Political Science* 52(3):504–519.

Staton, Jeffrey K., Varun Gauri, and Jorge Vargas Cullell. 2015. "The Costa Rican Supreme Court's Compliance Monitoring System." *Journal of Politics* 77(3): 774–786.

Stephenson, Matthew Caleb. 2003. "When the Devil Turns: The Political Foundations of Independent Judicial Review." *Journal of Legal Studies* 32(1):59–89.

Stephenson, Matthew Caleb, and Justin Fox. 2011. "Judicial Review as a Response to Political Posturing." *American Political Science Review* 105(2):397–414.

Stone Sweet, Alec. 2000. *Governing with Judges: Constitutional Politics in Europe*. Oxford University Press.

Stone Sweet, Alec, and Thomas L. Brunell. 2013. "Trustee Courts and the Judicialization of International Regimes: The Politics of Majoritarian Activism in the European Convention on Human Rights, the European Union, and the World Trade Organization." *Journal of Law and Courts* 1(1):61–88.

Svolik, Milan. 2008. "Authoritarian Reversals and Democratic Consolidation." *American Political Science Review* 102(2):153–168.

2012. *The Politics of Authoritarian Rule*. Cambridge University Press.

Tanner, Martin A. 1996. *Tools for Statistical Inference: Methods for the Exploration of Posterior Distributions and Likelihood Functions*. New York: Springer-Verlag.

Treier, Shawn, and Simon Jackman. 2008. "Democracy as a Latent Variable." *American Journal of Political Science* 52(1):201–217.

Tushnet, Mark. 2004. "Constitutional Hardball." *UIC John Marshall Law Review* 37(2):523–553.

Uprimny, Rodrigo. 2003. "The Constitutional Court and Control of Presidential Extraordinary Powers in Colombia." *Democratization* 10(4):46–69.

Vanberg, Georg. 1998. "Abstract Judicial Review, Legislative Bargaining, and Policy Compromise." *Journal of Theoretical Politics* 10(3):299–326.

2005. *The Politics of Constitutional Review in Germany*. New York: Cambridge University Press.

Vanhala, Lisa. 2012. "Legal Opportunity Structures and the Paradox of Legal Mobilization by the Environmental Movement in the UK." *Law and Society Review* 46(3):523–556.

Venice Commission. n.d. "Opinion on the Act of the Constitutional Tribunal."

Voigt, Stafan, Jerg Gutmann, and Lars P. Feld. 2015. "Economic Growth and Judicial Independence, a Dozen Years On: Cross-Country Evidence Using an Updated Set of Indicators." *European Journal of Political Economy* 38:197–211.

Weingast, Barry. 1997. "The Political Foundations of Democracy and the Rule of Law." *American Political Science Review* 91(2):245–263.

Whittington, Keith E. 2009. *Constitutional Construction: Divided Powers and Constitutional Meaning*. Cambridge, MA: Harvard University Press.

Wilson, Bruce M., and Juan Carlos Rodríguez Cordero. 2006. "Legal Opportunity Structures and Social Movements: The Effects of Institutional Change on Costa Rican Politics." *Comparative Political Studies* 39(3):325–351.

Index

In this index "t" refers to a table, "fig" refers to a figure, and "n" refers to a note

Acemoglu, Daron, 128
Adams, John, 140
Albanian transition to democracy, 43, 44, 46, 132
Alfonso XIII (King of Spain), 33
Alter, Karen J., 23
Apodaca, Claire, 36
appointments to judiciary. *See* judicial appointments
arbitrators, courts as, 23, 25–26
Archigos Project (database), 91
Argentinian Constitution, 17
attacks on judiciary. *See* judicial attacks
authority of judges, n12, 23, 29, 80
autocracy
  competition and, 48–50, 53–54
  courts as bulwarks and, 4
  judicial attacks and, 130
  judicial independence and, 39, 48*fig*, 48–49
  measurement of, 48*fig*, 44–50, 53–54
  scholarship on, 1
  states of emergency and, 92
  transitions to democracy and, 13, 41
autolimitation, 79
autonomy in modeling. *See* informational model of regime breakdown

Bacrach, Peter, 143
Bahry, Donna, 90–91
Barak, Aharon, 3–4
Baratz, Morton S., 143
Bardella, Kurt, 136
Barrett, Amy, 130
Basic Law (Germany), 5
Bass, Leeann, 137
Bavarian Constitutional Court, 5
Berlin Wall and judicial independence, 39, 44*fig*, 45*fig*, 41–47
Bjørnskov, Christian, 92
Blass, Abby, 28
Board of Immigration Appeals (BIA), 126–127
Boix, Carles, 99, 102
Bolivian Constitutional Tribunal, 7, 17, 88
Bonaparte, Napoleon, 60
breakdowns of democracy. *See* democratic breakdown
Brinks, Daniel, 28
Budowsky, Brent, 121
Bulgarian transition to democracy, 43, 44, 46
bulwarks of democracy. *See* courts as bulwarks of democracy
Bush, George W., 130, 131

Calvo, Ernesto, 89
Cane, Peter, 22
Carrubba, Clifford, 11, 24–26, 29, 61, 76–77
Chase, Amanda, 129
Chávez, Hugo, 107, 138, 143
Cheibub, José, 124
Chilean transition to democracy, 6, 51
Chilton, Adam, 69, 72
Citizens United v. *FEC* (2010), n121
Civic Platform (PO) (Poland), 6
civil society
  coups and, 87, 98, 100, 102
  judicial attacks and, 87
  judicial authority and, 29
  judicial independence and, 29, 86
  judicial review and, 69
  measurement of, 96, 100, 127*fig*
  prudence and, 86

public opinion and, 86
robust civil society, 29, 86, 96, 100, 127–128
V-Dem and, 100, 102, 127*fig*
Colombian Constitutional Court, 6, 17, 79
Comparative Constitutions Project (CCP), 37
competition
autocracy and, 48–50, 53–54
compromise and, 53, 124
courts as bulwarks and, 26, 124
democratic breakdown and, 107
economic development and, 122
fixed assets and, 50, 53
fluctuations in, 49, 53
identification analysis of, 50
incentives for, 27, 31, 46–47
interparty competition, 107, 144
investigation of political rivals and, 89–91
judicial attacks and, 135
judicial independence and, 13, 15, 27, 31, 39–41, 46–47, 48*fig*, 50, 51*t*, 52*t*, 51–53, 55–59, 144
measurement of, 48, 48*fig*, 50*t*, 51*t*, 52*t*, 45–53, 54, 55–59
prudence and, 28
regime stability and, 39–41
V-Dem and, 48, 50
compromise
competition and, 53, 124
conditions necessary for, 13, 28
constitutions and, 11, 19
courts as bulwarks and, 12–13, 26, 124
democracy and, 10, 19–20, 140
economic development and, 28
extraordinary actions and, 62
formal institutions and, 141
information and, 11, 28–29
judicial attacks and, 12
judicial independence and, 11–13, 28, 31, 141
limits on power and, 19
noncompliance and, 29
prudence and, 60
regime rules and, 60
regime stability and, 60
scholarship on, 140
Conaghan, Catherine, 90
constitutions
aims of, 20
compromise and, 11, 19
consent of governed and, 5–6
constitutional courts, 5, 11, 17–18, 21, 23, 46, 79
constitutional hardball, 129, 135
constitutional review, 4, 5, 22, 36, 144
courts as bulwarks and, 4–6, 26, 139
democracy and, 5–6, 17, 46
electoral reform and, 88
information and, 21
interpretative challenges of, 20, 76–77
judicial appointments and, 7
judicial attacks and, 7
judicial independence and, 46, 120
limits on power and, 20
measurement and, 46
mobilization of masses and, 69
organizational interests and, 69
regime rules and, 10, 19, 20, 46
scholarship on, 22
unconstitutional constitutional amendment doctrine, 89
Coppedge, Michael, 48
Costa Rican Supreme Court, 6, 8, 87, 104
coups
civil society and, 87, 98, 100, 102
definition of, 99
extraordinary actions and, 98
formal institutions and, 124
incentives for, 98
judicial attacks and, 87, 100, 101
judicial independence and, 14, 86, 98, 101–102
likelihood of, 101*fig*, 101–102, 112
measurement of, 100–101, 101*fig*, 112
noncompliance and, 100
overview of, 98–102
scholarship on, 99
V-Dem and, 100
Court of Justice of the European Union (CJEU), 24, 61
courts as arbitrators, 23, 25–26
courts as bulwarks of democracy
active role of courts as, 120, n120
argument overview for, 10–12, 26*fig*, 27*fig*, 26–29
autocracy and, 4
checking function of courts and, 120–121
competition and, 26, 124
compromise and, 12–13, 26, 124
constitutions and, 4–6, 26, 139
corruption and, 12
economic development and, 140
empirical challenges to, 12–13
failure cases of, 6–10, 12
historical context of, 3–4, 120
implications for, 14, 142–144
judicial appointments and, 7–10
judicial attacks and, 6–10
lack of guarantee of, 12
limits of, n12, 142–144
limits on power and, 12
methodological approach for, 12–13
noncompliance and, 5–6, 144
nonexistent bargains and, 142–143

open questions for, 144–145
overview of, 3–6, 13–14, 20, 26, 27*fig*, 29, 140–142
problem of governance and, 22–26
prudence and, 141, 143–145
regime stability and, 12, 20
requirements for, 11, 12, 26, 124
rule of law and, 4
scholarship on, 3, 11–12, 14, 26, 140, 143
states of emergency and, 4
success cases of, 4–6
tensions within, 4
transitions to democracy and, 5–6

democracy. *See also* courts as bulwarks of democracy; transitions to democracy
compromise and, 10, 19–20, 140
constitutions and, 5–6, 17, 46
contested status of, 15
definitions of, 10, 15–20
economic development and, 124, 140
global assault on, 1, 20–22, 140, 143
incentives for, 15
judicial review and, 22, 25
limits on power and, 10, 19
maximalist-substantive definition of, 15–19, 29
minimalist-procedural definition of, 15–19, 29
peaceful transfer of power and, 10, 12, 16, 19, 26, 141, 142
problem of governance in, 19–26, 29
regime rules and, 10, 19, 22
regime stability and, 15, 20
requirements of, 10
rule of law and, 16
scholarship on, 1, 10, 15, 140
uncertainty and, 22
values required for, 15, 18, 19, 29
democratic breakdown
competition and, 107
economic development and, 105
frailty model and, 104
global assault on democracy and, 1, 140, 143
judicial attacks and, 86, 87, 103, 104, 143
judicial independence and, 14, 39*fig*, 41*fig*, 86, 102–106, 122*fig*, 143
measurement of, 39*fig*, 41*fig*, 102–106, 113–117, 122*fig*
noncompliance and, 86, 103, 104
reverse causal account of, n105
scholarship on, 102
V-Dem and, 102, 103
Democratic Party (US), 130, 136, 138
Donnelly, Ann, 2
Doyle, Arthur Conan, 84
Duda, Andrzej, 7
Easterbrook, Frank, 127
Eastern Bloc states' judicial independence, 44*fig*, 45*fig*, 45*t*, 47*t*, 41–47
economic development
competition and, 122
compromise and, 28
courts as bulwarks and, 140
democracy and, 124, 140
democratic breakdown and, 105
fixed assets and, 124
judicial independence and, 28, 122
measurement of, 32, 96, 101, 103
regime stability and, 124
Egyptian Constitution, 17
election of 2020 (US), 121, 129, 137
electoral reform
constitutions and, 88
controversial nature of, 88–89
extraordinary actions and, 85
international examples of, 88–89
judicial attacks and, 106
judicial review and, 88
limits on power and, 85
measurement of, 89
overview of, 88–89
political context of, 85
presidential reelections and, 89
prudence and, 85
regime stability and, 89
V-Dem and, 89
Elkins, Zachary, 37, 39
Epperly, Brad, 13, 48, 91
Executive Order 13769 (2017), 2–3, 120
extraordinary actions. *See also* electoral reform; investigation of political rivals; states of emergency
compromise and, 62
coups and, 98
definition of, 85, 88
electoral reform and, 85
judicial attacks and, 106
judicial independence and, n87, 120–121
limits on power and, 88
overview of, 88–98
perceived necessity of, n87
prudence and, 84, 98
regime rules and, 77–78, 85
regime stability and, 84
scholarship on, 65

Fariss, Christopher, 92–93
FEC, *Citizens United* v. (2010), n121
Federalist 51, 15, 20
Federalist Society, 125

Feld, Lars, 33, 36
forbearance norm, 79, 121, 129–130
formal institutions, 39–41, 45–46, 53, 124–125, 141, 144–145
Fox, Justin, 62, 65
Fujimori, Alberto, 21, 89

Gabel, Matthew, 11, 24–26, 29, 61, 76–77
Garland, Merrick, 130, 137–138
German Federal Constitutional Court, 4–5
Ginsburg, Ruth Bader, 130, 137
Ginsburg, Tom, n12, 16, 22, 37, 39, 52, 129
Global Competitiveness Report (GCR), 33
Global Terrorism Database (2018), 97
Gorsuch, Neil, 130, 138

Hafner-Burton, Emilie, 92–93
Hamilton, Alexander, 1
Helfer, Laurence, 92–93
Historical Statistics (2012), 101, 103
Honduran democratic breakdown, 88, 138–139
human rights, 4, 36, 79, 92–93
Hungarian transition to democracy, 17, 44, 46
Huq, Aziz, n12, 16, 129

independence of judiciary. *See* judicial independence
information
  asymmetries in, 21, 21, 21, 24, 60
  compromise and, 11, 28–29
  constitutions and, 21
  court influence outside of, 79–80
  credibility of, 23–25
  deception through, 21, 24
  incentives for, 24, 61
  investigation of political rivals and, 85
  judicial appointments and, 79, 85
  judicial independence and, 11, 13, 15, 23, 26, 27, 77–78, 108, 141
  judicial review and, 24–26, 77–78
  limits on power and, 27
  noncompliance and, 26, 77–78, 107–108, 144
  private information, 10, 25–26, 61, 77–78
  problem of, 11, 20, 26, 76, 141
  regime rules and, 10, 11, 21, 61, 76–77
  regime stability and, 13, 27, 61, 77–80
  revealing of, 77–78
  sharing of, 11, 13, 15
  transmission of, 24–26, 61, 76–78, 108
  trust and, 24
  uncertainty and, 21
informational model of regime breakdown
  analysis of, 64
  baseline model of, 62–64, 66, 67*fig*, 71, 72*fig*
  communication in, 64
  definitions in, 64, 66
  equilibria in, 64–66, 67*fig*, 67, 71, 72*fig*
  extraordinary policies in, 64
  interpretation of results of, 67*fig*, 67–68, 71, 72*fig*
  judicial review model in, 71*fig*, 72*fig*, 68–76
  measurement in, 74*fig*
  opportunism in, 64–66
  overview of, 62
  political conflict in, 66–67
  political failure in, 64–66
  preferences in, 63
  probability of conflict in, 74*fig*
  propositions in, 65, 66
  regime rules and, 62, 65, 66
  responses available within, 64
international aid, 123
investigation of political rivals, 62, 85, 91, 88–91, 91
Irish Constitution, 17
Israeli High Court, 21

Jackman, Simon, 118
judges as mediators, 23–26
judges as trustees, 23, 76–77
judicial appointments
  blocking of, 129–130, 135
  blue slip and, 130
  constitutions and, 7
  courts as bulwarks and, 7–10
  information and, 79, 85
  judicial attacks and, 7
  measurement of, 35, 36
  overview of, 129–130
judicial attacks
  alternative interpretation of, 105–106
  autocracy and, 130
  civil society and, 87
  competition and, 135
  compromise and, 12
  constitutions and, 7
  coups and, 87, 100, 101
  courts as bulwarks and, 6–10
  democratic breakdown and, 86, 87, 103, 104, 143
  electoral reform and, 106
  extraordinary actions and, 106
  international examples of, 14, 132
  interpretation of, 135
  judicial appointments and, 7
  judicial independence and, 8*fig*, 7–10, 101, 106*fig*, 105–106
  measurement of, 8*fig*, 106*fig*, 130*fig*, 132*fig*, 132
  noncompliance and, 87
  prudence and, 106

regime stability and, 14, 104, 107, 143
V-Dem and, 102, 130*fig*
verbal attacks, 101, 132–135, 137
judicial authority, n12, 23, 29, 80
judicial autonomy, 32, 37
judicial decision-making, 8, 11, 125
judicial independence. *See also* measurement of judicial independence
autocracy and, 39, 48*fig*, 48–49
causes of, 13, 31, 41, 44, 46–47, 50, 53
civil society and, 29, 86
competition and, 13, 15, 27, 31, 39–41, 46–47, 48*fig*, 50, 51*t*, 52*t*, 51–53, 55–59, 144
compromise and, 11–13, 28, 31, 141
constitutions and, 46, 120
coups and, 14, 86, 98, 101–102
de facto independence, 8*fig*, 8, 13, 31–35, 44, 45*fig*, 45*t*, 47*t*, 46–47, 48*fig*, 50*t*, 50, 51*t*, 55–59, 110
de jure independence, 37*fig*, 35–38, 39*fig*, 39, 45*fig*, 46–47, 52*t*, 51–53, 144–145
democratic breakdown and, 14, 39*fig*, 41*fig*, 86, 102–106, 122*fig*, 143
economic development and, 28, 122
extraordinary actions and, n87, 120–121
incentives for, 11, 13–15, 27, 31
information and, 11, 13, 15, 23, 26, 27, 77–78, 108, 141
insurance model of, 11, 16, 28–29, 31, 39, 41, 53–54
judicial attacks and, 8*fig*, 7–10, 101, 106*fig*, 105–106
judicial review and, 25–26
limits on power and, 27, 29
natural disasters and, 96*fig*, 96, 110
noncompliance and, 8*fig*, 8, 13, 77–78
opportunism and, 76–77
prudence and, 12–13, 27, 60, 79, 84, 106–108, 120, 141
regime rules and, 11, 13, 23, 46, 76–80, 120–121, 144–145
regime stability and, 10, 13, 14, 25, 39–41, 76–80, 107, 120, 122, 142
requirements for, 11, 12, 27–29
rule of law and, 16
scholarship on, 8–12, 14, 16, 26, 36–38, 125, 141
states of emergency and, 93, 93*fig*, 94*fig*, 92–95, 95, 96*fig*, 110–117
terrorism and, 98*fig*, 98
judicial orders. *See* noncompliance with judicial orders
judicial review
civil society and, 69
democracy and, 22, 25
electoral reform and, 88
information and, 24–26, 77–78
judicial independence and, 25–26
jurisprudence and, 25–26
noncompliance and, 26, 29
political conflict reduced by, 25–26
regime rules and, 22, 26, 76–80
regime stability and, 26
scholarship on, 24–26
veto power and, 25–26
judicial review model
analysis in, 70–75
autonomy version of, 76
conflict reduction in, 74–75
definitions in, 70
equilibria in, 70–74, 76
extraordinary policies in, 70
interpretation of, 72–75
judicial strategies in, 74, 76
leader strategies in, 72, 74, 76
limits on power in, 75
mixed strategies in, 71–72
mobilization of masses in, 69
noncompliance in, 68–69, 75
opportunism and, 72, 74, 75
overview of, 68, 75
preferences in, 69–70
propositions in, 71–72
results in, 72, 74, 75
scholarship on, 69
timing and information in, 68
utility of court in, 70
jurisprudence, 11, 16, 24–26, 120

Keith, Linda, 36
Kim, Young Hum, 90–91
Kouba, Karel, 89

La Porta, Rafael, 36
Latin American electoral reform, 88–89, 124–125
Law and Justice Party (PiS) (Poland), 6
Law, David, n18
leadership forbearance, 79, 121, 129–130
Levitsky, Steven, 1, 2, 16, 79, 121, 129
limits on power
compromise and, 19
constitutions and, 20
courts as bulwarks and, 12
democracy and, 10, 19
electoral reform and, 85
extraordinary actions and, 88
information and, 27
judicial independence and, 27, 29
noncompliance and, 29

scholarship on, 125
separation of powers and, 36, 125
Lincoln, Abraham, 107–108, 144
Linzer, Drew, 32, 35, 41, 89, 91
LJI. *See* measurement of judicial independence

Madison, James, 15
Madison's Historical Statistics (2012), 101, 103
measurement of judicial independence. *See also* specific models, datasets, and concepts
autocracy and, 48*fig*, 44–50, 53–54
backdating data for, 33
challenges of, 16, 18–19, 35
civil society and, 96, 100, 127*fig*
competition and, 48, 48*fig*, 50*t*, 51*t*, 52*t*, 45–53, 54, 55–59
constitutions and, 46
coups and, 100–101, 101*fig*, 112
data availability and, 37*fig*
de facto independence and, 32–35, 43, 45, 53–54
de jure independence and, 35–38, 51–53
democratic breakdown and, 39*fig*, 41*fig*, 102–106, 113–117, 122*fig*
economic development and, 32, 96, 101, 103
electoral reform and, 89
identification analysis and, 50
inputs used for, 36–38
instrumental variables and, 48–53
international scores for, 125
judicial appointments and, 35, 36
judicial attacks and, 8*fig*, 102, 106*fig*, 130*fig*, 132, 132*fig*, 130–132, 135
limitations of, 32
measurement errors and, 118*fig*, 118–119
methodology for, 12–13, 18, 118
natural disasters and, n21, 96*fig*, 96, 110
noncompliance and, 8*fig*, 9, 86, 100, 102, 126–127
opportunism and, 64–66, 72, 74, 75
overview of, 16
regime rules and, 35, 76–80
regime stability and, 122
scholarship on, 32–38, 118
states of emergency and, 93, 94*fig*, 96*fig*, 110–117
terrorism and, 92–93, 98*fig*, 97–98
transitions to democracy and, 39*fig*, 41*fig*, 41–47
mediators, judges as, 23–26
Melton, James, 37, 39, 52, 118
Merryman, John, 107, 144
Meserve, Stephen, 118
models. *See* informational model of regime breakdown; judicial review model; measurement of judicial independence
Montesquieu, Baron de, 31
Morales, Evo, 8
Muslim travel ban (2007), 2, 3, 120, 134, 137
mutual toleration norm, 129–130

natural disasters
annual risk of, 96
constitutions and, n21
costs of, 96
human intervention and, 95–96
index of, 95
judicial independence and, 96*fig*, 96, 110
measurement of, n21, 96*fig*, 96, 110
opportunism and, 95–97
prudence and, 85
scholarship on, 93
states of emergency and, 85, 91, 93, 94*fig*, 96, 110
Negretto, Gabriel, 89
Netanyahu, Benjamin, 8, 87
New Deal policies, 131
Nixon, United States v. (1974), 121
noncompliance with judicial orders
compromise and, 29
consequences for, 29, 86
costly noncompliance, 29, 61–62, 69, 127, 144
coups and, 100
courts as bulwarks and, 5–6
democratic breakdown and, 86, 103, 104
dilemma posed by, 9
as healthy indicator, 14, 80, 86, 144
information and, 26, 77–78, 107–108, 144
judicial attacks and, 87
judicial independence and, 8*fig*, 8, 13, 77–78
judicial review and, 26, 29
limits on power and, 29
measurement of, 8*fig*, 9, 86, 100, 102, 126–127
prudence and, 86
public opinion and, 29
regime rules and, 61–62, 144
regime stability and, 12, 14, 26, 29, 79–80, 107–108, 144
risks involved with, 12, 107–108
rule of law and, 8, 87, 108
scholarship on, 29, 87
toleration by judges of, 29
V-Dem and, 8*fig*, 100, 102, 126*fig*, 126–127
vetoing policies and, 86

Obama, Barack
judicial appointments under, 125, 130, 137
lack of judicial comments under, 133
social media use by, 133*fig*, 133–134
Office of Democracy and Governance (USAID), 9, 87

opportunism
judicial independence and, 76–77
measurement of, 64–66, 72, 74, 75
natural disasters and, 95–97
regime rules and, 76–77
states of emergency and, 91–95
terrorism and, 97–98
Ortega, Daniel, 138

peaceful transfer of power, 10, 12, 16, 19, 26, 141, 142
Pemstein, Daniel, 118
Pinochet, Augusto, 6, 89
Polish Constitutional Tribunal (CT), 6, 8
Polish transition to democracy, 7–10, 43–44, 46, 132
political emergencies, 93*fig*, 94, 94*fig*, 93–95, 95, 97–98, 110
political reform. *See* electoral reform
politicization of courts, 90, 135, 144
Popova, Maria, 90
populism, 1, 129
Powell, Johnathan, 99
power. *See* limits on power
presidential election of 2020 (US), 121, 129, 137
Primo de Rivera, Miguel, 33
problem of democratic governance, 19–26, 29
prudence
civil society and, 86
competition and, 28
compromise and, 60
courts as bulwarks and, 141, 143–145
democratic regime collapse, 84
electoral reform and, 85
extraordinary actions and, 84, 98
forbearance norm and, 79, 121, 129–130
incentives for, 60, 79, 120, 141, 143–144
judicial attacks and, 106
judicial independence and, 12–13, 27, 60, 79, 84, 106–108, 120, 141
natural disasters and, 85
noncompliance and, 86
regime rules and, 60, 84
regime stability and, 11, 101–102, 120
stakes of holding power and, 28
states of emergency and, 91–92, 95
terrorism and, 85
transfer of power and, 106–108
Przeworski, Adam, 11, 19, 122
public opinion, 29, 86, 127, 136–137, 145

Radean, Marius, 122
Reenock, Christopher, 122
reforms. *See* electoral reform
Refugee Admissions Program (USRAP), 2
regime rules
compromise and, 60
constitutions and, 10, 19, 20, 46
context dependence of, 21
definition of, 10
democracy and, 10, 19, 22
disagreement over violations of, 60
extraordinary actions and, 77–78, 85
fundamental regime rules, 19, 22, 60
information and, 10, 11, 21, 61, 76–77
judges as trustees and, 23
judicial independence and, 11, 13, 23, 46, 76–80, 120–121, 144–145
judicial review and, 22, 26, 76–80
measurement of, 35, 76–80
nomination of judges as a, 46
noncompliance and, 61–62, 144
opportunism and, 76–77
opposition parties and, 79
policing of, 10, 11, 22, 79
policy failure and, 76–77
political conflict and, 76–77
prudence and, 60, 84
regime stability and, 10, 62
states of emergency and, 91
uncertainty of, 23, 76–77
undermining of, 108
violations of, 79, 84, 120–121
regime stability. *See also* democratic breakdown; informational model of regime breakdown; transitions to democracy
communication and, 27
competition and, 39–41
compromise and, 60
conditions necessary for, 25
constitutions and, 27
courts as bulwarks and, 12, 20
democracy and, 15, 20
destabilizing factors for, 14
economic development and, 124
economic factors in, 122
electoral reform and, 89
extraordinary actions and, 84
information and, 13, 27, 61, 77–80
international examples of, 79
judicial attacks and, 14, 104, 107, 143
judicial independence and, 10, 13, 14, 25, 39–41, 76–80, 107, 120, 122, 142
judicial review and, 26
measurement of, 122
noncompliance and, 12, 14, 26, 29, 79–80, 107–108, 144
prudence and, 11, 101–102, 120

regime rules and, 10, 62
scholarship on, 11, 79
transitions to democracy and, 39–41
uncertainty and, 25
Republican Party (US)
competition and, 135
election of 2020 and, 129, 137
judicial appointments and, 125, 129–130
Supreme Court as agent of, 135–137
Tea Party Republicans, 129
transfer of power and, 129
review by judiciary. *See* judicial review
Ríos-Figueroa, Julio, 11–12, 23–26, 29, 60
Robart, James L., 2, 134
Roberts, John, 120, 134
Robinson, James A., 128
Romanian transition to democracy, 43, 44, 132
Romero, Anthony, 2–3, 120, 143
Roosevelt, Franklin D., 131
Rosato, Sebastian, 99, 102
rule of law, 2, 4, 8, 10, 16, 79, 87, 108

Sanders, Bernie, 129
Scheppele, Kim, 6, 17, 19, 120
Schumpeter, Joseph, 15, 20
separation of powers, 36, 125
Sosa, Cecilia, 107, 143
Sotomayor, Sonia, 133
South African Constitutional Court, 5
states of emergency (SOE)
autocracy and, 92
coding of, 92–93
courts as bulwarks and, 4
declaring of, 92
definition of, 92–93
judicial independence and, 93, 93*fig*, 94*fig*, 92–95, 96*fig*, 110–117
measurement of, 92–93, 93, 94*fig*, 96*fig*, 110–117
natural disasters and, 85, 91, 93, 94*fig*, 96, 110
opportunism and, 91–95
overview of, 91–92
political emergencies and, 93*fig*, 94, 94*fig*, 93–95, 95, 97–98, 110
prudence and, 91–92, 95
regime rules and, 91
scholarship on, 92–93
terrorism and, 97
timing of, 94–95
types of, 93–95
Staton, Jeffrey, 32, 35, 41, 89, 91, 122
Steinburg, Bon, 129
Stephenson, Matthew, 62–63, 65
strategic deference of judges, 23, 107, 141
substantive values, 15, 18, 19, 29
Supreme Court (US)
election of 2020 and, 137
judicial appointments to, 129–130
legitimacy of, 127, 137, 138
media coverage of, 137
myth of legality and, 137
noncompliance of, 126–127, 138
politicization of, 138, 139
public opinion on, 127, 136–137
as Republican agent, 135–137
scholarship on, 127, 137
Svolik, Milan, 65

Tanner, Martin, 118
Tea Party Republicans, 129
Tenth Amendment, 17
terrorism
annual risk of, 97–98
definition of, 97
judicial independence and, 98*fig*, 98
measurement of, 92–93, 98*fig*, 97–98
opportunism and, 97–98
prudence and, 85
scholarship on, 97
states of emergency and, 97
Thyne, Clayton, 99, 100
transfer of power, 10, 12, 16, 19, 26, 141, 142
transitions to democracy
Albanian transition, 43, 44, 46, 132
autocracy and, 13, 41
Bulgarian transition, 43, 44, 46
Chilean transition, 6, 51
courts as bulwarks and, 5–6
Hungarian transition, 17, 44, 46
lag in process of, 46–47
measurement of, 39*fig*, 41*fig*, 41–47
overview of, 5–6, 39–41, 46
Polish transition, 7–10, 43–44, 46, 132
regime stability and, 39–41
Romanian transition, 43, 44, 132
travel ban (2017), 2, 3, 120, 134, 137
Treier, Shawn, 118
Trump, Donald J.
contested 2020 election and, 121, 129
coronavirus pandemic and, 123
disruptive effects of, 1
Executive Order 13769 of, 2–3, 120
extraordinary actions by, 129
judicial attacks by, 134, 131–135, 135
judicial independence under, 125
Muslim travel ban of, 2, 3, 120, 134, 137
social media use by, 133*fig*, 134*fig*, 132–135
trustees, judges as, 23, 76–77
Tushnet, Mark, 129

Tymoshenko, Julia, 90

United States
  caveats to courts as bulwarks in, 128–137
  checks and balances system in, 2
  civil society in, 127*fig*, 127–128
  competition in, 135
  compromise in, 124–125
  constitution of, 129, 135
  coronavirus pandemic and, 123
  coup potential in, 124, 131
  court failures in, 121
  courts as bulwarks in, 14, 121, 122, 124–128, 137–139
  democratic breakdown in, 129, 131, 135
  economic development in, 124
  extraordinary actions in, 129
  formal institutions in, 124–125
  immigration court in, 126–127
  income inequality in, 128
  judicial appointments in, 129–130
  judicial attacks in, 130–135
  limits on power in, 125
  military–civilian relationship in, 124
  noncompliance in, 126–127, 137
  overview of, 123, 137–139
  partisanship of judiciary in, 125
  politicization of the judiciary in, 139
  presidential system in, 2, 124–125
  prudence in, 121
  regime stability and, 122
  scholarship on, 123–125, 128
  stressors in, 123
  2020 election in, 121, 129, 137
United States v. *Nixon* (1974), 121

values, 15, 18, 19, 29
Varieties of Democracy (V-Dem) project. *See also* measurement of judicial independence
  civil society and, 100, 102, 127*fig*
  competition and, 48, 50
  coups and, 100
  democratic breakdown and, 102, 103
  electoral reform and, 89
  importance of data from, 19, 32–33
  judicial attacks and, 102, 130*fig*
  measurement errors and, 118*fig*, 118–119
  methodology for use of data from, 32, 34, 48, 50, 100
  noncompliance and, 8*fig*, 100, 102, 126*fig*, 126–127
  voter participation and, 48, 50
Venezuela Supreme Court, 107, 143
Versteeg, Mila, n18, 22, 69, 72
veto power of courts. *See* noncompliance with judicial orders
Voigt, Stefan, 33, 36, 92

Warren Court, 34, 126
Wooldridge, Jeffrey, 50

Yanukovych, Viktor, 90

Zelaya, Manuel, 88, 138–139
Ziblatt, Daniel, 1, 2, 16, 79, 121, 129

Printed by Integrated Books International,
United States of America